The Good-Natured

Feminist

CATRIONA SANDILANDS

The Good-Natured

Feminist

Ecofeminism and the

Quest for Democracy

UNIVERSITY OF MINNESOTA PRESS

MINNEAPOLIS

LONDON

An earlier version of chapter 4 appeared as "From Natural Identity to Radical
Democracy," in *Environmental Ethics* 17 (spring 1995): 75–91. Part of chapter 5 appeared
as "Mother Nature, the Cyborg, and the Queer: Ecofeminism and (More) Questions of
Identity," in *NWSA Journal*, 18–40; copyright 1998 *NWSA Journal*, reprinted with the
permission of Indiana University Press. Part of chapter 6 appeared as "Globalization
and Its Discontents: Ecofeminism and the Dilemma of 'Universal' Politics," in *Surviving
Globalism: The Social and Environmental Challenges*, edited by Ted Schrecker (Houndmills:
Macmillan Press, 1997), 199–213; copyright 1997 Macmillan and St. Martin's Press.
Part of chapter 7 appeared as "Is the Personal Always Political? Environmentalism in
Arendt's Age of 'the Social,'" in *Organizing Dissent: Contemporary Social Movements in Theory
and Practice*, 2d ed., edited by W. K. Carroll (Toronto: Garamond Press, 1997), 76–93;
copyright 1997 Garamond Press.

Published by the University of Minnesota Press
111 Third Avenue South, Suite 290
Minneapolis, MN 55401-2520
http://www.upress.umn.edu

Printed in the United States of America on acid-free paper

Library of Congress Cataloging-in-Publication Data
Sandilands, Catriona.
    The good-natured feminist : ecofeminism and the quest for democracy /
Catriona Sandilands.
        p.   cm.
    Includes bibliographical references and index.
    ISBN 0-8166-3096-8 (hc.). — ISBN 0-8166-3097-6 (pbk.)
        1. Ecofeminism. 2. Ecofeminism—Political aspects. 3. Human ecology.
    4. Feminist theory. 5. Green movement. 6. Environmental policy.
    7. Environmental ethics. I. Title.
    HQ1233.S213   1999
    305.42'01—dc21   98-54272

10 09 08 07 06 05 04 03 02 01 00 99   10 9 8 7 6 5 4 3 2 1

We are all the same, that is, human, in such a way that nobody is ever the same as anyone else who ever lived, lives, or will live.

Hannah Arendt, *The Human Condition*

To my parents, for both sameness and difference

Contents

Acknowledgments

This book began its life as a doctoral dissertation for the Graduate Programme in Sociology at York University in Toronto, Ontario. Many of its central arguments were born in the rich conversations I had with friends, advisors, and colleagues during my graduate work. Thus, I begin with thanks to those who sustained me in so many ways during that period. The Social Sciences and Humanities Research Council of Canada provided me with financial support, for which I am very grateful. I also thank my supervisory committee, Karen Anderson, Pat Armstrong, and especially Brian Singer, for their critical commentary on my work and for the latitude they gave me to find my own place in the literature. I also remember Patricia Cormack, Don Forgay, Kieran Keohane, Julian Knight, Kate Krug, Carmen Kuhling, and Matthew Trachman: thank you all.

My move from sociology to environmental studies—both institutionally and intellectually—has also had a profound impact on my ideas and commitments; I have found new questions and challenges in a variety of sources, many of which also trace their paths through this book. For their inspiration, dialogue, and traditions I thank my colleagues in the Faculty of Environmental Studies, especially Deborah Barndt, Mora Campbell, Leesa Fawcett, Roger Keil, and Joan Steigerwald. I also thank the many students who have spent long hours with me in our classrooms, in my office, and even in the pub taking up the political challenges of feminism, environmentalism, radical democracy, and postmodernism. In particular, I thank Rose Marie Kennedy for her unerring eye for paradox and irony, and Nick

Garside for his articulate commitment to democracy and his help in editing and clarifying the manuscript.

I also offer thanks to the many writers in the larger ecofeminist community whose work I address in these pages. Although I am often critical of that work, I firmly believe that it is through respectful debate that intellectual and political movements such as ecofeminism come to be able to address the complexities of the world they wish to understand and change. This book is thus a mark of my respect to them and my desire for an ongoing conversation with that community. I cannot thank all of these writers here, but I single out the following for special mention: Chaia Heller for really *showing* me social ecology and that there is a place for the erotic in political life; Greta Gaard for insisting on situated knowledges, democratic green politics, and the possibility of a queer ecofeminism, as well as for her excellent comments on the manuscript; Heather Eaton for her commitment to the conversation between the spirit and the polis (including the vicissitudes of childrearing); and Erica Bremner Kneipp and Tzeporah Berman for their determination to practice ecofeminism in nonacademic milieux. I am also grateful to Karen Warren and Irene Diamond for their respectful, insightful, and thorough comments on the manuscript, to Noël Sturgeon for her clear thinking about chapter 8, and to Sherilyn MacGregor for assuring me that the many questions I leave unanswered are being addressed very well indeed.

At the University of Minnesota Press, I am indebted to Carrie Mullen for her enthusiasm and rigor; both are aspects of her maieutic commitment to seeing this book enter the world in the healthiest possible condition. I am also grateful to Laura Westlund for her organizational care and acumen and to Jeanne Barker-Nunn for her sensitive editing of my unwieldy sentences and weeding out of my Canadian spellings.

Finally, I thank those whose love and attention are foundational to these pages in past, present, and future: David Swan, Eulala Mills Diment, Robert (Sandy) and June Sandilands, Solomon Chrom, and Hannah Sandilands.

Introduction

Mothers, Natures, and Ecofeminists

Women's concern for the natural environment is rooted in our concern for the health and well being of our family and community. . . . Because we have traditionally been mother, nurse, and guardian for the home and community, women have been quick to perceive the threat to the health and lives of our families and neighbours that is posed by nuclear power proliferation, polluted waters, and toxic chemicals.

Ontario Advisory Council on Women's Issues, *Women and the Environment*

This book begins with a message that may sound familiar to anyone in touch with the current trend toward the "greening" of social and political life: the environment is a mess, this story goes, and the catastrophe is so great that it is now being felt in that most intimate and sacred sphere of the contemporary social world, the family. In the context of all of this mess, women, the keepers of family sanctity and the doers of family work, are particularly aware of ecologically destructive events. This heightened awareness, the logic goes, nominates women as the vanguard speakers of environmental malaise, and perhaps also as the vanguard of the forthcoming ecological revolution to clean up the earth.

This pervasive message appears in all of these common interlocking assumptions. Women's concerns about the environment derive from their experiences of particular problems experienced in private. The environment becomes an important issue when it impinges on the security of the personal sphere, the home, the family. The personal, for women, is political. Politics, for women, are significantly expressed in private actions.

From assumption to fact: a whole raft of studies has "scientifically demonstrated" this perception of women's involvement in ecological politics. As Jan McStay and Riley Dunlap write,

> Although there have been numerous studies investigating sources of public concern for environmental quality, few have examined male-female differences. . . . Overall, the results indicate modest support for our prediction that women are more environmentally concerned than are men. . . . However, while females engage in *personal* behaviours on behalf of environmental quality significantly more often than do males, they are less likely than males to engage in *public* behaviours.[1]

From fact to action agenda: this message underpins the whole campaign for green consumerism. Women, the governors of family consumption, can transform their families' buying habits into an environmental campaign, into action for the future of the earth, without ever leaving the private sphere.[2] The concerned female consumer is enticed to purchase green goods through a strong rhetoric of virtue and fear that saturates contemporary advertising with moralizing images of saving the earth for the children. It doesn't really matter if the advertised goods *are* "environmentally friendly" because it's all in the image packaging. For example, in an Ontario Hydro advertisement selling nuclear power (of all things), a grandfather (kindly authority figure, obvious mother substitute) explains to his concerned granddaughter (well-informed for a four-year-old) how nuclear power does not cause acid rain or global warming (presumably, granddaughter can't yet pronounce "uranium tailings"), how the fragile tree they have planted together in an orgy of family values requires this so-called clean energy. The subtitle for the advertisement could well be "nuclear power for nuclear families."

Assumption, fact, and agenda agree: the private sphere is what counts. In green consumerism and the campaign around household ecology, action is located in the private domain; as evidence, one need only recite the eco-litany of saving, scrimping, buying, choosing, mulching, repairing, insulating, economizing, squashing, shoveling, reducing, reusing, and recycling.[3] In the supposedly scientific studies of women's environmental knowledge and participation, action is still located in the private sphere:

lifestyle changes, children's education. The Ontario Advisory Council (with whose quotation this book began)—and many other narratives that take Lois Gibbs of Love Canal and other homemaking eco-crusaders as their origin and idols—eventually includes other realms of environmental activism in the behavioral repertoire of the sensitive woman, like protesting hazardous wastes in the workplace and community, writing letters to politicians and newspapers, and holding public information meetings or demonstrations about environmental hazards.[4] But throughout these narratives, we still see the assumptions that women's concerns are particular, that women's actions are particular, and that women's awareness can be explained away by their apparently obvious epistemic grounding in specific private relations to natural events, or to threateningly unnatural ones.

This motherhood environmentalism, as I choose to call it, is only one of many ways that women are understood to have specific relations, as a group, to ecological awareness, action, or analysis. It is, however, a distressingly common discursive chain even within so-called Left environmentalist circles: women's concerns about nature, even if they have eventual public appearance and impact, boil down to an obvious manifestation of natural protective instincts toward home and family. It is all about threats to the children and self-sacrifice for the sake of future generations. (Sociobiologists would have a wonderful time with this stuff.) It is all about reacting to a crisis and has nothing to do with thinking or reasoning or aesthetics or ethics. It is all about immediate, selfish interests (which, if we are good mothers, are supposed to be identical to those of our children) and nothing to do with commitment to abstract principles like self-determination or democracy or liberty or inherent value or equality or even (bizarrely) ecology.

The neoconservative aroma of this discourse should be quite noticeable: a return to patriarchal and heterosexual "family values" will restore not only a healthy (natural) family but a healthy (natural) planet. This articulation of ecology with neoconservative discourses on the family is truly frightening in its implications for women. It is a naturalized morality tale of private women embodying particularistic, nuclear-family-oriented, antifeminist, heterosexist, and ultimately apolitical interests. Also important, however, are the equally frightening implications of this articulation for nature. The narrative is also a domestic morality tale of an unpredictable and threatening mutant nature in crisis that must be prohibited from entering the sacred home until it is appropriately purified. The earth, remember, must be saved for *human* children; nobody really cares about the rest until it becomes a human health problem.[5]

Yet what concerns me the most is the ease with which this narrative is passed off as feminist and ecological. While I may be filled with respect for the heroic and committed eco-crusaders who populate the now epic tales of women struggling over the health of their children, I think it rather important to consider them critically in relation to both feminist and ecological goals. In feminism, while it is certainly a frequent accident of political life that women may discover the limits of the private sphere as a result of environmentally induced experiential consciousness raising (Lois Gibbs claims, for example, to have discovered feminism through her ecological activism), the insistence in this narrative on the family as the primary site of value and validity mires women in a perpetual contradiction. As Helen MacDonald puts it, "It is concern for the family and community that catapults women into action in the first place, but in a pragmatic sense, home duties may become secondary as women become more active."[6] It is thus an irony of motherhood environmentalism that the home becomes the privileged site of feminine knowledge at the same time as it must be left behind en route to many types of action (especially feminist ones). It is also an irony of motherhood environmentalism that the metaphor for desired public action and outcome—cleaning up the mess—effectively reprivatizes political life and, along with it, naturalizes the gendered relations in which the terms are cast. The equivalential relation between recycling and demonstrating bypasses a problematization of gender; where is the feminism in this?

And where, one must also ask, is the ecology? In this epic form of maternal struggle, from private to (potential) public, women appear as caretakers only of *human* children and communities. There are no hands or ethics extended across species barriers; there are no women valorized for their abilities (experientially grounded or otherwise) to take, for example, the role of a natural Other to defend the right to life of the spotted owl; there is no ecocentrism even considered.[7] Women's knowledges of nature are reduced to a particular story about their children's health, and any other appearance of nature in human life (including the rather obvious fact that humans are part of nature) is rendered invisible and unnecessary to the homemaker's activist consciousness or practice. Of course, there is also a huge contradiction in this aspect of the narrative, as it is from other knowledges of nature—including, but not limited to, ecological science— that ecological activists draw their ideas on the ideal state of nature from which current conditions depart, but the narrative of motherhood environmentalism does not accept these plural knowledges as the "true" roots of women's environmental consciousness.[8] Whether or not ecocentrism is necessary to a "genuine" ecological politics is a question beyond the scope of this work;[9] what must be pointed out is that motherhood environmentalism ignores the question entirely.

I thus find it distressing that this narrative serves rather uncritically as a central one for so many discussions of feminism and ecology. The slippage from a critical position that insists on the problematization of gender relations alongside and through ecological questions to a motherhood position that considers both feminist and ecological any place where the words *women* and *nature* are mentioned together in a sentence is a powerful reminder of the need for a principled discursive vigilance. As Barbara Epstein notes, "In spite of the large numbers of women involved in the environmental movement, and their increasingly prominent roles in leadership, women in the [environmental justice] movement have not made issues of gender central to their political practice in the way people of colour have made issues of race."[10] Even worse, as Joni Seager writes,

> The problem that many feminists find with [motherhood environmentalism] is not that it's "not feminist" in a doctrinaire sense, but rather that it appears to undermine some of the basic understandings of Western feminism, and it comes uncomfortably close to countering the efforts of feminists who seek to reorder private and public gender assumptions and conventionally defined sex roles.[11]

As a discourse born of feminist politics (particularly situated in time, space, and intellectual/political traditions, of course), and necessarily distinct from motherhood environmentalism, ecofeminism, one would think, would retain a critical edge in the context of the both overt and veiled conservatism of the surrounding gendered and natured landscape. After all, as Karen Warren writes, "Eco-feminists take as their central project the unpacking of the connections between the *twin* oppressions of women and nature."[12] But evaluations of ecofeminism's critical successes have been profoundly mixed:

> Ecofeminism is a very important, energetic, and real social movement. I feel allied to it in many crucial ways—both as a critical project and in an emotional kind of way. . . . I think that ecofeminism, and the conceptions of nature being developed within this broad and complicated term, makes sense in a world under particular kinds of threats.[13]

> It had been my earnest hope that ecofeminism would draw on the best of social theory and meld it with radical concepts in ecology to produce a genuinely antihierarchical, enlightened, and broadly oppositional movement,

one that could oppose sexism and the many forces that are at work in destroying the biosphere and trammelling human freedom. . . . Recent ecofeminist literature does not fulfil this promise at all.[14]

Ecofeminist theory creates progressive dialogue which plays an important role in broadening the policy agenda of non-governmental and governmental institutions, reframes environmental issues to recognize gender implications, and questions the structure of the decision-making body.[15]

As a distinct stream or tendency within the women's movement, I think [ecofeminism] should die a quiet death.[16]

As these passages suggest, ecofeminism has become a movement and a theory capable of eliciting a broad range of responses. To some, it is vital, creative, and integrative; it is capable of confronting a wide range of social and environmental problems and offers a profound challenge to contemporary relations in which women and nature find themselves similarly, and relatedly, oppressed. To others, it is "dead in the water": reactionary, divisive, even destructive. To many of its advocates, ecofeminism is seen as an innovative response to contemporary relations of domination, a force with which to negotiate a new era of gendered and natured relations. To many of its critics, ecofeminism is seen as reinforcing, or even reproducing, the types of domination against which it purportedly struggles.

Of course, in its often noted diversity, ecofeminism contains all of these things at once: it is simultaneously innovative and reactionary, energetic and moribund. Paradoxical as this characterization may appear at first glance, it is both possible and necessary to identify the elements or *moments* of ecofeminist politics that should "die a quiet death" and to rescue from their ashes the promises of ecofeminism. Broadly speaking, ecofeminism is a movement and a current of analysis that attempts to link feminist struggles with ecological struggles; the range of possibilities within this general mandate is, therefore, considerable. There is much to be said in favor of ecofeminism's enunciation of gendered relations to nature. Not only is nature an important moment in feminist discourse, but gender is an important element in the social and political creation of nature. To understand the ways in which nature and gender are wielded as discursive constructs, to investigate the ways in which the oppression of women and the domination of nature are imbricated in a whole host of destructive relations and practices, and to create an oppositional framework capable of addressing their interrelations, it seems vital to explore the connections that ecofeminists examine between women/feminism and nature/ecology.

But these insights need to be unpacked from the considerable baggage that ecofeminism tends to carry. In large part, this baggage persists because ecofeminists (ironically) have been less than vigilant in their questioning of the gender and nature assumptions that are fundamental to the Western discursive landscape and that appear so unproblematically in motherhood environmentalism. Heroic mothers defending home and hearth against a nature deformed by multinationalist corporate practice may be a compelling story, but it is not the stuff of which good feminist or ecological critique is necessarily born. In this particular narrative, part of what is missing is, in Lee Quinby's terms, the interrogative element, an insistence on problematizing the whole ensemble of discursive relations that surrounds the phenomenon in question.[17] Also crucially missing is the democratic element, an insistence on bringing to public debate and contest precisely these discursive relations, in the hope of sloughing off their skin of naturalness. An ecofeminism that is both feminist and ecological must therefore, in my view, place at the center of its existence a commitment to good theory and good politics, in concert.

Entrance into Ecofeminism

The story about ecofeminism that I want to tell in this book concerns its existence as a body of political theory. My narrative begins with the premise that ecofeminism contains an inherently democratic political vision, even if that vision is not stated as explicitly as it might be. With this in mind, ecofeminism needs to be located in the context of contemporary democratic theory more generally in order to understand both how ecofeminism might be enriched by a conversation with democratic political principles and how it might contribute significantly to this ongoing conversation. My interest is thus to further ecofeminism as a politics, specifically a democratic politics, and to contribute more broadly to a democratic project that should, in my view, incorporate some of the insights of ecofeminism.

With this agenda in mind, I will examine some of the promises and problems of ecofeminism as a democratic political theory, with a focus on what I consider to be one of the most important tensions running through contemporary democratic struggles: identity's relation to democracy. It is in the context of the proliferation of democratic social movement struggles that ecofeminism appeared as a political vision focused on a particular kind of identification; it is because of ecofeminism's reliance on the language of identity that its political project is currently limited; it is in an interrogation of the democratic desires that lie behind identity that the promise of ecofeminist politics may be formulated; and it is through the kinds of democratic debate that have arisen as a result of critiques of identity politics that a revitalized ecofeminism may be shaped. In other words, this is a story about the past, present, and (I hope) future development of ecofeminism as a democratic theory, from its origins in identity politics to my desires for it as a post-identitarian, critical democratic project.

The book is divided into two sections. Part I discusses the development of identity within ecofeminism, the social movement context in which this development has taken place, problems it has created for ecofeminist theory and practice, and ways in which a focus on identity can be reoriented, via selected insights from Jacques Lacan and his political successors, to a more useful focus on radical democracy. In one sense, this deconstructive work is a prerequisite to the reconstructive work that begins in Part II; in another sense, it is a story unto itself concerning the ways in which ecofeminism is both produced by and contributes to a particular social and political milieu.

Part II explores points of transformative promise within ecofeminism that are highlighted when it is viewed as a radical democratic project; specifically, it is organized around a discussion of four tensions in ecofeminism that appear through a radically democratic lens. This discussion has us turn our attention from the obvious (and notably essentialist) limitations of much ecofeminist theory toward its movement in the direction of a broad and relatively sophisticated analysis of gender and nature in politics. It is this implicitly political element that strikes me as ecofeminism's greatest promise; the democratic politicization of gender and nature suggests a process of challenging hegemonic identifications, of opening up new spaces of social and political (and ecological) life to scrutiny and debate, and of tackling the discursive relations in which problematic gendered and ecological relations are embedded.

More specifically, Part I of this book is a story about ecofeminism told through its emphasis on identity politics, an emphasis that is largely a hangover from the U.S. cultural feminism from which it took much of its initial shape.[18] Notably, despite its official rejection of and multiplications beyond cultural feminism, ecofeminism has tended to reproduce, even magnify, fundamental problems in cultural feminist narratives about the relations between women and nature. These identity narratives for women and nature must be understood in the context of their appearance as representing a fundamentally democratic desire; at the same time, they are, in the context of the oft cited essentialist and reductionist limits of identity politics, highly problematic and must be rethought.

I state here (and will repeat) that this is only one story about ecofeminism and that there are many others that should also be told. But this account's specificity should not be a reason for its rejection. Throughout my interactions with ecofeminism, I have chafed—as I have seen many others do—against the narrow construction of identity (maternal and otherwise) that underlies ecofeminist attempts to combine a feminist with an environmental politics to provide a route to the liberation of both. While I think it is crucial to recognize and act from moments of political affinity grounded in the relation between the oppression of women and the domination of nature, I find it misguided to consider their coalition (as some ecofeminists have tended to do) in a way that reduces both women and nature to a very particular point of connection. Such a reduction essentializes women and domesticates nature, as if gender were a natural product and as if nature were describable in terms of particular cultural conventions of femininity.

Although ecofeminists such as Carolyn Merchant and Karen Warren[19] have developed a tradition of distinguishing ecofeminism from other feminisms and of differentiating among different kinds of ecofeminism (a tradition I will uphold as a crucial part of the story), it is my contention that most ecofeminist writing is imbricated in a cultural feminist logic of identity politics in which ontological claims to an essence—whether that essence is seen as biological or social—are understood necessarily to precede political claims. The particular form of this logic in ecofeminism derives from cultural feminist claims regarding women's "special" relation to nature; I will describe this logic and its procession through diverse ecofeminist visions in chapters 1 and 3. But it is also important to consider that this particular political focus on identity, however currently chafing, has both context and meaning. In my view, it is out of a profoundly democratic desire that social movements—ecofeminism not the least—have placed such an emphasis on identity within the context of a late capitalist deemphasis on the state as a container for politics. This focus is the subject of chapters 2 and 4, in which I weave (to use the faithful ecofeminist verb) my story about ecofeminism with a larger one about social movements, identity, nature, and democracy. With this broader narrative in mind, ecofeminism's problematic reliance on identity can be understood as a manifestation of a much larger democratic desire that can be rechanneled rather than as an essential limitation.

It is thus my hope in writing this book that ecofeminism can simultaneously cling to its liberatory democratic agenda and reject the identity politics with which it has generally entered democratic debate. To do this, I will argue, ecofeminism needs to take a close look at the limitations of its static notion of identity, especially its related claim to speak of and as nature, and to reject the notion of Cartesian subjectivity upon which this "speaking identity" is based. The exploration of a more flexible, open-ended version of subjectivity, such as the one offered in Lacanian-inspired psychoanalysis, in which a subject is constituted imperfectly *in* discourse rather than transparently prior *to* discourse, suggests a way out of ecofeminism's crisis of identity politics and points the way to a radical democratic vision.

The radical democratic writing of Ernesto Laclau and Chantal Mouffe, upon which I rely heavily in the new ecofeminist reading in Part II, is based on a notion of political subjectivity in which the subject is imperfectly constituted in discourse through the taking-up of multiple subject positions, discursive spaces describing shifting moments of symbolic representation derived from a temporary common understanding.[20] The categories "women" and "nature," in this formulation, appear as common (and possibly ironic) representations through which democratic politics can progress, rather than as statements about an inherent, oppositional identity. More generally, Laclau and Mouffe's political vision concerns the ways in which democracy constitutes politics itself as a perpetually open project: one can't "get democracy right," for the progressive inclusion of different voices undermines the fullness of the commonality through which their inclusion was solicited in the first place. Theirs is thus a vision of constant democratic movement: between conflict and coalition, between the common and the particular, between public and private, and between the political and the extra- or prepolitical.

For radical democratic politics, the loss of a sure grounding in a transparent identity requires a thorough analysis of the ways in which such a politics can be democratic, the ways in which the "death of the subject" is not a nihilistic statement of impossibility and inevitable lack (as many ecofeminist and other commentators seem to assume),[21] but a statement of political openness and democratic potential. Specifically, such an analysis includes an understanding of the tensions between antagonism (conflicts between or within subject positions) and equivalence (coalitional moments of affinity); between universality (the process by which a democratic common good is represented) and particularity (the moment at which the common good is constantly shown to be in need of reinterpretation); and between public life (the moment of the creation of a common political world) and private life (the moment outside publicity from which politics draws). Perhaps most importantly, such an analysis reveals the points where democracy experiences its own limits, i.e., the appearance, in Lacanian terms, of the Real, the unsymbolizable kernel around which discourse circulates but which it can never capture, including, as I argue here, nature itself.

Ecofeminism, while benefiting from such a perspective of perpetual openness and tension, also adds something very specific to these ideas about radical democracy. As a movement that has from its inception attempted to capture a moment of commonality between feminism and ecology, between women and nature as subject positions, ecofeminism has long revealed the importance of affinities within democratic conversations, a promising version of the equivalence that Laclau and Mouffe emphasize so strongly. In addition, ecofeminism points to the ways in which its specific agenda, the development of alternative relations to nature, would affect the shape of a radical democratic politics itself. Suggesting the need for distinctions among moments of human (and nonhuman) life, ecofeminism— although often reductive in its constructions of nature and women—contains within it the seeds of a radical democratic politics that includes both.

The point of this book is thus to show the specific trajectory of ecofeminism as a politics toward a radical democratic vision and the more general movement of radical democracy toward a horizon informed by the specific struggles of ecofeminism. Through the conversation between the two currents, space is created for the interdependent development of both. It is the intention of this book to develop this democratic interchange, to bring the subject of ecofeminism to a broader political quest.

PART I

On the Subject

of Ecofeminism

1

A Genealogy of Ecofeminism

I first encountered the word *ecofeminism* in 1987 when I was a master's student doing research for a term paper in a course in feminist sociology. Freshly arrived in the big city of Toronto, which I then perceived to be completely devoid of nature (I grew up in Victoria on Vancouver Island, where nature may not have been more plentiful but was certainly bigger), I was absolutely thrilled to discover that a word already existed to represent my deepest personal and political desire, the inclusion of an environmentalist perspective in feminist theory. I craved a language that would describe my growing sense that nature must be an important consideration in any feminist political vision; I remember devouring the first ecofeminist text I encountered—*Green Paradise Lost*, I think it was[1]—at the expense of the readings on public policy on which I was supposed to be focusing.

But the exhilaration I felt as a new convert was over quite soon, and I have never again felt quite so strongly that I belonged in ecofeminism, despite my increasing commitment to feminist ecological politics and theory. Certainly the gap between desire and realization is inevitable; certainly my sense of ecofeminism never being quite right has motivated me to spend years of my life practicing intervention into the discourse (which makes the desire/realization gap fundamental to democratic life, as I will describe at length later on). There are also more specific reasons for my ecofeminist malaise, almost all of them concerning the constructions of the relationship between women and nature that lie at the core of this particular feminist ecological project.

By no means do I suggest that ecofeminists, as a bloc, fall unthinking and unthoughtful prey to the neoconservative rhetoric of motherhood environmentalism, to the argument that women are better suited than men to cleaning up nature as an extension of their biology and their separate-but-equal household responsibilities. Indeed, it is because of ecofeminism's stated critique of such ideological linkages that I have remained involved and interested in its development. It has become increasingly clear to me over the years, however, that many ecofeminists do engage in a particular political logic, identity politics, that makes me singularly uncomfortable. Especially when combined with their inevitable forays into the place of nature in feminist and other politics, the tendency of many ecofeminists to place primary significance on identity opens up the real possibility of a kind of biological reductionism and essentialism that any feminism, in my view, ought to spend much of its time debunking.

Here's an example of what I understand as ecofeminism's logic of identity, which comes from a very recent (and generally very good) work by Carolyn Merchant:

> The word ecology derives from the Greek word "oikos," meaning house. Ecology, then, is the science of the household—the Earth's household. The connection between the Earth and the house has historically been mediated by women.[2]

In a book otherwise devoted to exploring a fairly full range of women's relations to nature and ecological activism, this passage proceeds to reduce this diversity to a highly problematic (if now rather familiar) relationship: ecology becomes home economics, the planet becomes a household, and women's complex relations to both of the above become, simply, "mediating." Which women are doing the mediating, what natures are involved in the mediation, and who is referred to by "women" and "nature" are questions left unasked, and Merchant (like many other ecofeminists) does not seem to feel compelled to interrogate them; the solid identity "women" becomes important through a specific relationship to a particular metaphoric "nature." This relationship is repeated and naturalized as the key narrative through which feminist relations to environmentalism are understood. Even if the relations producing the gendered specificity of this mediating labor are eventually called into question (as they are in places in Merchant's text), the fact remains that it is from this specificity that a primary and strongly normative relation between feminism and ecology is created.

In ecofeminism, the fact of being a woman is understood to lie at the base of one's experience of ecological degradation; of one's interests in ecological protection, preservation, and reconstruction; and of one's "special" ecological consciousness. Whether the important elements of that "being" are seen to reside in biological, social, ascribed, or imposed factors is immaterial to my argument; the crucial thing is that identity, similarity, and belonging to a specific group are the primary foci of political speech and the basis of political legitimacy, and that the achievement of the freedom to express that identity without oppression is a key political goal (as opposed to, say, a focus on individuality and a desire to put specific identity aside to achieve a common good, an equally problematic but nonetheless different political logic). While an obvious result of identity politics is an exclusionary logic—"you can't speak about this because you do not belong to the group"—there are other, deeper problems with the model. For example, identities are inevitably partial, and the relevant social categories on which identity politics are based can go only so far to describe a person; the reduction of any self to a list of categories replicates many of the problems that identity politics set out to address, including the socially experienced limits of the identity categories themselves. I will outline what I consider the logic and limits of identity politics later; what must be said at the outset is that ecofeminists, in basing their political specificity on an identitarian women's experience of nature or environmental degradation or on a specifically women's set of issues or principles or metaphors, assume a correspondence among ontology, epistemology, and politics—an identity politics—that reduces the relations between feminism and ecology to a highly problematic group experience for women and nature.

But I'm getting ahead of myself in the story. It's clearly the case that Merchant and others took this identitarian women/nature relationship from somewhere else, and it is the point of this chapter to tell a story about these origins. Ecofeminism claims originating sparks in a number of places— Ellen Swallow's home ecology, Lois Gibbs's struggles at Love Canal, feminist and maternalist pacifism and antimilitarism in North America and Europe, and the obvious gender gaps in environmental philosophy[3]—but it is my contention that ecofeminist theory has taken its specifically identitarian formulation of the relations between feminism and ecology from the radical and cultural feminist debates on nature of the 1970s and 1980s. While identity politics encompass much more than this debate (including democracy, as I will discuss in chapter 2), it is in their ideas of nature that some of the stickiest issues for ecofeminist identity are located.

Radical and Cultural Feminisms on "The Nature Question"

In 1974, French feminist Françoise d'Eaubonne published the word *eco-féminisme* for the first time to refer to the movement by women necessary to save the planet.[4] Despite the fact that almost every ecofeminist author who traces the movement back that far refers to this origin, d'Eaubonne's writing circulated in a different and particular context, and it was not until considerably later that the term *ecofeminism* came to refer to a distinct stream within U.S. feminist politics. Although it is vital to note other influences—as Rosi Braidotti, Ewa Charkiewicz, Sabine Häusler, and Saskia Wieringa observe,[5] these include ideas that were also present in the "natural womanhood" discourses of Nazi Germany—a far more important historical origin of ecofeminism is what has been called "the nature question" in the radical and cultural feminisms of the 1970s and 1980s U.S. political landscape; it is from there that the first authors who called themselves ecofeminists (or who otherwise specifically problematized ecological relations alongside gendered ones) took their language, logic, passions, and limitations.[6]

In 1974, Sherry Ortner wrote what were to become fighting words for a significant part of a generation of U.S. feminist theorists and activists:

> What could there be in the generalized structure and conditions of existence, common to every culture, that would lead every culture to place a lower value upon women? . . . My thesis is that woman is being identified with—or, if you will, seems to be a symbol of—something that every culture devalues, something that every culture defines as being of a lower order of existence than itself. Now it seems that there is only one thing that would fit that description, and that is "nature" in the most generalized sense.[7]

Ortner's project was to show how this (male) culturally defined connection was the universal underlying a range of misogynies, how woman's status in the middle position on a scale from culture down to nature or her role as a mediator between the two led to cultural assumptions and institutional mechanisms circumscribing her activities in the world. Ortner's political agenda was abundantly clear: "Ultimately, both men and women can and must be equally involved in projects of creativity and transcendence. Only then will women be seen as aligned with culture, in culture's ongoing dialectic with nature."[8]

Compare Ortner to d'Eaubonne: two radically opposed viewpoints in a single year. Where Ortner sought to eradicate the woman/nature connection, d'Eaubonne celebrated it as a means of revaluing those aspects of life degraded and distorted through centuries of patriarchal cultural and economic domination:

> Therefore, with a society at last in the feminine gender meaning non-power (and not power-to-the-women), it would be proved that no other human group could have brought about the ecological revolution; because none other was so directly concerned at all levels.

> And the planet in the feminine gender would become green again for all.[9]

D'Eaubonne's celebration of nature and the feminine was not unique; neither was Ortner's rejection of them. The juxtaposition of their views, however, makes it clear that the 1970s saw a particular rift developing in feminist thought: whether to welcome or renounce connections to nature. The polarized terms of the debate (and the failure to question the split itself) stemmed from a particular current of analysis, one developed largely if not entirely under the rubric of U.S. radical feminism. While the "nature question" has not always been the central preoccupation of radical feminism, as Alice Echols documents,[10] the line of continuity running from early radical feminist analyses of sex as class to cultural feminism and ecofeminism has been drawn through a terrain emphasizing difference. In turn, this focus on difference, largely based on analyses of reproduction, has exposed nature as a crucial trajectory of debate.

Following the lead of first-wave feminists and later theorists such as Simone de Beauvoir, 1970s radical feminist analyses focused on women's differences from men. This focus was born in part from a dissatisfaction with the ability of other progressive movements (notably the Students for a Democratic Society and other emerging socialist organizations) to incorporate women's concerns and in part from an increasing skepticism toward the equal rights orientation of groups such as the National Organization for Women. As exemplified in the following excerpt from the "Redstockings Manifesto," the agenda of these early analyses was to show the distinctly political and politically distinct character of women's oppression as women:

> Women are an oppressed class. Our oppression is total, affecting every facet of our lives. We are exploited as sex objects, breeders, domestic servants, and cheap labor. . . .

We identify the agents of our oppression as men. Male supremacy is the oldest, most basic form of domination. All other forms of exploitation and oppression (racism, capitalism, imperialism, etc.) are extensions of male supremacy.[11]

To find the origin of this primary male oppression of females, many radical feminist theorists turned, like Ortner, to the one thing that seemed constant across a variety of culturally specific manifestations of patriarchy: women's role in reproduction. Perhaps the most influential work of this genre, which shows both the grounding of feminist theory in Marxist concepts such as sex as class and the political agenda of exposing the oppression of women as women and not just incidentally as female members of other oppressed groups, was Shulamith Firestone's *The Dialectic of Sex*, published in 1970. In it, she documented the "natural origins" of patriarchy: "The natural reproductive difference between the sexes led directly to the first division of labor at the origins of class, as well as furnishing the paradigm of caste (discrimination based on biological characteristics)."[12] At the same time, however, Firestone asserted that there is a fundamental difference between humanity and nature; she wrote passionately that the eradication of women's oppression required the transcendence of this biologically derived division of labor. Her solution lay in "seizure of the means of reproduction," a revolution of women against the tyranny of biology made possible by claiming developing reproductive technologies. Her revolution, like Marx's, was based on the idea of eradicating the material conditions producing difference:

> Just as the end goal of socialist revolution was not only the elimination of class *privilege* but of the economic class *distinction* itself, so the end goal of feminist revolution must be, unlike that of the first feminist movement, not just the elimination of male *privilege* but of the sex *distinction* itself: genital differences between human beings would no longer matter culturally.[13]

The idea of biological difference as the source of women's oppression and the erasure of this oppression through the use of reproductive technologies generated considerable debate. Some radical feminists were justifiably skeptical about the liberatory possibility of artificial insemination and other reproductive technologies and concentrated on changing the form of reproductive organization, rather than the fact of reproduction itself. As Ti-Grace Atkinson put it, the question was not about biology, but about how "this biological classification . . . bec[a]me a political classification."[14]

Marge Piercy's influential 1976 novel, *Woman on the Edge of Time*, represented an interesting compromise between a biological and a sociological analysis. Her utopian world was organized according to a principle of genderlessness, and she suggested that the disconnection of women and reproduction was a necessary sacrifice made by women.[15] This move represented an interesting shift from Firestone's position but retained crucial elements of her analysis, including a certain faith in the liberatory potential of reproductive technologies. As one of the characters from Piercy's utopian world of Mattapoisett explains:

> It was part of women's long revolution. When we were breaking up the old hierarchies. Finally, there was that one thing we had to give up, too, the only power we ever had, in return for no more power for everyone. The original production: the power to give birth. Cause as long as we were biologically enchained, we'd never be equal. And males would never be humanized to be loving and tender.[16]

At the other end of the spectrum in the nature debates lay Mary Daly's "a-mazing" text, *Gyn/Ecology*. As far as Daly was concerned, reproductive technologies of all sorts were nothing short of misogynist violence and all arguments for women to renounce nature and biology nothing short of "male methods of mystification."[17] Taking her cue partly from d'Eaubonne's call for a feminist eco-revolution, Daly sought to cut through the "mind/spirit/body pollution inflicted through patriarchal myth and language on all levels," including their direct threat "to terminate all sentient life on this planet."[18] For her, the relationship among women and nature and biology was simple: where women embody the essence of life in all forms, patriarchal culture threatens to kill it through a legion of violent methods from clitoridectomy to language (she classifies these as erasure, reversal, polarization, and dividing and conquering). "The tree of life," she wrote, "has been replaced by the necrophilic symbol of a dead body hanging on dead wood" [i.e., Christ];[19] what women (or, rather, Hags) must do to dis-cover their inherent love for earth is break through the masks of patriarchal dis-ease and reclaim an inherently female integral identity.

Despite its many critics, Daly's text signaled a larger trend in 1970s feminism. Many feminists were beginning to explore the idea that women's difference from men might itself be a source of strength and that reproduction and nature might hold the key to women's power, not just women's oppression. In both European (particularly French) and North American feminisms, increasing dissatisfaction with what Yolande Cohen has since called a politics of assimilation,[20] a feminist agenda based on the achievement of equality in the traditionally male domains of politics and economics, led to a process in which alternatives to this so-called patriarchal culture were explored and celebrated. Women, an oppressed majority, were to look to their own experiences of nurturance, of caring, of connection as a way of beginning an affirmative culture outside the destructive proscriptions of "male-stream" society.[21]

The idea of this cultural feminism was to create an affirmative space for the creation of woman-centered literature, art, politics, and other pursuits in which women's differences from men would result in radically new modes of expression. The reasoning for this was twofold. First, this woman's culture was seen as a safe place for women to find and express their difference outside patriarchal definitions of quality or competence and to formulate from this exploration a distinct women's episteme. Second, this alternative culture was seen as the basis of a more authentic feminist politics, a site from which new women's definitions of political and social possibility would emerge to oppose hegemonic patriarchal conceptions of knowledge and politics. Women would find, or perhaps create, their true identity in spaces carefully separated from the distorting influences of patriarchy. New relations to nature were an integral part of this culture; women's "special" knowledges of reproduction and their experiences of mediating between nature and culture were part of their difference from men and thus needed to be discovered and freed.

In the midst of all of these "nature" debates, radical women of color and lesbians (among others) were becoming increasingly vocal about some of the shortcomings of radical feminist theory. In addition to overt instances of feminist racism and homophobia (black women being accused of false consciousness for allying with black men on some issues, lesbians being called enemies of feminism for simply being vocal), a feminist analysis that focused primarily on the dynamics of sex and gender—formulated as women's oppression as women by men—provided little space for an analysis of the dynamics of racism and heterosexism. Audre Lorde was especially critical of Mary Daly: "Why are her goddess-images only white, western-european, judeo-christian?"[22]

In the context of increasing fragmentation over issues of race, class, and sexuality, the version of radical feminism that focused on the creation of a women's "natural" culture eventually won preeminence. According to Echols, cultural feminism promised to unite a movement torn apart by differences among women: the creation of a "gynocracy," a world organized according to feminine principles, was a project that all women could participate in and consider their own. It also promised concrete gains despite the backlash against feminism: "Even if women's political, economic, and social gains were reversed, cultural feminism held out the possibility that women could build a culture, a space, uncontaminated by patriarchy."[23] In fact, as Josephine Donovan notes, lesbianism moved from a position of critique to become—with a little bit of conceptual massage and expansion from Adrienne Rich—one of the supposedly natural elements of women's culture and identity; as heterosexuality was one of the primary sites in which women were oppressed, becoming a woman-centered woman was a way of creating the conditions for freeing essential identity.[24]

Not surprisingly, cultural feminism turned to nature, both to underscore women's undeniable connections to each other irrespective of race, class, and sexual orientation and to define a difference around which to articulate a revolutionary femininity. Works such as Firestone's and Ortner's, despite their radically antinature conclusions, had already laid the groundwork for making this connection; Daly had turned it on its head to provide a template. Nature, in cultural feminism, referred to the experience of reproduction, the continuity of generations, the creation of life, the inherent bodily connection to the planet. Where men experienced separation from biology, disdaining the body and the material world (and oppressing women) en route to a necrophilic transcendence of nature, women, by virtue of their reproductive labor, lived their lives through nature, through a grounding in the body and the cycles of life.

Enter the Goddess

As Merchant notes, the feminist discourses on spirituality and theology that emerged in the early days of cultural feminism were also important to the development of specifically ecofeminist theory. First, the publication of a number of books exploring ancient matriarchies read of the split between male culture and female nature as *the* narrative of women's oppression, with the logical conclusion being to revalue the latter as a founding act of cultural creation. Merlin Stone's *When God Was A Woman*, one of the most detailed and contested explorations in this vein, investigated the development of goddess-centered cultures as a history of the interrelationships among their respect for reproduction, the high status of women in their social organizations, and the predominance of female divinities. While her project was overtly one of denaturalizing (Judeo-)Christian[25] conceptions of the relationships among God, man, woman, and nature, she ended up showing how in fact these conceptions were the result of perverting the connections made between women and nature in ancient goddess-centered religions.[26] The conclusion reached by many readers of

Stone's book was that these connections, twisted and destroyed by five thousand years or so of patriarchy, were in fact the utopian state from which humanity has deviated and to which it must return.

The logic of Stone's narrative is quite revealing. Although not original with her, there is a line of reasoning running through her accounts of ancient deities and civilizations that clearly states that women's lives were better when reproduction was respected by men. This does not mean just human reproduction, but also the reproduction of all life—the cycles of birth, death, and regeneration; the seasons; the lifespan. Her story of the destruction of ancient pastoral matriarchies by northern patriarchal invaders is itself a story of a "fall from grace," with all of its notions of innocence, utopia, and the effect of destructive knowledges on humanity's gardens of childhood; this time, however, the evil is patriarchy, the devaluation of women and women's relations to God.

The search for historical origins for the patriarchal degradation of women led to a considerable emphasis on tracing women's status—especially their relations to a degraded nature—in Western religion and philosophy. Rosemary Radford Ruether's 1975 book, *New Woman/New Earth*, was one of the first to outline explicitly the destructive significance of patriarchal religion for both women and nature; for Ruether, women in patriarchal societies are the primary symbolic repositories for all that such cultures see as wrong with the world, all that should be ignored or cut out of human life, especially nature.[27] With an interesting nod to the absence of a gender analysis in ecological thought, she writes,

> Since women in Western culture have been traditionally identified with nature, and nature, in turn, has been seen as an object of domination by man (males), it would seem almost a truism that the mentality that regarded the natural environment as an object of domination drew upon imagery and attitudes based on male domination of women. . . . Sexism and ecological destructiveness are related in the symbolic patterns of the patriarchal consciousness . . . [and] they take intensive socioeconomic form in modern industrial society.[28]

While Ruether does not suggest that women should find an oppositional or revolutionary consciousness in this symbolic placement next to nature—she is actually quite adamant that women should be extremely suspicious of anything that smacks of planetary housework or Mother Earth romanticism—she is very clear that patriarchy is historically and essentially antiecological and that ecological health requires the elimination of patriarchy. Calling for a genderless and quite materialist utopia (and predating object relations in her discussion of the relationship between parenting and caring for the earth), she still, ironically, creates a narrative by which the primary logic of women's oppression in Western societies operates through their conceptual linkage with nature and vice versa.

It is, from here, only a small step into an identity politics of gender and nature. One of the most influential and moving accounts to draw together elements of this woman/nature "herstory" and a specific revaluation of women's identitarian connections to nature is Susan Griffin's *Woman and Nature: The Roaring Inside Her.*[29] The book, an epic prose poem juxtaposing the development of religious, philosophical, and scientific discourses about nature with similar ideas on women, was written in two voices that Griffin describes as "the voice of authority—a male and patriarchal voice—attempt[ing] over and over again to dominate the female voice of the body, of forests, of wind, of mountains, of horses, of cows, of the earth."[30]

A very important shift occurred with Griffin's book. Whereas Ortner and earlier theorists saw women as mediators between nature and culture, as beings who, by virtue of their reproductive capacities and duties, were assigned natural status, and whereas Ruether saw naturalness as an ideology historically imposed on women and environmental degradation as justified by patriarchy, Griffin wrote as if nature were female and women would be natural if left to their own earth-loving devices. In this, Griffin's argument was quite similar to Daly's, but the centrality of nature to the analysis of women's oppression pushes her book into a different category, I think. To Griffin, woman represented nature not simply because of cultural assignment but because of an ongoing feminine embodied knowledge of nature that is a source of patriarchal jealousy and domination and that has remained "true" despite centuries of fundamentally misguided and destructive phallic attempts to capture, categorize, and subdue it. There is a spirit of woman and it is nature; where Daly would have women listen to other (Amazon) women to hear the truth of their identity, Griffin would have women listen to "the light in us," to a nature that has always been more ready to speak to and as women. "The earth is my sister; I love her daily grace, her silent daring, and how loved I am"; to find liberation from patriarchy and ecological devastation, Griffin advises, women must listen to their sister.[31]

It is easy to see the attraction of this text in the context of cultural feminism's development. If male culture is the problem, then arguing for the necessity of constructing or revealing a way of being somehow outside male culture suggests a reaffirmation of its opposite, the oppressed female

nature. Indeed, this notion of seeing nature as the terrain of female consciousness, with the corollary position of seeing femininity as natural, was
taken up by a number of feminists trying to build a female culture.
Women, they asserted, need to look to their nature, which is part of (and
therefore equivalent to) nature in general, in order to achieve women's and
the planet's liberation.

But there is also a second dimension of the women/nature question running through the works of Griffin and others. As an example, here is
Kathleen Barry's call for feminists to transcend their differences:

> We must look to our matriarchal past for guidance in defining a culture that
> is a logical extension of nature. With the essence of motherhood and a
> sense of the preservation of life imprinted in our genes, matrilineal descent
> will naturally become the organization of the society we envision.[32]

Especially in Barry, but also in Griffin and Daly, there is an interesting
tension between the need to look for a matriarchal past, thus implying that
women's identity is something to be achieved or at least uncovered, and
the claim that motherhood and ecological knowledge are imprinted in the
genes and presumably are readily (even naturally) accessible to everyday
consciousness. Thus, while women are supposed to look to nature for
knowledge, they may find that such knowledge of nature isn't too deeply
buried; nature is, at the very least, a sister with whose language women are
intimately acquainted. Women's nature thus becomes equivalent to nature
in general and is the thing that feminist activity should retrieve into political consciousness.

This cultural feminist construction of nature, emerging from and intertwined with explorations into reproduction and women's spirituality,
shaped both the political context and the analytical approach of ecofeminism. The view that nature was an epistemically transparent and positive
part of women's culture was clearly on the political agenda of a variety of
feminist thinkers, eco- and otherwise. The political significance of difference, especially a natural version of difference grounded in an episteme
beyond patriarchal culture, was also clear. Specifically, there was an assumption that an oppositional movement must be located in an alternative
culture, a new consciousness—or rather, in a revitalized old consciousness
suppressed by hierarchical and patriarchal power relations. There was a
strong notion that certain groups—i.e., men—have constructed human
value in terms opposite to a primal, organic state in their quest toward
transcendence, disembodiment, and the possession of "power over." And

there was a belief that conceptual structures—hierarchy, value, separation, independence—are the root of the problem and need to be remedied through a claiming of alternative experience. At the heart of that alternative was nature.

Ecofeminism and the Quest for Roots

Other than the often cited work of d'Eaubonne, it is difficult to pinpoint exactly the moment where ecofeminism first emerged as a current of thought distinct from cultural feminism. Indeed, Griffin's *Woman and Nature*, Daly's *Gyn/Ecology*, and Ruether's *New Woman/New Earth* are often cited as the first genuinely ecofeminist texts. Certainly, Ynestra King's 1981 manifesto "The Eco-Feminist Imperative" was also a key text that marked ecofeminism as both a distinct theoretical framework for feminist ecology and a distinct activist possibility for feminist writings on nature. King, though differing from Griffin and Daly in her emphasis on political activism, largely agreed with their diagnostic focus on patriarchal culture and their ground of resistance in women's identity:

> We believe that a culture against nature is a culture against women. We know we must get out from under the feet of men as they go about their projects of violence. In pursuing these projects men deny and dominate both women and nature. It is time to reconstitute our culture in the name of that nature, and of peace and freedom, and it is women who can show the way. We have to be the voice of the invisible, of nature who cannot speak for herself in the political arenas of our society.[33]

At the base of many early ecofeminist accounts of the origins of the interstructured identities and oppressions of women and nature (and apparent in a number of subsequent ones as well) is a notion of hierarchical dualism, an elaborate narrative of the development of difference into a hegemonic, patriarchal, antinature strategy. As Val Plumwood observes in a review essay on ecofeminist themes, in this approach "the problem for both women and Nature is their place as part of a set of dualisms which have their origins in classical philosophy and which can be traced through a complex history to the present."[34] The focus of these founding works is the historical polarization of humanity from nature, men from women, mind from body, and reason from emotion in the philosophical and religious development of ideals of transcendent humanity. As Ruether writes in a passage fairly typical of this analytic stream,

All the basic dualities—the alienation of the mind from the body; the alienation of the self from the objective world; the subjective retreat of the individual, alienated from the social community; the domination or rejection of nature by spirit—these all have roots in the apocalyptic-Platonic religious heritage of classical Christianity. But the alienation of the masculine from the feminine is the primary sexual symbolism that sums up all these alienations.[35]

Clearly, a number of cultural feminist assumptions inform this approach, notably the idea that the original difference informing the development of all others is sex. In addition, echoing Beauvoir is the notion that the supposedly lower halves of each dualism are not Other in their own right but are instead constructed as Other, as the negative reflection of true, transcendent humans. As Plumwood describes this process, in the philosophical logic of the operation of hierarchical dualism, these lower halves are also constructed as polarized from the upper halves. In addition, their existences are valued solely in terms of their instrumental value, as reflected in contemporary notions of so-called resources, a construction in which nature only has merit in terms of its use or exchange value to humans, and in definitions of women in terms of their relationships to men (as wives, mothers, virgins, whores, chattel).

What is interesting in these ecofeminist accounts of dualism is their transference of cultural feminist narratives of the historical oppression of women to ideas on nature. The form of the originating, sexual dualism in which "women's nature" is oppressed by "men's culture" is subtly transformed into a statement about all nature. Where Ortner wrote about cultural constructions of women as occupying particular locations in relation to children, the particular nature out of which male humans develop transcendence, many early ecofeminist authors (including Ruether) suggest that nature is oppressed because of its signification as female. It is not so much that certain divisions of labor condition male separation from natural processes but that men, philosophers in particular, form their opposition to nature in terms cast by their assertion of difference from women.

Hence, the emergence of nature as female (seen in terms such as Mother Earth, virgin forests, the rape of the wild) is understood to originate in the repudiation of woman; the construction of male separation from nature is justified in terms of nature's apparently feminine attributes. While there is a certain lack of clarity in these accounts about why the nature/woman connection was made in the first place (a number of authors cite Ortner's narrative on reproduction despite subtly altering her causal analysis), their histories of the domination of nature clearly suggest that the oppression of women has given form to all other hierarchical dualisms.[36]

"Naturism," whatever its origins, appears in these writings as a distinct form of oppression. In a 1981 special issue of *Heresies*, one of the first collections to specifically draw together a variety of writings on feminist and ecological themes, Joan Griscom asserts that naturism, as one of the four interlocking "pillars" of oppression (sexism, racism, class exploitation, and ecological destruction), "includes *speciesism*, the belief that humans are superior to other animals"[37] and other destructive beliefs that devalue the animal-like body in favor of the superior human mind. Although Griscom sees naturism as an expression of patriarchy, she also argues that it has a logic that needs to be explicitly challenged by feminist thinking. Its origins may be in sexual dualism, but ecological oppression has a separate dynamic and must be actively integrated into antioppressive politics.

Specifically, Griscom is critical of "social feminists," who have not paid sufficient attention to nature in their analyses of oppression, feminists who, "while they may discuss the ecological crisis, [do not] incorporate it into their full social analysis."[38] Interestingly, however, she is also critical of what she calls "nature feminists," those cultural feminists celebrating women's biology, whom she accuses of inadequate social analysis. Although the social analysis she then proposes as an integration of the two previous feminist streams resembles Ruether's theological and historical narrative of hierarchical dualism with a bit of social psychology thrown in, it is important to note that Griscom suggests the need for a new theory that incorporates different forms of oppression, beyond the insights of other feminisms.

At this point in the story it is possible to suggest that ecofeminism emerged as a feminist theoretical current grounded in but somewhat different from cultural feminism. In part, the terms of the separation were predicated on a rejection of cultural feminism's supposed claim that women are closer to nature than men in some natural, presocial, biologically immutable way. While I would argue that there was never a single position on this issue within cultural feminism, emerging ecofeminist thought (also not singular, of course) was formed with the explicit agenda of reconciling tensions among feminists on the nature question. This process took the form of a new synthesis of previous feminist positions (with the exception of liberal feminism, which was rejected as theoretically inadequate and, at its core, as antiwoman and antinature[39]).

Ynestra King located three distinct feminist responses to the nature question.[40] The first two approaches, both stemming from radical feminist analyses of biological difference and patriarchal oppression, took up opposite positions on the nature question (which she was later to call radical rationalist and radical culture feminist positions).[41] The choice between them was whether to embrace or repudiate the link with nature that had caused women's oppression, whether to organize separately from men to rediscover the true essence of womanness or to deny that there was a separate logic to women organizing as women. The third approach was socialist feminism, which King saw as "weak on radical cultural critique and strong on helping us understand how people's material situations condition their consciousnesses and their possibilities for social transformation."[42] She saw in socialist feminism an implicit alliance with rationalist views on severing the woman/nature connection and a general unease with the possibility of ecological feminism.

King's project was to transcend the "either/or" assumptions inherent in the debate between rationalist-materialist humanism and metaphysical-feminist naturalism,[43] to create a dialectical feminism that incorporates the best insights of both traditions, and to eventually resolve the nature/culture dualism. Although she saw an innate equation of women with nature as problematic (indeed, she saw the dissolution of ideologies of natural social orders as a precondition for women's questioning of their roles), she argued that feminists need to choose to work from a valuation of nature as part of a liberatory project for women:

> Acting on our own consciousness of our own needs, we act in the interests of all. We stand on the biological dividing line. We are the less rationalized side of humanity in an overly rationalized world, yet we can think as rationally as men and perhaps transform the idea of reason itself. As women, we are a naturalized culture in a culture defined against nature. If nature/culture antagonism is the primary contradiction of our time, it is also what weds feminism and ecology and makes women the historic subject.[44]

What emerges in King's work is an explicit political recognition that although woman may not equal nature, history has created a particular space for women that allows a connection between them to emerge that is repressed in male culture. Women's character or position in the social world may not be innate or natural, but their distance from the center of patriarchal culture conditions a critical distance from the ideologies, social practices, and interests lying at the root of ecological destruction. The way out, for King, was to develop an alternative rationality based on that distance, to self-consciously play with Otherness and engage in a form of transformation located in the historical experiences of the oppressed.

The notion of an ecofeminist marginal consciousness offered a certain resolution of the nature/culture debate: identification with nature was constructed as a rational choice, a political maneuver rather than an acceptance of patriarchal ideologies of nature. The focus of King's and others' analyses, however, was still located in a primary narrative of dualism, albeit an increasingly sophisticated one that took into account a wider range of historical phenomena. Carolyn Merchant's *The Death of Nature* and Brian Easlea's *Science and Sexual Oppression*, for example, focused on the rise of mechanistic science and technology during the Scientific Revolution.[45] Both suggested that it was the material conditions making widespread environmental manipulation possible that, in combination with dualistic discourses of individual mastery and scientific control, created the particular formations of domination and exploitation that characterize contemporary relations of sexism and ecological degradation. An organic worldview was replaced by a mechanical one; mystical and fearsome nature (to Merchant, characterized by a view of complementarity and interdependence, to Easlea, by the same irrationalities as modern science) was transformed into resources.[46]

Despite their more sophisticated and historical readings of the nature question in feminism, there are problems with all of these accounts. First, each in its own way oversimplifies the development of Western thought, many painting a monolithic picture of dualism or, in the case of Merchant and Easlea, an overly unified (not to mention, in Merchant's case, somewhat romantic) view of pre-Enlightenment perspectives on women and nature. Each creates, from a range of complex and often contradictory philosophical debates (covering a period of some centuries) a more or less linear narrative assuming the dominance of gender polarity in discourses about women and nature. As Prudence Allen's work illustrates, the period between pre-Aristotelian constructions and the ultimate triumph of polarity as a guiding construction of gender was by no means characterized by linear philosophical or theological development.[47] Nor has polarity ever been completely dominant in Western conceptions of gender; even in Christianity, there remains a tension between women's connection with Eve's sin and their equality with men in Christ.[48] Thus, although perceived differences between men and women may have gained ideological strength from associations with a nature/culture dualism, the fact remains that women have never become "only" nature, as these authors might suggest. It seems, then, problematic to assert that women and nature occupy the same conceptual space in a hegemonic notion of hierarchical dualism. Not only is dualism itself a historically contested concept, but the historical association of women and nature was never a question of complete identification. Similarly, it cannot be argued that a once harmonious identification was warped and inverted at a specific historical moment.

Second, these histories tend to take ideas of women and nature out of the particular social and ecological contexts in which they were created, as if such ideas could persist in a fairly linear way despite dramatic social, environmental, and political changes. This analysis, for all of King's desire to incorporate sophisticated social inquiry, always emphasizes particular sets of ideas, especially dualism. Specific social relations of domination or exploitation tend to be reduced to manifestations of the operation of dualistic ideologies. A primary focus on hierarchical dualism creates a grand narrative of how one framework of ideas has caused destruction; such narratives overlook, or at least deemphasize, the specific productive and reproductive relations in which conceptions of women and nature are always located, the specific discourses of gender and nature that adhere in different sociocultural locations and that may or may not play directly into hierarchical dualism.[49]

Third, and perhaps most importantly in their historical context, these accounts do not problematize the basis upon which the connections between women and nature were made in the first place. Instead, they tend to assume that there is some division between men and women (and, by extension, nature) that, if not essential, is at least historically unchallenged. From this starting assumption, these accounts seek to prove that the degradation of women and nature occurred as a result of the connection between the two and, tautologically, that there is now a connection between women and nature that men do not possess. What these accounts do offer is a narrative illustrating how the connections between women and nature have been devalued in Western thought. While this remains an interesting project, it inevitably elevates one oppression as most fundamental to the creation of hierarchical dualism, most often sex. This story does not question women's connection to nature, why women's bodies are seen as particular in their naturalness, or why it is that processes associated with birth are constructed as essentially more natural than those associated with eating, sleeping, or defecating; it assumes the connection and shows that its form has been oppressive to both women and nature under patriarchy.

In stories of historical dualism, the origin of woman's supposed connectedness to nature remained fundamentally unquestioned despite the fact that the narratives claimed to be about origins. This weakness, even if un-theorized, gnawed at the conceptual center of ecofeminist writing.

Given that most ecofeminists were extremely wary of making biologically reductionist claims about inherent sexual differences—this was, after all, their primary move beyond cultural feminism—a huge question remained: how was it possible to understand the reasons for women's and men's different relationships to nature? King's conscious choice, in its suggestion of an almost arbitrary constructivism, turned out to be fundamentally unsatisfying in light of so much historical dualism. Surely there was a good sociological explanation for women's degraded but fundamentally positive connections to nature?

Ecofeminism and Object Relations

For most ecofeminist writers of the 1980s, the pressing need to come up with a convincing and biologically nonreductionist origin story eventually faded away; the once plaguing question of which came first, the oppression of women or the domination of nature, just ceased to be asked.[50] Some writers, like Hazel Henderson, had no qualms at all about claiming that "biologically, most women in the world do still vividly experience their embeddedness in Nature, and can harbor few illusions concerning their freedom and separatedness from the cycles of birth and death."[51] More often, writers such as Karen Warren were far more concerned with describing the specific socially constructed dynamics of the present connection between the oppression of women and the domination of nature with the express purpose of either integrating ecological concerns into feminist politics (and feminist concerns into ecological politics) or deriving a critique and future-oriented ethic.[52] For this project, an analytic focus on what Warren called value-hierarchical thinking was ammunition enough (even if one might now accuse it of a certain idealism). Where Henderson's stance can now be included in the category of cultural ecofeminism and Warren's in the category of social ecofeminism (about which I will have more to say in chapter 3), there was one influential stream of ecofeminism that did attempt to find an appropriately sociological origin for the woman/nature connection: object relations. To the ecofeminist theory then developing, this version of psychoanalysis seemed to offer a way of explaining and problematizing the connection in a way that historical narratives of dualism had not.[53]

In 1978, Nancy Chodorow's book *The Reproduction of Mothering* explored, using object relations psychology, the psychosocial development of differences between male and female children as a way of explaining sexual divisions of labor beyond the apparently natural functions of the sexes.[54]

Chodorow's agenda was to explain gender in a way that did not posit femininity as an absence of masculinity and did not reduce the development of gendered personalities to the presence or absence of penises. She insisted on locating libidinal experiences, particularly Oedipal experiences, in a set of object relations occurring within specific mother-centered family forms. In particular, she questioned the biological imperative implicit in Freud's account of penis envy and stressed instead the power relations involved in associations of penises with male power:

> Girls, for many overdetermined reasons, do develop penis envy . . . because the penis symbolizes independence from the (internalized) powerful mother; as a defense against fantasies of acting on sexual desires for their father and anxiety at the possible consequences of this; because they have received either conscious or unconscious communication from their parents that penises (or being male) are better, or sensed maternal conflict about the mother's own genitals; and because the penis symbolizes the social privileges of their father and men.[55]

Instead of concentrating on castration complexes, Chodorow argued that the importance of the Oedipal period is not, as was the case in Freudian analyses focusing on penis envy and the development of the superego, "primarily in the development of gender identity and socially appropriate heterosexual genitality, but in the constitution of different forms of 'relational potential' in people of different genders."[56] She argued that mothers tend to experience their daughters as like, their sons as unlike. Girls, she claimed, are able to experience continuity from earlier pre-Oedipal identifications, but boys, particularly at the Oedipal stage, need to develop a stronger sense of difference from their mothers in denial of their pre-Oedipal modes of fusion. "Girls," in her view, "emerge from this period with a basis for 'empathy' built into their primary definition of self in a way that boys do not . . . [and] with a stronger basis for experiencing another's needs or feelings as one's own."[57] This process accounts for women's greater sense of connectedness to, and men's greater sense of separation from and denial of, the external object world and relations with other people, particularly women:

> Difference is psychologically salient for men in a way that it is not for women. . . . This salience . . . has become intertwined with and has helped to produce more general cultural notions, particularly that individualism, separateness, and distance from others are desirable and requisite to autonomy and human fulfillment. Throughout these processes, it is women, as

mothers, who become the objects apart from which separateness, difference, and autonomy are defined.[58]

Although Chodorow's primary concern was to change the social relations in which the gendered division of parenting labor leads to "the reproduction of mothering" and to girls' not experiencing full autonomy, ecofeminists were able to read into her analysis a psychosocial origin for women's connectedness and for men's separation and domination. As Ariel Salleh suggested in an essay along these lines, "Man's separation from Nature originates in recognition of [his] peripheral role in species creativity."[59] She notes that the biologies of male and female reproductive activities are such that women experience the value and continuity of life, in contrast to men, who experience separation from new life beginning at the moment of ejaculation and continuing through birth and suckling.[60] But the cultural taboos that exacerbate this biological separation and which do not provide the conditions to compensate for men's lack of direct procreative connection are located in the type of process outlined by Chodorow. Wrote Salleh,

> A boy child under the father's watchful eye must renounce his sensuous libidinal pleasure in his mother as he grows, and install her person with abstract love and respect in its place. The emotional cut establishes a dualism of natural and cultural orders; a disconnection that is crucially formative to the masculine ego under patriarchy. . . . This act of libidinal repression, the first break with Nature, psychologically prepares a mind for the detached, self-alienated thought mode of which the cogito, utilitarian calculus and scientific method are familiar forms.[61]

Thus, she argues, "the source of man's disorder is his recognition that he cannot bring forth new life. He cannot 'reproduce'; he can only 'produce.' So he does so with a vengeance."[62]

To object relations ecofeminists, the masculine separation from both human mother and Mother Earth, embodiments of dependency and the primal state that threaten masculine selfhood, results in men's vengeance, their desire to subdue both women and nature in a quest for individual potency and transcendence and the production of things. Dualism itself can be explained through object relations: the problem is not women's biology per se, but the ways in which sex becomes gender through psychosocial processes of differentiation. Domination over nature is part of the male separation that occurs within universal patriarchal family forms.

There is an interesting twist on the problem of gender difference here.

It is not simply that men have constructed biological differences between men and women as part of a strategy of domination, but that those very differences, at some level—here, Oedipal—create in men a greater propensity to see the world in terms of difference itself, to use difference as constructed into an elaborate series of hierarchical dualisms as a form of compensation for their inability to feel connected to women and/or nature. Not only is dualism a patriarchal *rationale* for domination, but it is a form of *rationality* born from a male experience of the world.

This theory also provides an account of the intertwined dominations of women and nature (which are, here, represented as the same thing: human origins) and a basis for an ecological politics for women. Unlike King's conscious choice model, ecofeminist object relations suggests that women are naturally more able to connect to nature because they have never been forced to separate from it and because their labor creates greater sensitivity to the needs of others. The implication is that women are not necessarily more natural than men but the conditions of their existence allow them to know nature in different ways than men: while men experience the world in terms of dualism and division (the source of the problem), women experience it in terms of continuity (the source of the solution). In a sense, this mode of thinking seemed to resolve the woman/nature connection problem, because embracing nature did not necessarily mean wallowing around in male-defined dualisms: this was "a different voice," a way of being in the world that already transcended dualism.

In addition, the central ecofeminist discourse of an ethic of care (which I will discuss in chapter 6) finds one of its theoretical origins in ecofeminist object relations, especially in the early work of Carol Gilligan.[63] Jim Cheney, for example, asserts that care and relationality should be central to ecofeminist ethics, which he describes as a highly contextual attempt to see clearly what a human being is and what the nonhuman world might be, morally speaking, for human beings—i.e., what kinds of care, regard, and responsiveness are appropriate in the particular conditions in which we find ourselves.[64]

While object relations has thus provoked some interesting trajectories, it remains a problematic account in many respects. First, while it does question the process of connection between women and nature, unlike many other ecofeminist accounts, it also assumes the construction of birth and mothering as essentially more natural than other biological events and processes. Why is it, for example, that the experience of separation from the M/Other is also seen as "the" experience of separation from nature? There seems to be no essential connection between the individual male's transcendence of his human M/Other and Mother Nature unless the connection between women and nature is already part of the historical, material, and cultural context in which individuation is created and expressed. Leaving aside a more general critique of the object relations upon which ecofeminist accounts of differentiation are based, there is nothing to suggest that the repudiation of the human mother necessarily includes the repudiation of nature. Psychosocial processes of individuation may lead the male child to separate from, and even seek dominance over, his own mother. It is, however, only in the context of other social relations that construct the mother/child bond as quintessentially more natural that this desire to dominate nature becomes connected to differentiation from the human mother.

Here, a tautology emerges: the primordial male desire to separate from the M/Other includes the repudiation of nature only in a context where that repudiation has already occurred. Questions this story does not ask concern the construction of the supposed naturalness of birth and childrearing, the discursive character of the development of self in relation to nature, and, perhaps most importantly, the flexibility of boundaries between nature and culture as they appear in and affect different social formations. The types of psychoanalytic accounts appropriated by ecofeminists have also been accused, more generally, of ahistoricism and Western centrism, largely because their versions of child development are based on a very particular model of the family and childrearing practices, one that ignores the effects of race and class in constructing the individual.

Isaac Balbus displays some sensitivity to this question and provides one of the most fully developed causal narratives of the oppression of nature in the ecofeminist object relations stream. While he still falls into the trap of assuming rather than problematizing the woman/nature connection, he constructs a model of history in which different modes of childrearing cultivate different ecological sensibilities in particular sociocultural contexts. He argues that certain practices such as earlier rites of passage into adulthood or more nurturing early childrearing modes, that are located primarily in what he unfortunately calls primitive cultures, do not give rise to the same sequence or intensity of separation between the male child and his mother as do Western practices. These different experiences of male children, he argues, result in different relationships between adult males and nature.

Balbus sees violence against women and violence against nature as partially separable: while women still represent the nature against which adult males rebel, the timing and intensity of the separation determine at whom the aggression will be directed. He sees the instrumentalization of nature as a relatively recent and developmentally particular phenomenon peculiar to societies in which childrearing is less nurturant (a twist on the profoundly racist assumption that "primitive" peoples are closer to nature). What he suggests we need, then, is a revolution in childrearing practices to complete a Hegelian synthesis between primitive and instrumental relations of childrearing that would foster new relations between men and nature. (It is to be assumed, it seems, that women are already connected to nature but that this sense is not passed on to male children.)[65]

While his argument is certainly creative, Balbus, in addition to perpetuating some extremely problematic assumptions about non-Western cultures, typifies the shortcomings of a theory that rests solely on object relations to explain complex sociohistorical processes. As Frank Adler notes, "Balbus replicates all the logical problems of orthodox Marxism; instead of fetishizing the mode of production, he fetishizes the mode of childrearing—everything else is epiphenomenal."[66] This approach ignores the effects of technology, of cultural specificity, and of power in the construction of relationships between women and men or between humans (variously situated) and nature. As Patricia Jagentowicz Mills argues, Balbus's argument also reifies nature and mystifies the processes by which a reconciliation with nature is to occur. "The 'meaningful experience' of the interaction between humans and nature in Balbus' work," she writes, "amounts to an elevation of nature 'itself' and a vagueness about how the 'natural' world is to be transformed through historical intervention."[67]

The Story So Far for an Ecofeminist Identity

In many respects, the use of object relations theory represented ecofeminists' last "grand" attempt to narrate not only the origins of the oppressed woman/nature connection, but a corresponding nonbiological singular identity for women in relation to nature. By this point, many ecofeminists were calling for "a central theoretical place for the diversity of women's experiences, even if this means abandoning the project of attempting to formulate one overarching feminist theory or one women's voice."[68] The universalizing voice called for in object relations fell from grace soon thereafter as its assumptions were called into question from a range of perspectives.

Despite these calls for diversity (which do not in themselves challenge identity politics, about which I say more in chapter 3), I contend that most ecofeminists remained strongly committed to a central logic of identity established in cultural feminism and borrowed into diverse ecofeminisms, even if that commitment is never again so clearly stated. Identity simply went underground and tends to be assumed in a great deal of subsequent ecofeminist writing. According to the logic of identity politics, women share a common experience of oppression, including relations to nature, that renders women a coherent group with a discernible set of interests, reveals a distinct set of women's experiences that are different from men's, and, in many understandings, represents women as privileged speakers of a new and unique transformative consciousness that includes nature. In the following chapters, I will argue that this logic does not work for feminism (especially ecofeminism) or for any politics of nature. But the purpose of challenging this logic is to reveal (or construct) what I understand to be positive and worth preserving from the desire to create an ecofeminist oppositional identity—its democratic impulse.

2

Identity: Another Genealogy

In her book *Earth Follies,* one of Joni Seager's chief criticisms of ecofeminism is "that it can lead to an apolitical ennui—it can be interpreted as undermining the rationale for women to take political action. If we humans are essentially or naturally dichotomized by sex-linked traits, there is a certain futility in trying to change human cultural practices."[1] While I have gone on record as a critic of certain apolitical tendencies in ecofeminism,[2] I think that Seager fundamentally misunderstands the fact that most ecofeminist invocations of identity, even many essentialist and naturalized ones, are very political indeed. The point of specifying or constructing a distinct connection between women and nature is not just to celebrate it or meditate on it (as Seager seems to think), but also to insist that its historical devaluation, silencing, and exclusion from public life is a fundamental problem for the future of the world and must be made a central topic of public conversation. There may be personal elements in this connection and a personal dimension to its discovery or construction, but the personal, in ecofeminism, is intended to be strongly political.

In its invocation of identity, ecofeminism is thus located in a tradition of democratic social movement politics. Since roughly the end of the Second World War (and certainly since the 1960s), so-called new social movements have appeared in order to facilitate the entry of oppressed groups into the mainstream of democratic political life and, crucially, to show the limitations of the mainstream in containing or representing these groups' interests and desires. But even earlier than that, identity—including many of its paradoxes and limitations—became an important element in radical political and economic discourses. In the socialist politics whose limits and categories remain a crucial part of the context for (and sometimes the content of) ecofeminism, the logic of identity in which so many social movements engage is already apparent. In order to contextualize ecofeminism's use of identity as a guarantor of speech and marker of specific political legitimacy, it thus seems fruitful to consider this other, earlier identity politics and to construct a story in which the relations between identity and politics are shown more clearly.

This chapter begins with the workers' movement and tells a story about the proliferation of democratic struggles that have arisen in the wake of its decline. This is an empirical story about the coming-to-prevalence of identity politics. Although there are other ways of thinking about this proliferation (some would call it fragmentation), the move toward questioning and democratizing an ever widening variety of social and political relations has led to a rejection of traditional political spaces and forms; identity has achieved a new prominence in this process of decentering the state as a political container.

This chapter also highlights the fundamental gap between the empirical people of the workers' movement and the representational category of the revolutionary class actor while simultaneously telling a story about the persistence of this gap in more recent democratic social movement politics. This is a conceptual story about the logic of identity politics in which the achievement of identity is understood as a necessary precondition for political speech. Although there are other ways of conceiving of and dealing with this gap (see chapter 5), identity politics, as exemplified by feminist standpoint epistemologies, mark an attempt to create a politically coherent bridge across the empirical fact of a group's existence and its political representation as a group with a particular set of knowledges and experiences. This view of identity politics highlights its paradox: the struggle for a standpoint cannot be seen as a struggle if its claims to ontological grounding are to be read as legitimate. Identity is thus an achievement of political representation, but one that must mask its constructive traces in order to appear authentic. And therein lies the problem for ecofeminists.

The Rise and Fall of the Ideal Class Subject

The rise of identity as a mode of political engagement is a process with multiple origins. One could point to the ways in which modernity strips away individuals' ability to locate themselves in a solid place in a clearly defined social hierarchy, spawning, perhaps, a desire to recreate some sort of semipermanent location in the world. One could also describe the rise of individualism as a foundational feature of capitalism or as an ethic accompanying social mobility, and the construction of group identity as an attempt to restore some sense of collective enterprise.

The appearance of identity as an element in political discourse thus did not begin with the workers' movement, but its genesis is important for at least two reasons. First, the shape of the workers' movement, constructing as it did a particular relationship between empirical social location and an ideal revolutionary consciousness or activity, has had a large impact on the logics and trajectories of subsequent social movements. Second, it is with the increasing gap between the actual working class and the ideal class subject as the bearer of revolutionary potential in the world that we see the beginnings of a proliferation of different social movement struggles, the beginnings of the quest for new revolutionary identities in which to locate and from which to generate the potential for social transformation. The two processes are intricately related; in many ways, it is the failure of the actual working class to embody idealized revolutionary consciousness that has led to both the decline of the workers' movement as a universal political body (if not the decline of the workers' movement as a particular political representative of some workers) and to the quest for new (if logically similar) actors to represent the possibility of transformation.

The narrative is a familiar one (for those on the Left, at least): workers, as a result of their relationship to the mode of production, are placed in a position of alienation (meaning alienation from the products of their labor, causing their alienation from themselves and their communities). The revolutionary task is to transform the capitalist mode of production into a socialist situation of collective ownership in which alienation is overcome. But therein lies the dilemma. In a fundamental condition of alienation and division (and particularly given the failure of the forces of capitalist production to drive their own demise), how is it possible to create a situation in which workers can realize their own revolutionary interests and overthrow capitalism? How is it possible to transform the *class an sich* into the *class für sich*, the working class (as an objective body) into the subject of the revolution (an ideal collective actor)?

The complexities of creating a "revolution before the revolution"—a revolution in consciousness to reveal to workers their commonality, their revolutionary identity—constitute a plaguing question to which there have been many answers: how does a political movement best intervene in the messy, diverse, empirical world of workers in order to create a movement of workers as workers? Marx and Engels, who were entirely aware of this problem, wrote that the "organization of the proletarians into a class . . . is continually being upset by competition between the workers themselves."[3] Proposing a mode of intervention, Gramsci spoke of education and "organic intellectuals," a leadership of the proletariat by segments of the proletariat who are able to "see" their class interests and show it to others.[4] Others have spoken of the representation of the proletariat in the political public sphere and the development of social democratic governments to act in workers' interests and simultaneously foster class solidarity. Still others have spoken of the importance of trade unionism as a way of showing day-to-day conflicts in the workplace, with unions acting both as representatives of workers' interests in the everyday world through collective bargaining and as a radicalizing force in the direction of wholesale social transformation.[5]

Identity is central to all of these visions. In order for the revolution to occur, it is not simply a question of showing an already obvious group of workers their so-called true interests or revolutionary destiny, but one of creating "workers" themselves out of a contradictory array of possibilities. Put bluntly, the revolution before the revolution is one of identification. It is no longer (if it ever was) the case that class identity appears easily out of capitalist industrial relations; one need only think of struggles within unions over racism, sexism, homophobia, and anti-Semitism. The invocation and politicization of identity is an attempt to construct class as a primary mode of social and political being in the context of a host of other social locations.

Alain Touraine goes one step further, arguing that the *class an sich* is an entirely mythical representation. To Touraine, the workers' movement is not about an economic or social situation, nor can the working class be defined objectively. "Let it be said here very clearly," he writes, "that *class in itself does not exist*, that there can be no class without consciousness of class."[6] It is thus the identity of "worker" and not an empirical set of people that defines the existence of the workers' movement, even if particular relations of production form the context in which this identity takes shape and meaning.

What Touraine suggests is that the workers' movement is, in fact, a social movement, not a natural embodiment of objective class struggle. As a social movement, workers' activism needs to appeal to a series of demands that carries them beyond self-interest; they need to refer to a mode of social transformation and a vision of solidarity that constitute, a posteriori, a revolutionary class subject. He writes:

> To go beyond the level of wage demands and bargaining requires the presence of "political" or "ideological" content in any action which is the vehicle for a social movement, although "political" and "ideological" are not the best words to use, as the issue is more utopian than ideological, more a challenge to social domination than a desire to seize political power.[7]

If class does not appear objectively, and if the workers' movement is an attempt to instill class into political and economic relations, then identity—class identity—becomes paramount. It is no longer the case, in most places, that workers' politics can refer to the defense of an easily discerned organic community; it is even less the case that the nature of work itself automatically opens up a space in workers' consciousness in which they see themselves primarily as workers. It is, rather, that workers' politics have as a primary task the creation of a community out of a variety of fragments. To transform trade unionism into socialism requires the invocation of a clear sense of political solidarity, not just a dawning recognition of self-interest. Thus, to Touraine, the workers' movement is about the formation of a community resisting a culture of aggression, not simply about the defense of economic interests, as if such a defense were always already part of workers' consciousness as workers.[8]

To put it slightly differently: identity is what lies in the space between the empirical working class and the revolutionary class actor. The space is created not by the empirical fact of class itself but by the intervention of a desire for a class actor to collect empirical struggles and interests, to embody a revolutionary challenge to contemporary relations of domination. As Laclau and Mouffe put it,

> if the unity of the working class were an infrastructural datum constituted *outside* the process of revolutionary overdetermination, the question concerning the class character of the revolutionary subject would not arise. Indeed, both political and economic struggle would be symmetrical expressions of a class subject constituted prior to the struggles themselves.[9]

But there is a paradox at the center of this construction: in order to appear as a revolutionary historical subject (one destined, for example, to achieve socialism), the creative and constructed class-as-identity cannot appear created and constructed. Class as created must appear to be class as given in social relations, revealed, and marching toward its socialist destiny or it cannot play the role of historically destined revolutionary subject; in Marxism, you may remember, "the history of all hitherto existing society is the history of class struggles."[10] Always already foregrounded in socialist discourse, class identity is assumed to be produced through objective relations to a mode of production; revolutionary identity is understood as an outgrowth of a historical narrative of changes in the mode of production, not a relatively conscious and deliberate creation at a particular point in time. The necessary fiction is that the identity of worker is not only paramount, but also given in historical relations, or at least there to be revealed. Neither is, in fact, the case.

In the empirical world, the workers' movement has generally failed to produce this revolutionary identity, justifiably concentrating instead on the defense of economic interests, collective bargaining, and job security; there has always been a tension between the universality of the working class in its embodiment of revolutionary potential and the particularity of workers' interests in everyday struggles within capitalist relations of production. Perhaps there is a question of multiple purposes to be explored here. Considering that trade unions have been the locus of revolutionary struggle as well as defensive organizations to ensure recognition of a particular set of interests, the revolutionary project, and the identity that it purportedly displays is always already entangled in a series of contradictory aims. There is an enormous gulf between trade unions (or social democratic parties) and revolutionary consciousness; in fact, the very relations that are seen to produce workers' consciousness are, generally, producing a much more limited version of economic self-interest, which suggests the need to inject workers' struggles with a more clearly political element.

But the fact remains: the workers' movement is no longer the central actor (revolutionary or otherwise) in the political landscape. Historically, as Touraine notes, workers' class consciousness arose in a particular industrial context and likewise has fallen away as "technological change removed the traditional categories of worker and replaced them with new figures."[11] Changes in production have negated the possibility of creating the worker as a transformative identity; indeed, the more the landscape changes, the less "the worker" is understood as a transformative universal subject and the more it is understood as a particular category representing particular interests. Thus, the decline of the workers' movement has resulted, at least in part, from a reduced possibility of creating a universal class identity or, more specifically, from the increasing gap between the workers' movement as the embodiment of universality and its status as a representative of what are now often perceived to be highly particular interests.

To speak of the decline of the workers' movement is not to speak of the death of socialism, or even of the decline of trade unionism. While it is certainly important to emphasize the economic and political relations that have stripped power from trade unions and the global changes in the structures of industry, it is more important, for the purposes of this chapter, to speak of this growing gap between trade unionism and revolutionary socialism. The class actor, the proletarian rebelling against an entire system of production (and not just particular relations in particular workplaces), is an increasingly rhetorical figure in socialist discourse, and "the revolution" is seldom a part of trade union or social democratic action.

The workers' movement has thus produced two trajectories that are of interest. First, the understanding of political identity suggested by this story is that social movements need to construct some sort of radical (i.e., revolutionary or resistant) commonality out of an array of possible horizons of significance and that identification bridges this gap between empirical reality and political representation. The process of foregrounding involved in the construction of political identities requires a sense of developing collective consciousness beyond immediate self-interest, a sense of deliberate opposition to cultures of domination, a sense that certain actors are embodiments of a broader radical consciousness. This is the logic of identity that has carried forward into so-called new social movements. Second, the decline of the workers' movement as a universal actor, the widening of the gap between responses to particular relations of production and revolutionary activity in the context of changes to capital, has created a large problem on the Left. If workers are "merely" particular, whither the revolution? Given material changes in the political landscape, there seems to be a need for the Left to identify and politicize a more complex array of social relations that could produce a more sophisticated, accurate, and inclusive revolutionary subject. In this sense, the notion of a universal class actor may be a mistake, not because class is not an important realm of conflict from which political identities emerge, but because this actor was always more complex than originally theorized.

A Proliferation of Social Movements

By way of an empirical explanation for the decentering of socialist politics, Carl Boggs suggests that a tendency toward productivism in Marxism has narrowed its ability to collect or represent an increasing plurality of popular struggles since the Second World War. He argues that political struggles in advanced capitalism can no longer be situated solely in terms of a bipolar vision of class and that economic relations can no longer be seen as the primary axis along which social conflicts can be aligned:

> There can be no denying that popular struggles grow out of real human needs, real historical processes, real social contradictions. Even though they interact with and are shaped by material factors, the economy as such has no automatic theoretical supremacy, no independent laws of development. In the final analysis, the new movements reflect a loosening of the (imputed) direct link between material necessity and political action, industrial expansion and human progress, the interests of the working class and the general struggle for social transformation.[12]

While Claus Offe would agree that these new social movements are in part the product of new contradictions, conflicts, and cleavages—new relations born from increasingly complex terrains of social conflict—he would also argue that they are the direct result of the decline of the revolutionary potential of the working class per se. With the development of the welfare state, class politics have become increasingly institutionalized; workers' parties (under the guise of social democracy) and workers' organizations (under the broad rubric of trade unions) have been incorporated into official systems of state management, thus blunting their radical edge.[13]

This incorporation, to Offe, has dulled the potential of the old paradigm of politics characterized by "collective bargaining, party competition, and representative party government"[14] to act as an effective realm of political conversation and of change for a growing number of demands and conflicts. In addition, it has prompted the emergence of an entirely new series of political forms in a space defined as outside the realm of institutional politics. The erosion of the universality of the workers' movement and its concomitant institutionalization in a much more particularistic form in the practices of the welfare state and collective bargaining has not just provided the need for new actors to represent a proliferation of social conflicts, but has also given a particular character to new social movements.

"The new movements," he writes, "politicize themes which cannot easily be 'coded' within the binary universe of social action that underlies liberal political theory."[15] Not simply are there new actors in political conflict, but conflict itself is actively defined against the containers of institutional politics, notably against its categorization of certain actions as public or private. The new movements, he asserts,

> claim a type of issue for themselves, one that is neither "private" (in the sense of being no legitimate concern for others), nor "public" (in the sense of being recognized as the legitimate object of official institutions and actors), but which consists in collectively "relevant" results and side effects of either private or institutional political actors for which these actors, however, cannot be held responsible nor made responsive by available legal or institutional means.[16]

Offe describes the new social movements as inhabiting a space that is self-consciously outside the parameters of traditional politics; in this way, such new politics challenge the legitimacy of existing formal political arrangements to define what constitutes the political. The decline of workers' movements has brought about both a loss of faith in the class actor and a growing concern that the traditional political arrangements representing the class actor do not contain the types of politics necessary to stage contemporary forms of social movement conflict. Indeed, as Alberto Melucci adds, struggles for mainstream citizenship, for inclusion in the formalized structures of power and politics, have become increasingly separated from struggles for the democratic transformation of social life. Writes Melucci:

> Social conflicts—in the strict sense of conflicts concerning social relationships constituting a given system and struggles for the extension of citizenship: that is, for the inclusion of excluded or underprivileged groups in the domain of rights and the rules of the political game—have become quite distinct and involve quite different actors and forms of action.[17]

Thus, while it is useful to follow Boggs's suggestion that the increasing complexity of social conflict under capitalism has produced an explosion of potential points of transformation, it is also necessary to think of proliferation as a response to the limitations inherent both in class as a position and in the institutionalization of class politics. The term *proliferation* expresses not just the multiplication of political struggles, but an expansion of horizons away from political forms that have traditionally acted as containers for the expression of politics. In the context of this proliferation, I would like to suggest, the construction and recognition of identity became increasingly important to these new social movements, partly as a result of their movement away from a focus on enfranchisement, partly because of class identity's becoming more and more obviously inadequate to collect or represent the specific needs and desires of oppressed peoples (especially, but not only, women and people of color), and partly because of the rapid social, political and technological changes occurring in late capitalism.

According to Melucci, all of these factors contributed to the new social movements' desire for and practice of "the democratization of everyday life." Although many social movement struggles began by organizing around questions of inclusion, equality, and enfranchisement (black civil rights struggles of the 1960s are exemplary in this regard), subsequent developments have tended to concentrate on the creation of new political and cultural forms and new practices of meaning. He writes:

> In the collective action of women, for example, the problem of rights, inequality and exclusion constitutes a large part of the mobilization process. But what women, along with other contemporary collective actors, have achieved is above all to practise alternative definitions of sense: in other words, they have created meanings and definitions of identity which contrast with the increasing determination of individual and collective life by impersonal technocratic power.[18]

Particularly in a context where power does not operate simply at the level of the economy (or, for that matter, of formal democracy), the practice of alternative definitions of sense is a direct challenge to oppressive social relations. As Melucci argues, new social movements must be viewed as signs that "translate their action into symbolic challenges that upset the dominant cultural codes."[19] The act of definition—especially self-definition—is thus paramount to the work of social movements. To transform social relations, it becomes necessary to define them in a way that accurately reflects the positions and desires of the group for which the transformation is to occur. The act of definition, then, requires the creation of a group itself—in other words, the creation of a new and meaningful identity.

Identity has thus itself become a political goal for social movements; alternative definitions of sense are not simply the means to achieve a revolutionary end but are ends in and of themselves. The practice of an alternative identity marks a moment of resistance to and relief from the destructive hegemonic codes of the dominant society. In the context of alienating and destructive social relations, such politics mark a space of authenticity, of the possibility of a nonalienated speech, of particular challenge to the very legitimacy of a hegemonic social order that claims to represent universal interests. The achievement of identification marks a belonging to a political community that speaks in a resistant language and that derives its knowledge from experiences that have long gone unspoken or that lie outside the cultural horizons of dominant cultural forms. Identity challenges even the ability of liberal democratic institutions to own and represent democracy.

Standpoint Epistemologies and Identity Politics

So there are now two main components to the story. In one, social movements have—for a variety of reasons—come to place increasing focus on identity; the practice of alternative definitions of sense is not only means but end in a multiple political world. But in the other, the conceptual logic of identity born in the workers' movement has been, to a large extent, maintained; there remains a fundamental space between empirical people and group representation, and identity is the term creating a political linkage between them. Together, these components suggest that identity politics are not only extremely urgent, but extremely paradoxical.

I would like in this section to show how feminist standpoint epistemologies and politics as articulated by Nancy Hartsock exemplify both the significance and the paradox of identity as a form of political representation for social movements such as ecofeminism. While the content of her account of the feminist standpoint is clearly significant for ecofeminists, as it echoes and foreshadows central ecofeminist themes, it is the way in which the form of her account reveals the central problems of identity politics that most interests me here.

Hartsock writes that "a standpoint . . . carries with it the contention that there are some perspectives on society from which, however well-intentioned one may be, the real relations of humans with each other and with the natural world are not visible."[20] Much like Marx (save for his class analysis and her gender one), Hartsock insists that women's everyday experience of reality is profoundly alienated, and that in order to examine their "true" condition they must look to the social and economic conditions that make them "women" in capitalist society. Specifically, this means looking at their "sensuous human activity"—their childbearing experiences, their daily contact with concrete material life, their labor in reproducing men (on a daily basis) and children (daily and generationally)—in addition to their different experiences of childhood personality development (à la Chodorow) and denigration at the hands of dualistic ideologies and philosophies. This specific experience of being women, to Hartsock, "has important epistemological and ontological consequences for both the understanding and construction of social relations."[21]

Also much like Marx, Hartsock understands that a true knowledge of this essential (her term) experience—a standpoint, a "real" material identity—"not only inverts that of the male, but forms a basis on which to expose abstract masculinity as both partial and fundamentally perverse, as not only occupying only one side of the dualities it has constructed, but reversing the proper valuation of human activity."[22] Thus, still like Marx, Hartsock understands that women's conscious achievement of a truthful women's identity has a historical and universal destiny: "generalizing the activity of women to the social system as a whole would raise, for the first time in human history, the possibility of a fully human community, a community structured by connection rather than separation and opposition."[23]

Hartsock is extremely clear that women's identity is an achievement of feminist politics and not something of which women are transparently aware in day-to-day life (at least, not without some consciousness-raising). She is equally clear that this identity lies at the core of an alternative and transformative definition of sense, not just for women but for the world. It is thus relatively easy to see that there is a gap between empirical female actors and the revolutionary feminist standpoint; the true identity of women as women is a constructed—nurtured?—identity, a knowledgeable and politicized intervention into the lives of a specific group of people with the express purpose of developing a specific and transformative epistemology.

But here's the paradox: despite her central admission that identity is achieved, Hartsock argues that the essence of that identity lies not in the conscious and creative political act of constructing an identity (which would seem arbitrary), but in the particular reproductive activities of daily life (even the biological differences) that define an objective group of women in capitalist society. Despite her astute awareness that politics are a necessary intervention into women's lives in order for them to become "women," she writes as if the significant process by which one becomes a woman is actually prepolitical. To put it differently, if the experiences that form the essence of a distinctly women's standpoint lie in everyday life, why do we need a political movement like feminism to show us that they form a coherent standpoint or identity?

Identity, in Hartsock's standpoint epistemology, is an intentional and creative political construction of a significant category of social actors that does not and cannot appear to be an intentional and creative political construction. The category "women" must, it seems, appear to precede its politicization, even if (as Hartsock suggests) it achieves meaning only after it has been truthfully named and described. More generally, I see this (with variations) as the central logic of all identity politics. The desire for a revolutionary gendered subject is an intervention into the messy world of empirical gendered people, socially organized in conflicting ways through multiple and often oppressive social and political relations. This intervention, while it certainly collects and represents real and nonarbitrary power relations (Laclau and Mouffe call them nodal points), creates a coherent collective actor—"women"—that is necessarily re-signified as historical, as objectively given in social relations and not at all a construction born of political desire. The identity also represents more than itself; the movement in which it is organized must negotiate between representing the specific and messy needs and interests of the gendered actors who are understood to belong to the identity, and it must fulfill the feminist transformative and utopian desire from which the identity was born.

Melucci argues that alternative identities are present in a culture to the extent that there are latent moments of social movement action existing prior to their politicization through particular events (what he calls their visibility).[24] I would argue something slightly different, that identity is seen to preexist its politicization in social movement action around issues of conflict; latent networks are not given in social relations (rather, these networks are the result of political work outside the realm of formal politics), but visible confrontation requires that the actors be understood as existing before they are mobilized. To Melucci, latent networks are a prerequisite to the appearance of their visible outgrowths; where he sees the work of creating a network as highly political (the democratization of everyday life), I would like to add that it tends to appear as if it were not, as if the identity produced were not "produced" at all.

What we have is a situation in which identity exists as part of politics but should not be seen as deriving from politics. In order to appear politically legitimate, an identity cannot be viewed as an arbitrary production; it must be seen as something hidden and later revealed, not as something constructed in a particular context and out of particular conditions. An example might clarify this argument. Some gay, bisexual, and lesbian advocates have actively embraced biomedical research that suggests that there is a "gay gene." This apparent capitulation to otherwise highly problematic stories about the origins of homosexuality only makes sense when it is understood in terms of this identity politics. The identity "gay" seems to carry no political legitimacy if it is seen as a choice, as a lifestyle, as a form of resistance to heterosexual domination, or as a result of political struggles around sexuality. If "gay" is genetic, then not only can one not be "converted," but one has recourse to a logic of political appearance that constructs the origin of the collective actor outside of the realm of the political itself. Political appearance here involves the construction of a story about the "cause" of identity in which that identity must be seen as pre-political and specifically *not* constructed or chosen.

Identity, Democracy, and Misrecognition

Despite this central paradox, the unfixity of identity in late capitalism (i.e., that identities are not overdetermined by class relations) points to the importance of developing identity in contemporary social movement struggles. With the decline of an obvious, singular actor in transformative struggle (although one could argue that the obviousness of that actor was never fixed in the first place), a wide variety of potential spaces has been opened to contestation and a wide range of potential political identities has been created. Clearly, the transformation of social life itself has had a great deal to do with this process, but changes in economic relations, for example, cannot explain the proliferation of politics that has arisen under the guise of new social movements. The movement from a singular focus on economic life as the basis for identity and on the state as a realm of political action has caused a veritable explosion of points of conflict and a considerable focus on noninstitutional forms of politics. These two factors have led to a situation in which politics are profoundly uncertain, a situation in which struggles for identity have arisen as especially significant, in that the realization of identity itself has become increasingly the horizon of achievement for democracy.

Magnusson and Walker argue that critical social movements are a response "not to the dumb universality of the proletariat, nor to the identities established for capital, but to the new subjects freed by the re-articulation of capital."[25] In their view, new identities are not created as resources to be tapped by social movements so much as they are a goal in and of themselves. They argue that social movements transect bourgeois definitions of political space and by their challenging such definitions defy "a false opposition between identity and community within [the state], difference and anarchy without."[26] The process of building identity is itself seen as a transformative act; new networks of solidarity in defiance of the categories mandated in capitalist relations are the hope of the future. In this process, they write,

> people are led to rethink what we mean by community, or power, or energy, or security, or development, or democracy. . . . People probe their own identities and their relations to others, to discover ways of thinking, acting, and being in the world that are appropriate to the reality they have to confront.[27]

Thus, to Magnusson and Walker the building of new identities is itself a radical action. In some respects, Melucci would agree; in that the process of new collective identity formation creates new systems of representation, struggles for identity are profoundly *democratic* struggles. Decision making and sense making are pluralized; collective demands are formulated in a broader array of social spaces; new identities mark alternative sources of strength and legitimacy to some extent outside (or at least on the margins of) the reaches of dominant codes of meaning. Identity politics are in this way a profound and democratic challenge.

It is thus vital to consider identity as an element in a democratic politics, insofar as it represents a moment not only of proliferation, of "freeing," but of claiming a potentially transgressive power. As Touraine writes,

> In the case of most societies, the appeal to identity relies upon a metasocial guarantor of social order, such as the essence of humanity or, more simply, one's belonging to a community defined by certain values or by a natural or historical attribute. But in our society the appeal to identity seems more often to refer not to a metasocial guarantor but to an infrasocial and natural force. The appeal to identity becomes an appeal, against social roles, to life, freedom, and creativity.[28]

More specifically, he argues that in the context of postindustrial social formations identity has two faces: a defensive one in which communities define themselves in terms of some presocial (particularly preindustrial) state of being as a counteroffensive against crisis and complexity, and an offensive one in which identities represent the "capacity for autonomous intervention by collectivities and individuals,"[29] the potential for democratic struggle against the forces acting to dominate them. In drawing this distinction between the two faces of identity, he argues that although social movements may have identity as a core component, they must somehow transcend such a singular focus in favor of "an appeal to the collective control of some cultural orientations and of the great means by which society produces itself."[30]

But this duality also points to problems: although identity may represent an important gesture in the development of democratic social movement politics, this very focus embodies the potential danger of sectarianism. In its appeal to "life, freedom, and creativity," identity can (and does) vivify collective struggle; in its appeal to a realm of life somehow outside the social, identity can (and does) represent a problematic "fundamentalist and communitarian tendency."[31] Identity politics can be seen as a profoundly democratic moment in the politicization of a wide range of struggles, a way of reconceiving power away from technocratic and invasive forms of social control. Unfortunately, in the very act of formulating politics around a core idea of identity, the potential for an antidemocratic sectarianism looms large insofar as the desire for difference overshadows the desire for political challenge.

Returning to Hartsock's example, the appeal to a common identity, "women," has us think about the crystallization of a set of issues of power and control around a specific subject position, around a specific picture of experience. Very clearly, this mode of framing social life has important political consequences; Hartsock's invocation of a subject position as particular, as excluded, calls into question the universality of dominant traditions of thought and practice. There is, according to Hartsock, a different way of understanding the world; that difference has been excluded from dominant systems of representation and thus forms the basis for a reconfiguration of social life away from its current destructive trajectory. Writes Micheline de Sève, in the same vein:

> The false neutrality of traditional politics is thereby exposed. From the moment women begin to speak out [as women], to contemplate their own independent views as men do, the usual norms based on exclusively male conceptions of rationality and forms of social organization prove inadequate; they are unable to accurately describe, let alone transcend, the variety and richness of both the male *and* the female life experiences.[32]

Although it represents a democratizing moment, political identity tends to view itself as originating outside processes of democratic representation: it must be portrayed as "an infrasocial and natural force" if it is to have meaning. For feminism (and especially ecofeminism), the charge of essentialism has cast a significant shadow over its democratic theorizing for precisely this reason. As Touraine notes, identity is not instrumental, yet is used instrumentally; in the process of politicizing identity, the politics must be put in parentheses so as to appear to reveal the origins of the struggle in some organization of concrete "being." And at the point where identity politics fail to make this process of production apparent, identity's invocation of a prepolitical cause (and sometimes a presocial one) involves a misrecognition of its origins.

As a political genre, identity is, as this chapter has suggested, quite historically specific, yet it seems, from the standpoint of identity politics, to have existed all along, waiting to be retrieved from oppressed obscurity in order to achieve its rightful place in the public realm. In a similar vein, each individual political identity appears as if it has been in some sense a constant, inhabiting the margins of social life until its relatively recent emergence as a political entity. Yet this appearance is really not a moment of revelation; it is a moment of constitution insofar as the character of new social movements revolves around a certain notion of what politics are and how they are related to identity. In short, identity as a political construct is constituted retroactively; this retroactive moment collects a variety of potential representations of social life and ties them together around specific constellations of issues. But this act of tying appears invisible; it is as if the social fabric naturally brought given subject positions to light or revealed a clear actor to represent the possibility of change.

Laclau and Mouffe call this process one of articulation. "The practice of articulation," they write, "consists in the construction of nodal points which partially fix meaning."[33] Social identities, in their terms, are not fixed but appear overdetermined and preconstituted as a result of the intervention of certain chains of meaning into a polysemic social fabric. These nodal points, which may or may not be of a specifically political character, collect elements of potential meaning and give rise to an appearance of natural progression when that progression is, in fact, produced by a process of retroactive signification. Social identities are thus, in their own terms, neither inevitable nor the result of some great overarching progression of historical meaning; they are, instead, highly contingent, dependent on the collective representation of a variety of floating signifiers through a particular discursive framework.

If this contingency is the ontological ground of social movement politics in the late twentieth century, why is the identity of identity politics not seen as a political construct? Especially in the context of the proliferation of social movements discussed earlier, liberation has increasingly come to signify the ability of a social group, a collective subject position if you will, to represent itself in a way that is not simply the negative reflection of the judgments of the dominant group, the group that is seen to constitute these oppressed subject positions as Other. A certain version of community is invoked, which frequently involves the signification of the group to be constituted in terms of their particularity, their difference from the dominant group; ecofeminism, in its call for women's knowledge of nature to serve as a template for future human/nature relations, is exemplary in this respect. In its difference, identity excludes from itself the traces of its "contamination" by the relations that produced it; if it is to express a genuine difference, then that difference cannot be seen to be a transient phenomenon.

The process of revealing (actually constructing) a subject position to be liberated from its subjugation involves the creation of a chain of meaning in which this particular subject position is seen to be oppressed or prevented from coming into full being. Laclau and Mouffe call this type of conflict *antagonism* and suggest that the character of contemporary social conflict involves an ever increasing field of antagonisms. "The presence of the other," this stance declares, "prevents me from being totally myself";[34] it is actually the presence of the antagonistic other that gives shape and meaning to the group (mis)identified as the origin of identity. Identity as a political form results from the attempt to become "ourselves" despite the presence of the other, even if that other is implicated in the process of giving the "us" meaning in the first place.

But the goal of full transparency, the creation of a self liberated from the antagonistic presence of the Other, is a fiction; antagonism "arises not from full totalities, but from the impossibility of their constitution."[35] This impossibility lies at the heart of the problem of misrecognition. For an identity to appear as a basis for political action, it must claim origins beyond the political or, in Laclau and Mouffe's terms, beyond the antagonistic presence of the Other. It is not that identities don't exist as important modes of social presence; it is that they tend, in this political context, to produce an account of themselves through a story that locates their origins beyond the antagonisms from which they emerge.

Thus, the standpoint or identity is not original; it is constituted in the process of conflict itself. Yet in order to appear as coherent, it must invoke a version of order that transcends its own contingency (in Touraine's language, so it appears as natural or inevitable). That order is represented as internal to the subject position itself, not as the external effect of dominant systems of representation; it is authentic, not simply the illegitimate residue of oppressive significations. It is different, not because it has been constituted as different in particular discursive systems but because it actually *is* different, because it actually *does* refer to a slice of a natural order silenced or rendered invisible through domination.

What is important to note is that the very solidity apparently called for in identity politics—the choosing of a horizon of significance, the revelation of its fundamentality—is, in fact, a representation produced in the same conditions as the identity it is meant to challenge. Political identity is produced through the very antagonistic relations that are viewed as blocking the identity's full constitution. What this suggests is that identity politics represent the desire for identity rather than the revelation of identity; the misrecognition of its origins bespeaks a process of looking beyond the social for solidity, beyond the political for a form of legitimacy and certainty to act as a guarantor of rights or truth previously denied.

A whole or complete identity may be constitutively impossible, but the claim to identity is a powerful political force in the context of a lack of clear boundaries to the political, in the context of dispersion of political power away from the state (at least in terms of social movements' perceptions of the state's illegitimacy to define politics), and in the context of a broad proliferation of potential points of social conflict. In this way, identity represents the potential for solidity when all else seems to have melted into air; it constitutes horizons of significance in the absence of otherwise potent metanarratives, and it offers a political story in the absence of clear boundaries around the political.

What is also important to note is that no identity manages to fully suture the polysemy of the social. Given the reference to a certain version of order, identity shapes itself according to a notion of what elements of life are integral to that order and what elements are merely noise. Of course, these constructions are always already partial and contingent, produced in the context of historically specific discursive constellations. The desire for order within obscures diversity, obscures the moments where floating signifiers are articulated with other elements in a different (and potentially conflicting) chain of meaning. In other words, we never inhabit only one subject position; different constitutive possibilities are constantly at play in both politics and everyday life. Not only are certain possibilities excluded as a result of the lingering effects of old forms of domination. Instead, no identity can ever fully capture the multiplicity of potential horizons of meaning, nowhere more so than in the context of the broadening and deepening of points of political conflict.

Iris Marion Young suggests that the version of community underscoring identity politics creates part of this problem; identity, in this view, attempts to suture the social at the expense of flexibility and respect for diversity. She writes:

> The ideal of community . . . privileges unity over difference, immediacy over mediation, sympathy over recognition of the limits of one's understanding of others from their point of view. Community is an understandable dream, expressing a desire for selves that are transparent to one another, relationships of mutual identification, social closeness and comfort. The dream is understandable, but politically problematic . . . because those motivated by it will tend to suppress differences among themselves or implicitly to exclude from their political groups persons with whom they do not identify.[36]

Young's argument is an important one: identity, as a goal, suppresses difference, halts the multiplicity of the social, and creates a situation in which
claims of exclusion are not only likely but almost inevitable. Identity is
both politically problematic and based on a foundational narrowing of the
horizons of identificatory possibilities. Multiplicity can never be captured
through the invocation of a single notion of community; again, insofar as
identity is seen to be based on a difference whose origins reside outside
the political world of its antagonistic construction, that difference will be
exclusive.

Finally, it should be noted that identity politics based on difference and
the search for homogeneous community fail at precisely the task that
Marx set for the working class: the production of a universal actor to embody revolutionary ideals. So long as the quest for identity rests in a defensive moment as opposed to a disruptive one, and so long as identity itself and not its subversive potential is the founding moment of identity
politics, then movements for the revelation of a particular marginalized
identity will never succeed in their transformative task. The solidification
of identity results in politics of exclusion (and the further fragmentation of
identities themselves in search of a truer representation, a truer difference)
as well as in a withdrawal into the particular. Although new social movements have emerged to fill the gap between the status of the workers'
movement as a particular representative and as a universal actor, they have
not done any better at being universal precisely because they have taken
up identity's defensive moment over its democratizing one.

That the workers' movement could never capture the growing multiplicity of new identities is thus not only the result of a growing tension between everyday struggles and revolutionary possibilities. This is an empirical tension, and a very important one, but it must be augmented by the
observation that any identity necessarily fails to reach its desire of self-
completion and that identity itself cannot be the point of politics. The
desire continues, however, engendered by a version of identity politics
created from the gap between empirical class and ideal class. With the increasing proliferation of points of social conflict and with the decentrali-
zation of political power in the direction of creating new definitions of
sense, new codes of meaning to resist institutionalized political forms, it
seems clear that democracy is also heavily involved in the process associated with new social movements. Identity is only one highly problematic
political genre; in subsequent chapters, I will argue that it is not the only
option, even for movements as strongly tied to identity as ecofeminism
seems to have been.

3

From Difference to Differences:

A Proliferation of Ecofeminisms

In his ambitious 1994 text outlining the shape of radical ecological movements in postmodernity, Michael Zimmerman argues that "of the three
branches of radical ecology" he considers, the other two being social and
deep ecology, "ecofeminism is the most complex. During the past decade
it has become increasingly sophisticated and self-critical."[1] I couldn't agree
more: in the realm of theory alone, ecofeminists have taken diverse strands
from feminist spirituality, social ecology, transpersonal psychology,
Foucauldian genealogical criticism, Heideggerian philosophy, antiracist
pedagogy, postcolonial literary criticism, and gay and lesbian history (to
name but a few) and have woven from them a vibrant and genuinely inter-
disciplinary tapestry of ideas and debates.

In the midst of all of this diversity, however, there has been an interesting absence: feminist postmodernist critiques of the limits of identity as a
political form. As Zimmerman points out,

> Feminists influenced by postmodern theory emphasize that the concept of
> invariant identity is linked with the idea that there is one truth about the
> world. Supposedly, "true" statements simply mirror a pre-given, self-identical
> reality. Concealing the fact that knowledge involves interpretation, such an

epistemology privileges one truth, while marginalizing alternative interpretations of the world.[2]

Although the precise meaning of *postmodern theory* is subject to both confusion and debate, there are rather fundamental differences of emphasis and opinion between most ecofeminist and feminist postmodernist thinkers on the issue of identity. On one side, Carolyn Merchant asserts that ecofeminist thought offers a "standpoint from which to analyze social and ecological transformations, and to suggest social actions that will lead to the sustainability of life and a just society";[3] on the other, Donna Haraway argues that "the feminist dream of a common language, like all dreams for a perfectly true language, a perfectly faithful naming of experience, is a totalizing and imperialist one."[4] Indeed, Zimmerman goes on to show that there is, in certain corners of (especially cultural) ecofeminism, an outright hostility to so-called deconstructive postmodernism, claiming that Charlene Spretnak even sees it as "the latest version of a longstanding effort by men to construct disembodied abstractions in order to negate the elemental power of the female body."[5]

It is my eventual contention in this book (especially chapter 5) that ecofeminists and feminist postmodernists have a great number of productive things to say to one another—even that the influence of certain postmodernist ideas is already present in ecofeminism and should be nurtured. Before this conversation can happen, however, ecofeminists need to take more seriously the feminist postmodernist assertion that identity politics (of which standpoint epistemologies are an important part), although perhaps grounded in the best of democratic intentions, don't work. While there are certainly ecofeminists who avoid the *practice* of identity politics in their writing, they have not embraced the critique of the ability of identity to capture or represent the crucial problems of gender, nature, and democracy that are the central terrain of ecofeminist political theory. And this, to me, is an odd absence, given that the important calls for diversity within ecofeminism come very close to recognizing that no identity will ever capture the fullness of the relations between women and nature.

But I'm getting ahead of myself again. Among other things, I have yet to show how the logic of identity has acted as a thread running through the diverse positions that make up the contemporary ecofeminist tapestry. In this chapter, I argue that during the 1980s, a proliferation of diverse ecofeminisms burst forth on the political scene; by and large, this proliferation circulated around the problem of developing a better standpoint from which ecofeminists could speak of the specific relations between women and nature.

Two currents were apparent in this proliferation of ecofeminisms, both proceeding from similar critiques of cultural ecofeminism's primary emphasis upon women's difference from men. The first was ecofeminism's need to include experiences of oppression that could not be reduced to sexual dualism. Race, class, and colonialism became important inclusions in ecofeminist discussions of women's relations to nature (sexual orientation has taken much longer to "come out" into the theoretical center of ecofeminist debate). The second current was more a response to theoretical adequacy than to political inclusivity: as ecofeminism grew, it also diversified as a result of the influence of socialist, social ecological, and postcolonialist insights. As Zimmerman argues, an especially significant shift was from biological essentialism to social constructivism in the formulation of a distinct ecofeminist standpoint epistemology. While it is important to trace the ways in which these different currents affected the development of ecofeminist thought, I will argue that neither of these diversifying tendencies—including the growing emphasis on the socially constructed character of women's relations to nature—sufficiently questioned the limits of identity as a political form. In part, I argue, this is because a profoundly dualistic and identitarian construction of nature remained at the core of ecofeminist theory long after "women" had been recognized as a diverse, socially produced group.

This chapter thus continues my version of the identity story in ecofeminism (roughly to the late 1980s and early 1990s), but it is quite clear that other stories can and should be told (especially by and about those ecofeminist authors who have managed to avoid the logic of identity politics). As I will relate in the book's second half, the process of proliferation apparent in ecofeminism has given rise in the 1990s both to attempts to specify and solidify identity and to new visions that work with the lack of fit of any identity (i.e., the beginnings of a postmodernist conversation). Although the story is far from linear, this chapter will relate the first and more problematic (and still existing) of these tendencies, leaving the alternative (and chronologically more recent) reinscription to the discussion of radical democracy that focuses the second half of the book.

Proliferations and Challenges to Racism and Colonialism

As early as 1983, questions were raised about the ability of ecofeminism to incorporate experiences of environmental degradation from outside the confines of white, middle-class, North American culture. In her essay "Roots: Black Ghetto Ecology," Wilmette Brown suggested that feminist ecological celebrations of the holistic health movement both failed to address the inaccessibility of this natural health solution to poor black women and completely ignored the holistic healing traditions of other cultures.[6] In her critique, Brown thus foreshadowed two important developmental threads in future ecofeminist writing. First, it became increasingly apparent that race and class needed to be considered alongside gender and nature in ecofeminist analyses of oppression and programs for political change. Second, it appeared that not all women were affected in the same ways by ecological degradation and that not all women viewed nature through the same lens. The first of these problems was initially glossed over through a simplistic "add race and stir" approach in which some authors included racism in their lists of interlocking oppressions that ecofeminism should combat. The changes wrought by the second took a much longer time to develop.

In part a response to the need to include considerations of racism and colonialism, Vandana Shiva's 1988 book, *Staying Alive*, represented an important moment in the unfolding of ecofeminist analysis.[7] In it, Shiva argued that development was a project of Western patriarchy. Relying heavily on earlier ecofeminist analyses of dualism and difference but adding a significant analysis of development as one of the logics of patriarchy thus far relatively unaddressed by ecofeminists, Shiva maintained that not only could the oppressions of women and nature be linked to oppressive dualistic constructions of the Other, but so too could racism and colonialism. Development, she argued, was in fact "mal(e)development," the domination of the feminine principle by the masculine. All problems of oppression, including the physical destruction of the earth apparent in most development projects, could be traced to capitalist-embedded dualism; women, as the sustainers of life—most obviously in countries of the South—needed to be empowered in order to reassert the importance of the devalued feminine principle against the overvalued patriarchal logic of technological development and economic growth.

This discourse about race and colonialism was tied to ecofeminist principles in a rather interesting way. Where Brown's article, for example, called into question the universality of the women's experience of nature described by earlier ecofeminists, Shiva's writings asserted that dualism could still be used to explain problems of oppression and that diversity was, ultimately, a question of degree rather than kind. It may also be the case that different women respond in different ways to environmental

threat; it may also be the case that different women are affected differently by relations of domination; but it is clearly the case that all of these oppressions share a root cause: patriarchal dualism and the relations of domination that spring from it. Thus, the important problem to which Brown
alluded in 1981—that women's experiences of nature are organized differently according to different needs, agendas, oppressions, and histories and
that no single causal thread can collect them all—was not really addressed
in Shiva's analysis.

At the same time as some ecofeminists had come to see the need to include more and different voices, the problems about which these voices
were expected to speak became in Shiva's text increasingly tied to a notion
of gender difference. While responses to environmental threats came increasingly to be characterized as diverse, Shiva's analysis of the root problem for all of them was, perhaps ironically, quite monolithic:

> Limited patriarchal thought and action . . . regards its self-interest as uni-
> versal and imposes it on others in total disregard of the needs of other be-
> ings in nature and society.[8]

Thus, while racism and colonialism were included in Shiva's analysis of the
domination of women and nature, the possibility of their different (if interrelated) logics and origins was not highlighted. A patriarchal root remained quite solidly agreed upon as the source of the problem for women
and nature, and it was characterized in much the same way as it had been
in earlier ecofeminist analyses. Cultural feminist formulations of women,
nature, and dualism were still strongly present.

Another exemplary logic at work in Shiva's analysis was her characterization of the standpoint from which to understand the experiences of
women and nature and to locate resistance to the root patriarchal problem
as a space marginal to patriarchal practices. This logic came to have an
important influence on much subsequent ecofeminist work. Rather than
consider the feminist ecological standpoint an achievement of political intervention (as would be Hartsock's argument, however ultimately contradictory), Shiva's analysis held that such a standpoint could be accessed
quite directly in the daily lives and ecological knowledges of the women
most marginalized and oppressed by patriarchal domination. For women
living their lives in the proverbial belly of the Western patriarchal beast,
such direct access was not likely. For women whose lives were most marginal to and oppressed by the power and temptations of capitalist development and whose practices in relation to nature were not yet fully conta-
minated by them, an "ecofeminist" (I use the label gingerly) standpoint was

far more transparent, and even far more truthful, than those of Western women.

The combination of a continued reliance on an analytic frame that prioritized sexual dualism with a growing search for an ecofeminist standpoint on the margins of capitalist patriarchy created some acute problems in ecofeminist analyses, especially (and ironically) in those that attempted to take seriously issues of racism and colonialism. First, there was a contradictory logic of reversal at work: if ecofeminists argue that patriarchal dualism is the cause of the problem for women and nature because it marginalizes a crucial set of experiences, doesn't the affirmation of precisely that marginalization seem odd? For Shiva, the dualistic separation of the world into positive masculine and negative feminine principles is a fundamentally false and oppressive creation of Western patriarchy, yet it is by believing and embracing precisely this dualism that a transformative consciousness can be discovered. This presents an interesting irony: only by appropriating dualism can dualism be opposed.

Second, as evident in early ecofeminist writings and later in Shiva's, the ideal standpoint for ecofeminism was constructed in a way that focused on dualized characteristics considered feminine in contemporary white Western middle-class heterosexual discursive ideals and on experiences understood as generally shared among white Western middle-class heterosexual women (which was, of course, not Shiva's intent). The reliance on images of nurturance, healing, and empathy supposedly grounded in a particular experience of reproductive labor was especially telling; even if these images are the product of a particularly Western patriarchy, they are somehow real and valuable and relatively universal women's experiences of nature throughout the world. Again, this set of assumptions clearly finds its roots in cultural feminism.

While the incorporation of the work of women of color such as Rachel Bagby in some anthologies published at about this time altered (to some extent, at least) the authorial face of ecofeminism, the problematic logic and content of the analytic focus on reversal remained throughout.[9] Many ecofeminist authors, even after clearly acknowledging the profound diversity of women's experiences of nature, ended up deriving their normative ecofeminist principles from an understanding of a relatively essentialized women's character that suspiciously resembled the supposed Western dualistic ideal. There was, however, an interesting twist: as part of a desire for diversity and plurality, there was an active attempt to incorporate the perspectives of women of color, especially North American First Nations women, into the privileged ecofeminist standpoint. Ynestra King, for example, hoped as much:

> The collision of modern industrial society with indigenous cultures has decimated these ancestral forms, but it may have brought white westerners into contact with forms of knowledge useful to us as we try to imagine our way beyond dualism, to understand what it means to be embodied human beings on this planet.[10]

In works by those ecofeminists who attempted to incorporate racism and colonialism into their analysis in this period, including collected volumes that included First Nations or so-called Third World contributors (e.g., Plant's *Healing the Wounds* and Diamond and Orenstein's *Reweaving the World*), this was the type of place given to women writing from cultural traditions other than those imputed to be North American, white, heterosexual, and middle class. Somehow, such women were seen as particularly privileged repositories of knowledge about nature. The inclusion of race was not especially analytical; it did not, in most cases, suggest ways in which women may have different relations to particular ecological issues or problems, and it did not look deeply at the ways in which these traditions have themselves been lost or reconstructed in particular social contexts. Rather, these traditional knowledges became somehow sacred *because of* their marginal location in relation to the dominant culture, even though they often echoed the contents of the ecofeminist standpoint, which in turn frequently had the effect of naturalizing that standpoint. In many ways, the ecofeminist project of oppositional identity found its ultimate source in the voices of First Nations women and women from the South.

Even Karen Warren, who has been more careful than most to avoid universalizing identity proscriptions, fell into this trap in one of her outlines of standpoint ecofeminist ethical principles, as is apparent in the juxtaposition of the following passages:

> Fourth, since a feminist ethic is structurally pluralistic, one way to evaluate a feminist ethic is in terms of its *inclusiveness*: Those claims, voices, or patterns of voices are morally and epistemologically favored (better, preferred, less partial, less biased) which are more inclusive of the felt experiences, contributions, and perspectives ("the realities") of oppressed persons. . . . It requires that the diverse voices of women be given central legitimacy in ethical theory-building. . . .

And on the next page:

Sixth, a feminist ethic is embedded in such concrete values as care, friend-ship, appropriate trust, and reciprocity, values often overlooked and under-valued in mainstream ethical discussions.

And finally:

Lastly, a feminist ethic provides a guide to action in the pre-feminist pre-sent. The Chipko Movement provides a wonderful example of the sort of action women can take to prevent the mutual destruction of the natural en-vironment and their livelihood.[11]

The essay in which these passages appear begins with the Chipko move-ment of Northern India, moves into a broader discussion of gender and feminist issues in forestry that includes a critique of (among other things) the dualism of patriarchal conceptual frameworks, and ends with a norma-tive feminist ethic that is, in part, generalized from the concrete Chipko experience of resisting this dualism.[12] Although there are other threads in her argument, the logic described above is, unfortunately, also quite clear in her story: patriarchy devalues a certain set of traits and knowledges; these knowledges are the key to the development of a "morally and episte-mologically favored" ecofeminist standpoint; diversity is a key part of femi-nist ethics and requires that we look to oppressed women's experiences in particular; the ethics we find at the end of our search resemble, rather suspiciously, the ones we understood as feminine before we began; these ethics are legitimated (even naturalized) by their exemplary presence in the Chipko movement.

There is nothing inherently wrong with—and we certainly have a great deal to learn from—the project of looking to other cultures for examples of alternative ways of knowing and being in the world. What was prob-lematic about many ecofeminist appropriations of indigenous or tradi-tional knowledges was their characterization of them as somehow pure, somehow dissociable from what colonization has actually done to those different cultures and social practices. Also problematic was their general assumption that all "women's" practices in nature are (at their core at least) benign, caring, and respectful. It is as if women from the South were not alienated from nature, despite living their lives in patriarchal and increas-ingly capitalist cultures; it is as if First Nations women have never engaged in unecological practices. Even given her careful discussion of the ways in which Chipko women's labor is alienated (my term), Warren gives no sense that Chipko women's consciousness of nature is anything but holis-tic and positive, that their interests are nature's interests. There was little acknowledgment within ecofeminist literature of First Nations struggles for self-determination or of ecological contradictions in non-Western societies; there was only the "traditional" woman whose experience of nature was, underneath it all, epistemologically unpolluted. This glorification went hand in hand with a relative absence of critical polylogue among women from different perspectives and a dearth of political alliances between antisexism and antiracism. The two problems were strongly connected: what First Nations and Southern women were to do was to show white Western women how to reconnect with a part of themselves (the ecofeminist standpoint) that was already there, but unexpressed or unformulated. There was precious little discussion of colonized women as whole people who may have conflictual relations with nonhuman beings in their struggles against particular conditions of existence and oppression.

By and large, First Nations and Southern women did not claim this space for themselves. Irene Dankelman and Joan Davidson's *Women and the Environment in the Third World*, for example, had much more to do with the struggles of women to influence decision-making processes in development than it had to do with retrieving a genuine ecofeminist standpoint buried under or marginalized by patriarchal culture.[13] But even with the addition of new voices and the specification of new relations that intersect with those primarily centered on gender and nature, the singular ecofeminist standpoint remained intact, largely because the dualism upon which the model was constructed in the first place had not been challenged. One cannot find "woman" simply by reversing "man," even if one takes intersecting relations into account. What was once a single mirror may have been replaced by a large room of differently focused ones, but none of them challenged the assumptions producing the desire for reflection. Thus even though ecofeminism seemed to diversify its perspectives with the increasing presence of a variety of different voices, the diversity was illusory, at least in terms of analytic complexity. In the context of a desire for one true story about domination, the stories told by Southern and First Nations women could only be seen as somehow purer accounts of the same narrative experienced by all women.

But (I'm very happy to say) this mode of discussion is no longer predominant in ecofeminist literatures that question racism and colonialism. In 1993, for example, Huey-li Li published an article that called into serious question the assumptions about gender and nature upon which ecofeminist analyses of dualism rested.[14] In other cultures, it pointed out, there were other discourses of gender and nature; in other cultures, power was organized differently and could not be understood through a narrative that focused on a very particular Western cultural logic; in other cultures, there may have been different contradictions.

It thus took ten years for the full implications of Brown's early article to be considered. As the next section will address, only after the emphasis on dualism in cultural feminism was seriously challenged by different analytic currents—notably socialist ecofeminism—was it possible to include a narrative about racism and colonialism that was not simply a magnification of processes already described in early ecofeminist accounts.

Movements into Socialist Ecofeminism

The earliest socialist ecofeminist text was probably Carolyn Merchant's *The Death of Nature* (1980). The book presented a detailed history of Western social practices around nature and described a transition from an organic orientation to a mechanical one, the latter heralded by the Scientific Revolution. Where once Mother Earth was a source of awe and reverence—Merchant insisted that the earth was considered female and that this gendering worked to the advantage of women before the Scientific Revolution—it has now come to be seen as an inert entity to be controlled. This control is made possible by technological development and made desirable by the advent of ideologies of mechanistic and rational "management."[15]

Merchant (apparently influenced by a reading of Horkheimer and Adorno) was highly critical of the Enlightenment. While she noted that the mathematical traditions upon which mechanistic objectivist science were built dated as far back as Plato, it wasn't until the seventeenth century that the organism was finally supplanted by the machine as the hegemonic metaphor for nature. In the context of growing capitalist economic and social relations, Merchant wrote, this "death" of nature was disastrous for the natural world:

> Because nature was now viewed as a system of dead, inert particles moved by external, rather than inherent, forces, the mechanical framework itself could legitimate the manipulation of nature. Moreover, as a conceptual framework, the mechanical order had associated with it a framework of values based on power, fully compatible with the directions taken by commerical capitalism.[16]

What Merchant added to ecofeminism was a specific recognition of the relationships among prevailing ideologies and forces of production and reproduction. To Merchant, it wasn't simply a dualistic worldview that represented the source of the problem for women and nature (although, as I noted in chapter 1, dualism remained at the center of this text); it was a complex series of technological, social, and perceptual relations summed up in the post-Enlightenment transition to industrial capitalism.

In her subsequent writings, Merchant's emphasis shifted somewhat from the death of nature at the hands of mechanization to the destruction of the biosphere by capitalist forces and relations of production. In these later texts, she made her socialist feminist claims more central: reproduction has also been exploited by the processes of capitalist production. Thus, her claim to a socialist ecofeminism came to be based on the recognition of the effects of post-Enlightenment capitalist expansion shared by women and nature. In 1992, she defined socialist ecofeminism as

> not yet a movement, but rather a feminist transformation of socialist ecology that makes the category of reproduction, rather than production, central to the concept of a just, sustainable world. . . . It goes beyond cultural ecofeminism in offering a critique of capitalist patriarchy that focuses on the dialectical relationships between production and reproduction, and between production and ecology.[17]

Beginning with Engels's insights on the production and reproduction of life, Merchant's socialist ecofeminism came to focus on the ways in which patriarchal domination has circumscribed and eroded women's traditional activities in nature: production of immediate needs, reproduction of daily life, and reproduction of the species itself, all as mediated by productive relations. In this regard, Merchant's analysis represented an important divergence from cultural ecofeminism. It was no longer enough to speak of patriarchy, because capitalism was clearly a crucial element in the oppressions of both women and nature. In addition, Merchant's view of reproduction was quite different from that of her predecessors and clearly more oriented to survival than to some inherently nurturant set of properties. For example, Merchant did not consider reproduction to be a site of nature; she emphasized the ways in which reproduction is a social process and involves a transformation of nature, but in a way different from production.

While clearly critical of and more sophisticated than accounts focused on patriarchal dualism, and while leading away from biologically reductionist accounts of women's relations to nature, Merchant's analysis remained grounded in a logic of identity that is very similar to the one expressed in earlier ecofeminist writings. In fact, Merchant's analysis is strikingly similar to Hartsock's in its particular invocation of a feminist standpoint based on experiences of reproductive labor, here extended to include the ways in which women's labor includes a specific series of relations to nonhuman nature:

> As producers and reproducers of life, women in tribal and traditional cultures over the centuries have had highly significant interactions with the environment. As gatherers of food, fuel, and medicinal herbs; fabricators of clothing; planters, weeders, and harvesters of horticultural crops; tenders of poultry; preparers and preservers of food; and bearers and caretakers of young children, women's intimate knowledge of nature has helped to sustain life in every global human habitat.[18]

Given that reproduction, to Merchant, was simultaneously biological and social, she saw reproduction and nature existing in a rather harmonious dialectical relationship, with both affected negatively by the advent of capitalism's productive orientation. Her socialist ecofeminism would thus "reverse the priorities of capitalism, making production subordinate to reproduction and ecology."[19] As continual bearers of degraded knowledges of nature, it is up to women (especially so-called tribal and traditional women) to struggle for the survival of these knowledges against capitalist productivism and to lead the way toward the reversal of capitalism's priorities.

Apart from the problems I have already pointed out with the assumption that all reproductive practices, traditional or otherwise, are inherently good for nature (or, for that matter, for women), Merchant maintains the fundamental logic that all women do or can share an ecofeminist standpoint, that this standpoint is relatively transparent in the daily practices of women especially marginalized from (if oppressed by) the history of patriarchal capitalist social relations, and that the core of an ecofeminist politics is a revelation, not a construction, of the inherently ecologically sound consciousness of at least some women. Even if white Western women need to do some work to achieve an ecofeminist identity, the practices of survival in which many Southern women engage form the voice from which a nonalienated nature already speaks. As Merchant writes:

> Women in the Third World . . . are working to maintain their own life-support systems through forest and waste conservation, to rebuild soil fertility, and to preserve ecological diversity. In doing so, they are assuming leadership in their own communities . . . [and] they are slowly achieving the goals of ecofeminism—the liberation of women and nature.[20]

Again, I should emphasize that there is much to be gained by looking to struggles in different parts of the world for examples of principled, effective, and sophisticated environmental activism. The problem is not the desire for a conversation or the act of creating international linkages among movements with structural links or family resemblances; the problem is the assumption that such desires and acts must be legitimated or connected by assumptions of identity, especially in the form of a marginal standpoint epistemology. Merchant replaced a cultural feminist model of resistant Otherness with another, socialist one: it may not be the case that women are closer to nature, but they are certainly further from culture (if culture means patriarchal capitalist productive relations), and therein lies the truthful place from which to speak.

Socialist ecofeminism did, however, move away from an analysis centered on sexual difference as the primary logic of the oppression of women and nature. In doing so, spaces were opened up for an analysis of racism and colonialism that was not already overdetermined by earlier ecofeminist work on sexual dualism. One of the best examples of this type of analysis came from Bina Agarwal, who wrote about the specific and local conditions affecting women and nature in India as part of a critique of North American cultural ecofeminism.[21]

Agarwal's analysis centered on the ways in which material conditions (especially immediate ecological degradation) adversely affect, and thus politicize, poor peasant women in India. She suggested that

> the processes of environmental degradation and appropriation of natural
> resources by the few have specific class-gender as well as locational impli-
> cations—it is women of poor, rural households who are most adversely af-
> fected by and who have participated actively in ecology movements.[22]

Empirically, environmental "adverse effects" are experienced generally by a class or caste of people, but particularly by women, who do not have males' access to property and power. Thus, women's grassroots activism, in Agarwal's estimation, is not so much about preserving women's subsistence activities as it is about questioning the relations of structural inequality in which specific women experience environmental degradation on a daily basis.

As a result of her research, Agarwal produced a rather paradoxical argument. First, she suggested that "women" is not a unitary category and that North American ecofeminism's characterization of women's relations to nature completely misses the class/caste and local roots of women's environmental struggles. This is an important argument, as it calls into question the possibility of a single ecofeminist identity. At the same time, however, she argued that women's activism in Indian ecology movements is distinct from men's and has to do with family survival to a much greater extent, which echoes a very familiar notion of a women's standpoint. She argued that, as a result of poor women's position in both a patriarchal and a class/caste hierarchy, implicit in Indian women's ecological struggles is "an attempt to carve out a space for an alternative existence that is based on equality, not dominance over people, and on cooperation with and not dominance over nature."[23]

Agarwal's account, like Merchant's, explicitly rejected any sort of biological determinism and attempted to call into question the idea of a transcendent women's voice with which to speak of nature. Agarwal was actually more careful than was Merchant in the texts I have mentioned here to speak about the importance of understanding constellations of local conditions.[24] But both Merchant's and Agarwal's arguments fall prey to the same problem: women, as women, struggle in the name of reproduction, the family, and, in Agarwal's terms, cooperation with nature. Try as she may to challenge cultural ecofeminism's emphasis on difference, Agarwal's picture of difference and identity remains intact: "women" may not be a unitary category, but women still struggle *as women*, and at the moment at which they do so, they are struggling for feminine values remarkably similar to those sketched out in, say, ecofeminisms inspired by feminist object relations. Resistance to ecological degradation inhabits a space that is posited as the obverse of the developmental trends produced by patriarchal capitalism, local conditions notwithstanding. Where capitalism emphasizes production and competition, socialist ecofeminism emphasizes all that capitalism has marginalized in the course of pursuing this emphasis: reproduction, cooperation, and ecology. And women remain "the bearers of the revolution," their activities the ground in which an ecofeminist standpoint can be revealed (not constructed), their claims to a genuine ecofeminist identity the basis for political representation.

Thus, despite its careful consideration of the ways in which capitalist productive relations create specific and local conditions of oppression and revolt, socialist ecofeminism remained largely, if not entirely or irrevocably, trapped in a notion of identity based on difference. It is the moments when women differ from men that are seen as the crucial moment of politicization, despite the inclusion of other fault lines along which resistances could erupt. Class/caste, poverty, race, and colonialism specify the women who may be most at risk in ecological catastrophe, but it is the fact of being a woman in these contexts that shapes the experience of oppression and the identity to be claimed in struggles against oppression.

This stance is stated quite clearly in Mary Mellor's text *Breaking the*

Boundaries.[25] While she argues that women are not biologically inscribed as nurturant, she also insists that "a feminist green socialism must be underpinned by those values that have hitherto been imposed on women: altruism, selfless caring, the desire to help other people realise their potential."[26] After a careful analysis of the ways in which capitalism fetishizes production and expansion at the expense of ecological concerns, Mellor reverts to a phenomenally simplistic distinction: where capitalism emphasizes the "me" world, a world of individuals struggling to maximize their resources, women have at their disposal a "we" world, a world of community and caring. Mellor argues that although oppressed communities have at their disposal this communal model of existence, it is largely women who do the work of caring; this work is the hope of the world, and women are the revolutionary vanguard.

The assumption that it is those who are most oppressed who will struggle for themselves and for nature is also telling. Agarwal is clearest among the authors mentioned on this: poor and tribal Indian women are involved in ecology movements because they exist on the fringes of power and influence, because their "critical otherness" allows a truer or more cooperative social world to emerge, because they feel the effects of ecological degradation most strongly. These assumptions, all excellent examples of the logic of identity politics described in chapter 2, are highly questionable but pervasive in socialist ecofeminism: the inclusion of class/caste, race, and colonialism serves to specify the most precise Other, the one whose voice is most necessary to visions of liberation, the one whose difference is most in need of democratic telling.

Movements into Social Ecofeminism

Social ecofeminism, like socialist ecofeminism, originally proceeded from a critique of cultural ecofeminism. In fact, I would argue that cultural ecofeminism came to be categorized as a distinct strand of ecofeminism *because* of the critical constructions of social ecofeminists. Janet Biehl's *Finding Our Way,* for example, calls into question what she sees as cultural (or psychobiologistic) ecofeminism's reliance on a mythical and irrational notion of the feminine, which she describes as a "pestilential breeding ground for reaction as well as romanticism."[27] Her major critique of ecofeminism is that, in its reliance on (debatably) deep ecological notions of human/nature relations—and, I would add, cultural feminist assumptions about the woman/nature connection—human subjectivity is erased and politics are left to irrational forces, a result, in part, of an uncritical reliance on reversal as a strategy. What she offers as an alternative, an explicitly rational politics, is based strongly on social ecological (or, to be more precise, Murray Bookchin's) notions of democratic political participation in a community polis, in which various communities of interest would be heard without granting epistemic privilege to any one community.[28]

Biehl's analysis rests on the idea that social practices of domination—including, but not limited to, the domination of women by men—lead human beings to practice the domination of nature. In this, she differs from both Ortner, for whom the devaluation of nature lies at the origin of women's oppression, and from ecofeminists who assert that patriarchy is the root cause of all subsequent oppressions. Overcoming patriarchy, in her view, does not spell the end of other social hierarchies such as racism and "classism," thus an ecofeminist analytic focus on the dualistic operations of patriarchy leaves most relations of domination unchallenged. Even more problematic for Biehl is the logic in ecofeminism, including socialist ecofeminism, that women are somehow closer to nature, even if the relationship is socially constructed.

> Ecofeminist images of women . . . retain the patriarchal stereotypes of what men expect women to be. These stereotypes freeze women as merely caring and nurturant beings, instead of expanding the full range of women's human potentialities and abilities. To focus overwhelmingly on women's "caring nature" as the source of ecological values easily leads to the notion that women are to remain intuitive and discourages them from expanding their human horizons and capacities.[29]

Although there are many important points to Biehl's critique of ecofeminists' reliance on the results of dualism for a standpoint, her complete rejection of their *oikos* in favor of her *polis* ironically negates the transgressive potential of a feminist ecological politics for showing the arbitrariness of a delineation between the two (as I will discuss at greater length in chapter 7). For Biehl, the human (rational, deliberative) standpoint that women are to attain is as strongly attached to the top half of a hierarchical dualism as Merchant's socialist ecofeminist one is to the bottom. Biehl's rather dogmatic insistence on direct democracy as a rational form of political participation leaves no space for a critique of the gendered constitution of rationality; her insistence on particular boundaries for the social does nothing, in the end, to destabilize the reification of nature; and her denial of the possibility of legitimacy for any gendered specificity does not question the processes that constitute particular definitions of the universal. She does not consider feminist ecology's potential for redefining democratic subjectivity itself or allow that ecofeminism might represent a moment in a process of democratization. In short, while she is critical of ecofeminism's inhabitance of a particular moment of dualism, in her emphatic but uncritical inhabitance of an opposite moment she fails to critique the division itself and produces a political vision that does as much to reify organic dualism as any cultural ecofeminist work.

Social ecofeminist Val Plumwood might call Biehl's project a feminism of uncritical equality, which she argues has been a major rival to feminisms of uncritical reversal. In the former category, she includes liberal feminism, some forms of socialist and Marxist feminism, and some forms of social ecology; she suggests that their strategy has been one of equal admittance into the privileged, male realms of "objectivity, abstractness, rationality and suppression of emotionality" as well as to "the masculine virtues of transcendence of, control of and struggle with nature."[30] On the other side, the reversal feminists—mostly cultural ecofeminists—agree with the analysis of women's exclusion from patriarchal structures of power and knowledge but contend that liberation should proceed through an opposition to this male culture, an opposition grounded in valuing more highly women's experiences of nature, their alternative culture.

Plumwood rejects both poles of this debate and sees a social ecofeminism as taking elements of each to form what she calls a third wave. To Plumwood, this wave requires a thorough analysis of how dualism is implicated in the devaluation of women and nature as "a way of construing difference in terms of the logic of hierarchy where the more highly valued side (for example, males or humans) is construed as alien to and of a different nature or order of being than the lower side (woman, nature) and each is treated as lacking in qualities which make possible overlap, kinship, and continuity."[31]

This third wave requires both a questioning and transcendence of dualism in addition to a reaffirmation of women's standpoint as part of a genuinely liberating strategy that goes beyond mere reversal. While the passage I included in chapter 1 from Ynestra King's work suggesting that women are the bearers of revolutionary potential in the world states this logic exceptionally clearly, Karen Warren's transformative feminism is also an excellent example of this strategy. Warren is, like Plumwood, critical of both cultural and socialist ecofeminisms (not to mention liberal feminism) and calls for a new vision integrating the positive qualities of both analytic streams while transcending their weaknesses. She is explicit in her recognition of the social construction of women's knowledges and experiences of nature; she is also clear about the need for a transformative feminism that respects and preserves diversity, acknowledging that there may be more than one women's voice and more than one feminist theory. Moving into standpoint logic, however, she locates resistance to a logic of domination in a "call for oppressed groups to collectively assert for themselves their felt experiences, needs, and distinctiveness," a collective project that leads to the "rejection of a logic of domination and the patriarchal framework which gives rise to it," to a "rethinking of what it means to be human."[32] Although Warren does not argue that the critical edge of ecofeminism derives directly from women's experiences, she does so implicitly in her reluctance to problematize the relationship between oppressed experience and transformative consciousness. It is the point of view of the oppressed that gives rise—transparently—to the knowledges upon which a transformative feminism is to act. As she writes in a later article, ecofeminism

> emerges from the voices of women who experience the harmful domination of nature and the way that domination is tied to their domination as women. It emerges from listening to the voices of indigenous peoples such as Native Americans who have been dislocated from their land and have witnessed the attendant undermining of such values as appropriate reciprocity, sharing and kinship that characterize traditional Indian culture.[33]

There is thus a certain paradox in social ecofeminisms such as Plumwood's and Warren's. On the one hand their analysis is of the social construction of women as "closer to nature" as an oppressive fiction, part of a series of practices of power and hierarchy that also includes racism and classism, part of a series of discourses by which women are contained. While Biehl is probably the most vocal proponent of this view, it has become almost a truism of social ecofeminism that the connection is a social construction. On the other hand, its constructed location of women *as if they were* closer to nature grounds the standpoint of social ecofeminism, its ability to suggest out of women's (and sometimes other groups') direct experiences of nature an alternative vision.

This apparent paradox, I would argue, is born out of social ecofeminism's insistence on integrating into itself the "good" parts of other ecofeminisms, taking an emphasis on equality from liberal or socialist feminism and an insistence on difference from cultural ecofeminism and combining them into an agenda that cannot be other than paradoxical. Here's the logic: ecofeminists cannot simply accept the patriarchal idea that women are closer to nature than men. Instead, what they need to do is stand outside the hierarchical dualisms that have created or shaped this destructive dualism in order to find a new series of concepts and practices to guide relations between men and women and between humanity and nature. Given that patriarchal capitalist relations are the problem, and given that these same relations have placed women and nature in a space in which a different form of conversation is possible than that between men and nature, these new concepts and practices are to be found in, or perhaps created from, women's experiences with nature. To social eco-feminists, this practice does not mean that women are closer to nature than men; it means that, for a variety of reasons, women have been placed as Others in a position that does not produce the same destructive separation from nature, the other Other, that men experience. Thus, a process of re-specting, and working from, the voice of this connected Otherness is the key to a new ecological and social ethic. To quote Plumwood again,

> An approach critical of dualism would . . . insist that women must be treat-
> ed as fully human and as fully part of culture as men, but that both sexes
> must challenge this dualized conception of human identity and develop an
> alternative culture which fully recognizes *human* identity as continuous
> with, not alien from, nature.[34]

Social ecofeminists like Plumwood may claim that they have somehow resolved the tension between equality versus difference found in other ver-sions of ecofeminist politics. But the statement that women are both equal and different, even if that difference is socially produced, keeps ecofemi-nism locked in a destructively essentialist mode of analysis and politics. The problem, for Plumwood as for all the other authors I have described so far, is that ecofeminism is a politics of identity. Despite the efforts of anti-racist, socialist, and social ecofeminists to problematize cultural ecofemi-nist assumptions about woman in her relationship to nature, all of these variants remain committed to the discovery of a position from which to speak of oppression, an existing and coherent standpoint from which to describe another way of being in the world.

It is the desire for a revolutionary Other that has tended to drive ecofeminist proliferation, a desire for an identity not just to protect itself, but to act as a focal point for all ecofeminist struggles. Despite its prolif-eration, despite the inclusion of issues of race and colonialism, despite the development of more sophisticated analyses of capitalist economic and so-cial structures, despite an attempt to transcend dualism, ecofeminism has often remained caught in the original question posed by identity politics: Where do we find a revolutionary Other to reveal, and struggle for, a bet-ter life for women and nature?

Nature and the Problem of Identity

To most ecofeminists—cultural, socialist, *and* social—it is generally quite clear that it is no longer (if it ever was) reasonable or accurate to speak of a singular and monolithic group of women. To a greater or lesser extent, ecofeminists have noticed (or been forced to notice) that different women have different lives and that the experiences of racism and caste/class position (many have mentioned but few have analyzed sexual orientation) are at least as important as sex/gender in shaping relations to nature. Women have become a rather more diverse lot than originally theorized in radical and cultural feminist works on nature, and Wilmette Brown's declaration that this diversity must be considered more fully in ecofeminist theory has, it seems, been heard if not fully realized.

But in the midst of all of this diversity, many ecofeminists from a variety of currents remained in the 1980s and early 1990s quite strongly committed to a standpoint epistemology that privileged a particular set of activities and attributes, to an identity that ironically invoked a femininity that was, supposedly, highly problematic. The answer to the question of locating an analytic ground and standpoint for ecofeminism, wrote socialist ecofeminist Mary Mellor, lies "in the material limitations of the need to secure human reproduction and survival and the parameters it places upon human (in practice, women's) activity."[35] Or, as Brian Swimme rather less subtly wrote, "I would simply point to the [holistic] perspective, awareness, and consciousness found most clearly in primal peoples and women generally."[36]

While I do not wish to lump the growing number of ecofeminist positions into a single category, I think there is something that Mellor and Swimme share, and that is their idea of nature. Indeed, although there are certainly exceptions, this logic is pervasive in much historical and current ecofeminist writing. This logic holds that while oppressed peoples may be diversely situated in relation to nature as a result of their diverse material and conceptual positions and activities, what they share is a supposedly direct experience of nature that is the thing that patriarchal culture has historically devalued and continues to oppress and exploit. Even more important to their view, perhaps, it is from such experience that an ecofeminist identity politics emerges; however socially constructed human beings might be in their relations to nature, nature lies somehow beyond the oppressive and patriarchal constructions that threaten to destroy it. Thus, the people who feel nature more directly or fully in their productive and reproductive activities or in their biological bodies—in other words, the ones who are furthest from the temptations and obfuscations of patriarchal-capitalist culture and power—are the ones whose identities express eco-feminist "nature" the best.

In this logic, nature became a primary category linking together a vast diversity of oppressed and resistant social positions. As an element tying together some of the proliferation of ecofeminisms in the context of the increasing unhomogeneity of women (or, rather, the realization of this fact by white Western ecofeminists), what but nature could stand as the "thing" to specify ecofeminism? Although many (if not most) ecofeminists gave tacit assent to the idea that nature is in part a social construct, most notably in the assertion that contemporary Western relations to nature involve a highly destructive social creation in which nature is understood as evil, base, and/or mechanistic, there was not then (and is now only in places) a strong sense that all relations to nature are partly socially produced, including the ones that ecofeminists envision as utopian.

The social construction of nature upon which many ecofeminists relied was generally the product of precisely the same reversal that seemed so problematic as a construction of women. In accounts that emphasized dualistic conceptual frameworks, such as that in which what is "not masculine" became the truth of essential femininity, so too did that which is "not culture" become the natural state from which we came and toward which we must aspire. Nature was viewed as the obverse of all that is wrong with civilization. As patriarchal culture was individuated, nature was interconnected. As androcentric institutions emphasized rationality, nature was mysterious. As capitalism was inherently crisis-driven and unsustainable, nature was inherently stable, balanced, and sustaining. Nature was defined in terms of stereotypical femininity because contemporary culture was the manifestation of all that is quintessentially male. And if nature is all of these things, then it is not surprising that women and other oppressed peoples, who have privileged access to nature in their daily activities and/or are excluded from the false consciousness of patriarchal culture, are more likely to display these characteristics of nature even if they do not do so as a *result* of nature.

What is perhaps most significant about this commonly held idea of a natural ecofeminist standpoint is that it is to be found or discovered through an act of distancing from patriarchal capitalist culture. It is here that we see most clearly displayed the logic that political identity must conceal its origins. Rather than understand all activities in nature to be socially located and contestable, and rather than understand the knowledges of nature that derive from these activities to be equally social, many ecofeminists saw nature as an original place from which to derive experiences and ideas of sustainability. Reproductive or subsistence practices in nature were thus a particularly authentic route to finding that place.

To put it differently, the particular social creation of nature that many ecofeminists wanted to promote and politicize was misrecognized as a nature given *in* nature. That nature was seen as simply more accessible by women doing particular tasks. While I think there is much to be said for the project of revaluing the kinds of tasks in which, empirically, women tend to engage on a daily basis more than men, and while I think that there is a dire need for a more democratic exploration of diverse relations and possible relations between and among humans and nonhuman nature, I do not think it at all fruitful to construct an ecofeminist politics that naturalizes its assumptions about nature and that does so backhandedly by naturalizing a particular gendered division of labor. If natural identity is only "truly" accessible through particular kinds of reproductive or subsistence practice, then ecofeminists—if they want to speak as this authentic nature—are locked into an analysis that privileges a narrow and limiting identity.

The quest for an ecofeminist standpoint was clearly oriented to a space beyond the social, sometimes described as a form of spiritual connection. Especially in some spiritual ecofeminist discourses that hold that connectedness to the earth is a form of knowledge superior to abstracting and alienating patriarchal cultural, social, and economic structures, the distancing of the self from that culture becomes part of the process of connection. That is, the natural aspects of the self become privileged over the social, even though that natural self is clearly a social construct; nature represents a voice that can only be heard if one somehow listens beyond patriarchal culture and all of the individualistic, rational layers of false consciousness implied thereby. Joanna Macy, for example, suggests that the discovery of the ecological self requires the experience of being acted through, the dissolution of the individuated self into the interconnected web of natural being.[37]

In this version, ecofeminism is focused on women's empathy with nature, women's identification with nature, women's self-identification as natural. This privileging of connection with nature, this desire to be nature at the apparent expense of human subjectivity, represents an interesting construction of a politics of identity. In this construction, the oppression of nature becomes part of women's experience; the experience of oppression—of women as nature—is countered by reappropriating a set of negative definitions and turning it on its head. By emphasizing the connections between women and nature, by asserting the primacy of the natural aspects of the self, by the fusion of the social actor with the natural world in an attempt to become a natural actor, ecofeminists assert that nature is identity and that the strengthening of that identity will form an effective opposition to contemporary exploitations of women and nature, even (though it is seldom expressed so directly) in the face of the other forms of epistemic diversity that sexuality, race, class, and caste might produce.

While many ecofeminists problematize culture by looking at how particular patterns of thought have led to the repudiation of human and non-human nature, while many ecofeminists have actively embraced the idea of women's diversity, and while some ecofeminists have even produced relatively sophisticated accounts of the intersections of race, class, and gender, nature itself is still very often characterized as a primordial, stable, and pure entity which, by some means, must be allowed to emerge if we are to survive. Nature is original; culture is superimposed on that biological web, with devastating results. In short, this thread of ecofeminism advocates a "natural standpoint," a view from nature as if it were a singular entity, as if it had an ontology independent of society that society perverts and as if that natural being could be directly accessed through a specific series of everyday practices.

In this way, a fundamental problem many ecofeminist writers share is that they fail to assert strongly enough that ecofeminist nature is a social nature.[38] Ecofeminist myths of unity rest on the idea that humans can return to an organic state of grace by transcending the ways in which nature has been constructed in patriarchal development. Such a quest for organic harmony is impossible and dangerous: impossible because we can never know nature apart from culture, wilderness experiences notwithstanding; we cannot return to an organic state of grace because it has never existed. We may once have done less damage, but that is a question of social organization—of technology, of ideas, of social divisions—in relation to what gets constructed as nature, not a question of nature itself. And it is dangerous because it draws attention away from the fact that ecological degradation is a complex social problem. Instead, the task of ecology must be to question if not transcend the fundamentally misleading nature/culture split, to show that division as arbitrary, to come to new realizations of humans as always already simultaneously natural and cultural beings, and to work in the world aware of our limitations.

Also worth noting is the idea that if nature is the basis of identity, then even women, diverse and differently located though they may be, can be seen as unified from the perspective of this natural self. While some authors repudiate the idea of the naturalness of women, the idea that women are somehow more natural than men, there is within ecofeminism a moment that insists on carving out a distinct terrain of womanhood in which connections to nature are made. Whether that terrain is defined in terms of experiences of reproduction and hence knowledge of the continuity of life; whether that terrain is formed by different processes of ego development and hence a greater capacity to connect and nurture and less need to separate from primordial natural bonds; whether woman is more distant from male culture and hence closer to nature by virtue of exclusion; or even whether women, differently situated, are the mutual subjects of a naturalized gaze, there is a distinct thread that suggests a unified meaning to femininity. From my view, this is a misrecognized view of an uncreated and prepolitical identity that locates women and nature closer together.

The Charge of Essentialism

The language of essentialism has, over the years, become an important component of ecofeminist discussions. It has been used to distinguish an evolutionary trend in ecofeminism from biological determinism to social constructivism. It is a way for ecofeminists—accurately and inaccurately—to distance themselves from analytic tendencies that they see as dangerous and problematic. Although some critics wield the label as a blunt instrument and although some ecofeminists seem to think they are being nonessentialist as long as they are not biological determinists[39] (which I trust I have made clear is not the case; social construction and essentialism are not necessarily opposed concepts[40]), some recent discussions on this theme have produced exciting twists and turns in ecofeminist theory.

I will return to those twists in chapter 5, but would like to suggest here that it is around the charge of essentialism that ecofeminists have the most to gain by conversing with feminist postmodernism. It is not enough to critique biological determinism; the point is to question the origins and significance of any invocation of "women" (or of "nature") as a relatively stable or coherent category. As Denise Riley would point out, ecofeminist invocations of a specific identity for women—as opposed to men, for example—need to be questioned not only for their empirical exclusion of the experiences of particular women but for their own imbrication in the discursive operations of power. "Women," writes Riley, "is a volatile collectivity in which female persons can be very differently positioned";[41] part of the very practice of domination is the invocation of this category as if it were stable, as if it could be tied to a series of natural (and therefore, un-natural) practices of gender.

The ecofeminist assertion of distinct essences for women and nature is, in these terms, implicated in the very forms of power that ecofeminists see as problems. "Women" and "nature" are social constructs, discursive cate-gories produced in and through social practice in particular contexts, yet their ecofeminist representation as coherent, stable, and inherently mean-ingful reinforces their definitional power. The interesting thing in eco-feminism is that both representations tend to take the same shape: as characteristics of the self oppressed by and devalued in monolithic andro-centric culture, as aspects of living in the world that have always been pre-sent but are marginalized within dominant institutions. In other words, the ecofeminist usage of the categories "woman" and "nature" takes the partic-ular form of an identity politics based on a notion of stable difference, a difference that resides, very explicitly, in a nature that not only lies but should lie outside social life.

Reversal is not, if one is to take Riley's argument seriously, a sufficient sabotage. If "women" and "nature" are unstable discursive categories, them-selves crucial parts of the operations of the destructive forms of power that ecofeminists are trying to address, then reliance on highly stable notions of their meaning, on essences, would seem to detract from the potential of ecofeminism to change them. In ecofeminism, the binary oppositional structure that is seen as the source of the problem remains intact, which suggests that a process of questioning the forms of the dualism itself does not lie within the parameters of this ecofeminist strategy. Thus, King and others are led to a point where the woman/nature connection may not be biologically determined but that leaves the only possibilities for transfor-mation in an act of choosing to embrace the devalued pole and the prac-tices that this entails. An assumption of the stability of "women" and "na-ture" throughout historical, philosophical, and psychosocial developments renders ecofeminism a somewhat crude theoretical tool for the necessary destabilization process as complex configurations of social life are molded into a relatively unidimensional picture of dualism. What is necessary is a more thoroughly transgressive politics, one that shows the wielding of woman and nature as part of systems of domination, that shows dualism to be an oppressive fiction rather than a fact of nature itself.

Donna Haraway suggests that if organic dualism were ever an accurate depiction of social and natural life, it is not now. In her accounts of con-temporary "informatics of domination," she describes a world in which di-visions between male and female, between human and animal, and between nature and technology are breaking down: organic dualisms are no longer adequate to describe oppression or resistance. Her image of the cyborg, a boundary creature expressing this ambiguity, represents an attempt to go beyond these dualisms toward a political project based on the argument that:

> (1) the production of universal, totalizing theory is a major mistake that misses most of reality, probably always, but certainly now; (2) taking responsibility for the social relations of science and technology means refusing an anti-science metaphysics, a demonology of technology, and so means embracing the skilful task of *reconstructing* the boundaries of daily life, in partial connection with others, in communication with all our parts.[42]

This reconstruction, this process of showing discursive ambiguities, underscores a politics based more on transgression than on reification of organic boundaries. In order to understand environmentalism and feminism as related moments in a process of social transformation, but without the constraining—and, eventually, ineffective—limits of binary discourses of reversal, focus needs to be placed on some form of politics other than identity. Identities need to be questioned for their productive role in the creation and perpetuation of power relations, not assumed as privileged positions from which to view power relations.

In a very favorable reading of the potential of ecofeminism, Lee Quinby suggests that this interrogative form of resistance is already present within ecofeminist politics:

> Ecofeminism as a politics of resistance forces us to question the categories of experience that order the world and the truths we have come to know, even the truths of our radical politics, by confronting us with the truths of other women and men, differently acculturated, fighting against specific threats to their particular lands and bodies. This questioning must also extend to the anthropocentric assumption that only human beings have truths to tell about their and our experiences. The cries of factory farm animals, the suffocation of fish in poisoned waters, the sounds of flood waters rushing over deforested land—these are also voices we need to heed.[43]

Quinby's decentered politics represents a reading of parts of ecofeminism as specifically opposed to the problematic master narratives she sees in other political forms. While she notes the existence of essentialist ecofeminism, she shows a moment within contemporary feminist/ecological convergences that explicitly challenges the formulation of ecofeminism as a complete and coherent narrative of domination. I agree with Quinby wholeheartedly on this point; the seeds of alternative configurations of politics lie within the parameters of a feminist/ecological problematic. But the form of analysis needs to shift, certainly in the direction that Quinby suggests—a questioning of specificities through the recognition of poly-vocality—but also toward a direct confrontation with the bifurcating categories of human and nonhuman experience that order the world in oppositional pairs. Thus, Quinby's prescriptions might not go far enough; the idea of local truths in confrontation does not necessarily suggest rearranging the codes of human/natural understanding, or the challenge to natural identity that radical ecology so desperately needs to do.

4

From Natural Identity to Radical Democracy

In a 1990 essay exploring the relations between ecofeminism and deep ecology, Marti Kheel observed the following:

> It is out of women's unique, felt sense of connection to the natural world that an ecofeminist philosophy must be forged. Identification may, in fact, enter into this philosophy, but only to the extent that it flows from an existing connection with individual lives. Individual beings must not be used in a kind of psychological instrumentalism to help establish a feeling of connection that in fact does not exist. Our sense of oneness with nature must be connected with concrete, loving actions.[1]

In a 1994 essay evaluating ecofeminism's feminism, Victoria Davion had this to say about Kheel:

> If Kheel is right, much more needs to be said. Not all women feel connected to nature. Furthermore, some men may feel this more than many women. Hence, we should not assume that (1) all women feel this connection with nature or (2) the connections women do feel are healthy.[2]

As the preceding chapter demonstrated, there has been a great deal of work within recent feminist theory—including some ecofeminist theory—to problematize essentialist understandings of women's identity, including their relations to nature. But the problem of essentialism does not sum up the shortcomings of identity politics, and these feminist insights into it unfortunately are not always heeded. Even as identity politics come under scrutiny in some feminist circles, many radical ecological theories, including some ecofeminist ones, have gone to great lengths to create an identity for nature and to debate the authenticity and representativeness of the ones that other radical ecologies have asserted. Perhaps it is ecofeminism's position within both of these fields that has lent it such an ambivalent attitude toward identity, one in which a natural feminist standpoint is adored one moment and hated the next, sometimes even in the same article. My view is that there is also a larger question at stake: What if the radical ecological project of creating or discovering an identity for nature is both the apex of the democratic desire of identity politics *and* its final limit?

Nature, Voice, and the Subject

In her analysis of human voice-overs in wildlife documentaries, Margot La Rocque notes that the authoritarian and disembodied (usually male) voice is "primarily responsible for guiding the apparent haphazardness of natural events toward an intended meaning."[3] This problem of translation, the creation of sense from a world of possibly random events and processes, is a problem of all discourse but is perhaps most obvious when it is nature that is to be somehow ordered. This Other, this series of relationships and events, is both a constant presence in everyday human life and a politically charged entity in popular North American consciousness. It is, however, an enigma.

In contemporary environmental discourses, it is largely the voices of authority that guide our understandings of nature, of environmental crisis, and of any progress in halting ecological degradation. To cite an obvious example, witness the recent discussions of ozone depletion. Ultraviolet radiation, intangible and unknowable as it is in everyday consciousness, could appear on the front page of the *Globe and Mail* only through the voice of a science that could see nature for what it really is and translate it into a form that could be readily perceived. That the dire warnings of ozone depletion over the Arctic are subject to a variety of political agendas is irrelevant, if important, the fact of this environmental hazard lurks in everyday human consciousness as the product of a scientific voice that can experience nature tangibly and translate it into other realms of human comprehension.

One could argue (and many have) that ecology, a scientific field dealing with living organisms' relations to their surroundings, should be particularly influential in defining the nature of environmental crisis and in outlining the proper behavior of humans—as a species—for moving toward a more natural state, toward a series of social relations that more accurately reflects what our species would be doing under natural conditions, toward a less destructive vision. Unfortunately, as Neil Evernden notes, nature provides ecologists with (or, more accurately, ecologists read nature through) a number of conflicting versions of what the human species should be doing naturally. As he writes,

> We have [at least] three forms of belief about the action proper to human beings, all apparently justified by the insights of ecology. We can live "in harmony" with nature, which to some is clearly the "natural" thing to do; or we can expand our domain by direct competition with other species, which certainly seems (since Darwin) a "natural" enough thing to do; or we can [following the example of the spruce budworm] endorse the overexploitation of nature in certain knowledge that through our destruction we are doing nature's work, just as we were "naturally" meant to do.[4]

The idea that the wanton devastation of nature could be vindicated by the insights of ecological science is a clear expression of the message of environmentalism: "nature justifies nothing, or anything."[5] Models for human behavior are not given in nature; our understanding of ourselves as a species cannot be derived from ecological inquiry, as if ecology had a clear insight into the truth of human (or nonhuman) nature. Instead, as Evernden suggests, ideas of nature tell us far more about human social values and ideals than they tell us about human or nonhuman nature itself.

There is thus a considerable political problem involved in widespread and too often unquestioned reliance on science to guide ecological consciousness. The construction of nature as an object for methodical inquiry does little to change the social relations that many environmentalists see as part of the source of contemporary environmental malaise, of the alienation of humanity from nonhuman nature. Indeed, many currents of the environmentalist movement propose that alternative ways of knowing nature are crucial for any lasting reconciliation between human and nonhuman nature; the hegemonic epistemological filter of science, ecological or otherwise, needs to be supplanted by a variety of alternative experiences of nature, as part of both a short-term and a long-term project.

It is important to note, however, that all environmental discourse contains a moment of filtration, some point where nature is made knowable and meaningful; these discourses are not merely convenient descriptive fictions, but carry important implications for the prescribed relations between humans and nonhuman nature. For example, La Rocque notes that the contemporary wildlife voice-over "authorizes and sustains a limited number of relationships between human and nonhuman nature: by speaking *through* animals, *about* animals, or *for* animals, but rarely *as* animal."[6] The primacy of the first three modes of speech, she argues, maintains a series of relationships in which the privilege of the human species is guaranteed. All three represent the erasure of nonhuman nature and the replacement of its independent existence with fundamentally human projections of ontology as if they originated in the nature about which the speech is concerned.

In part as a result of these dominant discourses, much contemporary ecological philosophy and activism concerns itself with the construction of alternative modes of "speaking" nature that challenge these hierarchical constructs; these are political and epistemic projects to make nature known in ways consistent with the democratic discourses in which environmentalism is located. Indeed, La Rocque's project of "speaking as animals" has been taken up in a variety of ways within radical environmentalism. The recognition of the human being as animal is the goal of ecological theorists who locate human existence within complex ecospheric interactions. The construction of human beings as parts of nature who happen to speak is also the goal of ecophilosophers who would have us reconnect to the so-called natural aspects of ourselves as a way of addressing the ecological crisis and of finding speech for nonspeaking nature. Perhaps most importantly, the creation of an equivalence between the speech of oppressed humans and the speech of an oppressed nature suggests a relation in which democratic norms of listening are in operation; this is implicitly and sometimes explicitly the goal of many ecofeminists.

Consider another issue appearing on the front pages of the *Globe and Mail*: the authenticity of voice, an important element in the identity politics discussed in chapter 2. In the debates surrounding the question of who may or may not speak for whom, one side argues that the authentic speaker relies on direct experience of being a member of a relevant identity group; this version of authentic speech relies on identity, as speech is legitimated by belonging to or by being constructed within a consciousness created by social location.[7] The other side of the authenticity debate asserts that speech is enriched by taking the role of the Other, by constructing the Other through a projected "universal" experiencing of the world in which all speakers may find resonance as members of a speaking community. The process of writing or speaking through (not as) the Other is seen as part of a "journey to understand the works of humankind"[8] rather than as a quest for authenticity. But the politics of this position are complex: as Alan Hutcheon explains especially clearly, "In the same way that it is mistaken to believe that an author's identity has nothing to do with a work's authenticity, it is wrong to assume that it has everything to do with it. We should listen closely to the voice of oppression without mistaking it for an absolute truth."[9] The issue here is the presumed truth of any speaker as a perfect representative of a series of experiences; truth becomes imbricated in a politics of authenticity, and speech and writing become wrapped in a specific logic of identity and representation.

Rather than take sides in this debate, I would like to point out a dilemma: in identitarian logic, what is the "authentic" voice of nature? While La Rocque justifiably asserts that the limited perspective of the contemporary wildlife voice-over tends to reinforce hierarchical human/nature relationships through the construction of the Other in particular ways—making nature knowable via gross anthropomorphism or under the pretext of objective, distant knowledge, for example—it cannot be argued, as it has been in the controversy over the authenticity of voice, that we should simply let this oppressed voice speak itself. La Rocque's call to speak as nature may be useful in that it reinforces the idea that humans are animals, but it does not solve the problem of authentic speech for nonspeaking nature.[10] It seems more likely that humans who write or speak nature, whether that be through, about, for, or as nature, are embarked upon a journey to understand the works of nature through representing or taking the place of this Other in some way, and perhaps recognizing the self as part of nature as a result. But is this speech "authentic"?

This problem of voice, this problem of speaking nature, is at its core a problem of the subject. *Webster's* notes the polysemy of the word: "a topic; a theme; a person or idea being discussed. One who is under the authority of another. . . . The word representing the person or thing acting." Rendering nature knowable involves a process of subjectivation; constructing nature as a subject—in all of *Webster's* senses—is the task of environmentalism: by bringing up the topic of nature, by showing its subjection to an external authority, and by representing nature itself as an active subject. This last form of subjectivation is crucial; arguments oriented toward the eradication of hierarchical constructions of humans and nonhuman nature have concentrated on showing nature to be in and of itself an actor, a presence, a subject that needs to be taken into consideration as an equal rather than an object, as integral rather than background. And there are thus important moral and ethical considerations involved in any such construction.

But the problem of subjectivation is, fundamentally, a democratic one, as it is the political context of democracy that requires the public creation or representation of a speaking subject. It is through speech that actors reveal their interests and needs to one another; it is through political rhetoric that persuasion and negotiation take place. It is thus the speaker who is the fundamental actor of democratic public life. How, then, does nature speak—reveal and persuade—for itself? Similarly, a persistent problem is that nature is not a singular coherent entity; even as a single ecoregion, so often the subject of environmentalist controversy, is not necessarily authentically spoken as a solo voice. Furthermore, are humans part of the nature that gets spoken or not?[11] The forms of speech that are given legitimacy in political discourse, the realm in which environmentalism represents itself, always requires some form of translation; problems of objectification, of affirmative action, of construction, and of appropriation are therefore also involved. Even if humans speak as animals, as singular parts of a plural nature; even if we choose not to represent difference of speech as lack of speech; even if we represent ourselves as speakers of human relations to nonhuman nature (productive, reproductive, or metaphoric), it cannot be said that nature is spoken comprehensively as an identity in and for the political realm in which it must be represented. In the terms of argument cast by contemporary politics of identity, speaking nature is impossible: there cannot be an authentic voice of nature without profound revision of either the notion of speech or the notion of the speaking subject. The "I" that speaks in environmentalist discourse cannot speak as the subject in these terms: it is always already something else, subject to a process of translation through other identities, through myriad relationships and interactions, through other forms of language.

More broadly, however, what the idea of speech in identity politics highlights is a form of democratic subjectivation—the construction of political consciousness, an "I," through the necessary uncovering and reconstruction of ways of being in the world oppressed and marginalized by hegemonic political and cultural formations. For a woman, for example, the right to speak differently and not be spoken for is not merely a question of claiming equal power in the privileged male domain of speech but a way of discovering or creating a new voice to express experiences not apprehensible through dominant constructs; democracy requires a different kind of speech, not just more of the same. This process represents both means and ends: the creation of a new series of codes through which to perceive and act in the world and through which to challenge and therefore change dominant and oppressive constructions of sense.

Aspects of identity politics are increasingly prevalent in environmentalist discourses. For example, as I described earlier, ecofeminism has been centered on a theoretical construction in which women and nature are constructed as related identities through a process of historical association, psychosocial development, and marginalization from androcentric culture. It is in deep ecology, however, that the appearance of an environmental identity politics—including an authentic nature speech—is most visible, even if the genesis of this identity is not overtly democratic. The phrase "thinking like a mountain" suggests a process in which the empathetic relation to nature, the recognition of the self as natural (or nature as self), forms the terrain upon which legitimate and progressive speech is grounded. The speech of human beings *as* nature, as not over and above other species but as part of the ecosphere, is seen as a way of reconnecting both to the nature outside and to the natural parts of ourselves that have been suppressed through centuries of environmental devaluation and degradation. The reintegration of this aspect of ourselves to other aspects of nature is seen as a way of creating new ways of living in, on, and as parts of the earth. For example, Theodore Roszak notes the centrality of reintegrating to ecological living:

> The core of the mind is the ecological unconscious. For ecopsychology, repression of the ecological unconscious is the deepest root of collusive madness in industrial society; open access to the ecological unconscious is the path to sanity. . . . Ecopsychology seeks to heal the more fundamental alienation between the person and the natural environment.[12]

Although the word *democracy* is seldom uttered in deep ecological circles, the democratic logic of identity is quite apparent in their calls for nature's representation; one of the end results of this search for an ecological unconscious is a voice for nature. For many deep ecologists, the work of listening to nature is a fundamental act of overcoming an essential human alienation from nature; for others, overcoming alienation nominates the self as a privileged natural speaker. As John Seed puts it, "I try to remember that it's not me, John Seed, trying to protect the rainforest. Rather I am part of the rainforest protecting myself, I am that part of the rainforest recently emerged into human thinking."[13] Self-questioning and the exploration of ego boundaries to cultivate a different sense of ecological awareness is potentially seen as part of a legitimating act for political representation.

The notion of the subject at the base of identity politics—ecological and otherwise—is highly problematic. For example, the call for authenticity by deep and other ecologies underlies an identity politics that finds its legitimacy in prepolitical rather than political life. Authenticity is the rhetorical veil over misrecognition; it is only with an idea of a foundational experiential (prepolitical) truth that there can be any debate about the "right" to take up a particular voice in political discussion. The assumption is that there is a difference that must be represented, and that only those who experience that difference before and outside the act of its revelation (actually its constitution) in speech are legitimately able to engage in any representational practice. There can be no appearance of construction, no appearance of imagination, no appearance of taking the role of the Other; there can only be expression, even though the appearance of expression might serve to reify the identity and experience being spoken.

When it is nature that is being spoken, the claim to authenticity transports the speaker into a form of prepolitical legitimation that can be exceedingly dangerous. Even if deep ecological and other claims to listen to, know, and speak nature are intended as a challenge to hegemonic scientific epistemological relations (which they often are), any claim to represent nature fully—as identity—bears with it shades of a potentially authoritarian naturalism. Given that claims to nature are often used to legitimate particular social relations (like the supposed naturalness of patriarchy and the supposed unnaturalness of homosexuality), some deep ecologists end up nominating themselves as the only legitimate speakers of either nonhuman or human life. Deep ecology contains within it the seeds of a truly problematic (not just undemocratic but antidemocratic) authoritarianism; even if few actually engage in it; how else is it possible to explain a certain deep ecologist's assertion that AIDS is nature's revenge on humanity? The claim to know, when unaccountable and naturalized, is a dangerous thing indeed.

The identity of environmental identity politics is closed, fixed, beyond the social, and, most importantly, completed and speakable. The "I" who speaks is seen as a coherent totality, a representative of an identity, a post-Cartesian ego that, in Lacanian terms, is "a fixed, whole, entity that is innate or instinctual, and—if not divinely—then genetically, neurophysiologically, chemically, or developmentally determined."[14] The fact that the environmental subject can never be that speaking "I" not only calls into question the applicability of identity politics to ecological struggle, but reaffirms the idea that this identity is not the only possible form of political subjectivity and that the subject is always already more complex than this singular form of representation admits. In order to rescue democratic desire from the limitations of identity politics—including the limits shown to us so clearly in nature representation—it is necessary to look to other ways of theorizing democratic subjectivity.

Critiques of and alternatives to the post-Cartesian subject are numerous. Ecological philosophy itself has been adamant that the dualistic basis of this form of thought results in the polarization of conceptions of human and nature, nature being not human and therefore inferior. Indeed, even in deep ecology there is a certain tension between an idealized speaking self and a critique of humanistic overvaluation of speech and language. But perhaps the most sustained critique of the a priori, empirical subject comes from psychoanalysis.[15] Particularly in the works of French analyst Jacques Lacan and his followers, the subject is shown to be more fiction than positivity; in fact, Lacan's conception of the subject as "the empty place of the structure" views the Cartesian subject not as simply incomplete, but as impossible.[16]

Briefly, Lacan sees the subject as characterized by a fundamental, insoluble alienation. In what he calls the mirror stage of development, in which the child recognizes the self as distinct from the (m)Other, the theme of absence is fundamental. The construction of the self as an active social agent is dependent on the recognition that the world does not belong to the child. Elizabeth Grosz describes the significance of this process to the developing ego:

> From this time on, lack, gap, splitting will be its mode of being. It will attempt to fill its (impossible, unfillable) lack. Its recognition of lack signals an ontological rift with nature or the Real. This gap will propel it into seeking an identificatory image of its own stability and permanence (the imaginary), and eventually language (the symbolic) by which it hopes to fill the lack.[17]

The subject per se (and not just the ego) emerges with the insertion of the individual into the Symbolic order, the gaze of the Other, the totality of signifiers. What is important to note in Lacan is that the Symbolic order is also marked by a fundamental lack, a core of representational impossibility; the production of meaning is, as a result, permanently contingent, as there is no fixed anchoring point to the signifier. The signifier cannot perfectly correspond to the signified; instead, meaning is partially and momentarily fixed through a retroactive process in which a *point de capiton* (literally, "upholstery button") temporarily halts the sliding of meaning of signifiers and signifieds. Thus, the agent is involved in a process of trying to compensate for the fundamental lack marking it through the construction of a self spoken through these sliding meanings; she or he can never completely do so, however, as "the subject of the signifier is precisely . . . this impossibility of finding a signifier which would be 'its own.'"[18] The process of subjectivation, the process through which the agent finds imaginary and symbolic identifications in the taking up of different subject positions, does not produce a subject. To quote Slavoj Žižek,

> If we make an abstraction, if we subtract all the richness of the different modes of subjectivation, all the fullness present in the way individuals are 'living' their subject-positions, what remains is an empty place which was filled out with this richness; this original void, this lack of symbolic structure, is the subject, the subject of the signifier.[19]

The subject, then, is opposed to identity; it is, instead, the point of failure of identification. The subject marks the failure of the Symbolic, the limits of signification; the Symbolic, in turn, produces the subject as the effect of its own constitutive lack. Or, as Lacan puts it in his typical style, "the subject is born in so far as the signifier emerges in the field of the Other. But, by this very fact, the subject—which was previously nothing if not a subject coming into being—solidifies into a signifier."[20]

What we have is a radical contingency in which signifier and signified cannot correspond, in which identification is produced through the taking up of subject positions to mask the lack in the subject, and in which the meaning of these subject positions is determined not by some reference to positive realities but to an arbitrary and external anchoring point that temporarily fixes the continual sliding of meaning of signifiers and signifieds. It is a dynamic notion of the subject, in which identification cannot be fixed. It is also a reversal of contemporary understandings: politics do not emerge from identity, but identity, incomplete, partial, and transient, emerges from politics.

Perhaps this is the "real" logic of the misrecognition of identity, in which an act of masking—representing a coherent self in language in order to bypass lack—bears particular societal and political meaning. Where identity politics show a relationship between identity and politics that traces a path from the former to the latter, it seems instead that the reverse is closer to the truth. Identity involves the intervention of a nodal point that collects a certain set of interpreted experiences and produces from them a sense of coherence as if the identity in question emerged from somewhere else. It is not that identity doesn't exist; it is that it is an intrasocial process that actually masks the impossibility of its completion, its fullness, of overcoming its constitutive lack.

The implications of this version of the subject for environmental politics are significant for a number of reasons. Among other things, the lack of correspondence between subject and subject position—including nature's—underlies the particular vision of radical democracy that is the focus of the second half of this book and which includes the constitutive tensions and exclusions engendered in relations of lack. For now, though, what is most important to note is that the impossibility of identity—the process of identification as masking the fundamental alienation of the subject—implies a profound critique of the project of finding a speaking subject for nature. The creation of the subject of environmentalism is, in this schema, not about speech and expression; it is about a process of contingency in which the emergence of this subject within the Symbolic order is always already part of a chain of meaning created by the anchoring of particular signifiers through a *point de capiton*. More specifically, there is a fundamental tension between the emergence of the subject of environmentalism in a particular sociopolitical context that stresses the importance of identity as politics and the limits of that project that are inherent not only in the notion of the subject upon which these politics are based but in environmentalism itself.

Ecology and Political Subjectivity

Laclau and Mouffe have examined these insights of Lacan in terms of their political potential, specifically for a "post-Marxist" politics that acknowledges a diversity of contemporary social movement struggles. They have postulated that the notion of antagonism contains a recognition of the lack characterizing both the subject and the Symbolic order. Arguing against the transparent "class" subject described earlier, one capable of recognizing and acting upon its objective interests in confrontation with an equally transparent enemy, Laclau and Mouffe argue that antagonism represents the process through which the Other's existence bars the full constitution of identity for the agent. (Likewise, the Other is also marked by limits.) Social conflict, then, is not a battle among identities but is organized around the impossibility of the constitution of identities.

Society itself is marked by the sliding of meaning around a constitutive lack that is the limit of the social, of the Symbolic. Indeed, it is traversed by a variety of antagonisms, a variety of places where the presence of some Other prevents the constitution of complete identity. These antagonistic identifications, to Laclau and Mouffe, are the loci of political struggle, of struggles for identity in the face of the Other. Such identifications do not exist in isolation, but emerge as political struggles within a certain discursive context—specifically, within a chain of equivalences that temporarily fixes specific struggles, specific political identifications, as related. This process is one of articulation, in which each element in the signifying network achieves precise meaning only in relation to other elements, and only temporarily. Thus, the meaning of any political struggle, any antagonism, exists only in relation to other political struggles; as no social identity is ever totally achieved, each is subject to the effects of its changing meaning in discursive space.

The radical potential of any political identification, then, is neither determined in advance nor fixed into the future; it depends on its articulation with other struggles, on its location in a chain of equivalences among subject positions, on the creation of a new subject position capable of creating affinities among a diverse range of antagonisms. Žižek gives a most relevant example, which I will cite at length to illustrate a crucial point:

> Insofar as the participant in the struggle for democracy "finds out by experience" that there is no real democracy without the emancipation of women, insofar as the participant in the ecological struggle "finds out by experience" that there is no real reconciliation with nature without abandoning the aggressive-masculine attitude towards nature, insofar as the participant in the peace-movement "finds out by experience" that there is no real peace without radical democratization, etc., that is to say, insofar as the identity of each of the . . . above-mentioned positions is marked by the metaphorical surplus of the other . . . positions, we can say that something like a unified subject-position is being constructed: to be a democrat means at the same time to be a feminist, etc. What we must not overlook is, of course, that such a unity is always radically contingent, the result of symbolic condensation, and not an expression of some kind of internal necessity according to which the interests of all the above-mentioned positions would in the long run "objectively convene." It is quite possible, for example, to imagine an ecological position which sees the only solution in a strong anti-democratic, authoritarian state resuming control over the exploitation of natural resources, etc.[21]

I have argued elsewhere that ecology must include this type of radical democratic articulation among a diverse range of subject positions in order to challenge dominant notions of the environment as an object and in order to transcend the version of environmental politics offered to us by states and corporations that unproblematically link a shallow "green" agenda with a continued project of economic growth and exploitation.[22] I would like to argue here, perhaps even more strongly, that the subject of environmentalism is always contingent on its articulation with other subject positions in some chain of equivalences. None is a "true" representation, as a subject cannot be completely captured in a subject position, but the ability of an environmental subject position to effectively challenge dominant discursive formations depends on its articulation with other democratic struggles.

Radical ecologies in various incarnations are located within a chain of equivalences emphasizing the relatedness of a variety of forms of oppression and liberation. To take the example provided by ecofeminism, it is not simply that feminism and environmentalism are allied struggles, but that the very antagonistic forces of oppression that are seen to prevent women's full identity as women and nature's full realization as nature are one and the same; the fantasy is that women's full identity is, in part, *as* a self-realized nature. In this construction of political affinity, the two subjects exist as equivalences, occupying the same space in relation to the antifeminist, antiecological Other that prevents the full constitution of either identity.

But the emergence of the subject of environmentalism is not only conditioned by equivalence of position in a chain of contingent meaning; the form in which political subjectivity is expressed is also influenced by other struggles.[23] Specifically, the radical ecological notion of nature as speaking identity has emerged as a democratic subject position conditioned by notions of democracy already present in the other social movement struggles with which it is not only contemporary but articulated. As described earlier, these notions of democracy have been shaped by ideas emphasizing the need to value those identities repressed by the dominant culture. Democracy therefore involves the creation of new codes and meanings, new modes of speech, from these repressed identities to represent and construct alternative, liberatory ways of being in the world for that oppressed group. Democracy is contingent not just on the ability to speak, but on the mode of speech itself.

The radical potential of environmentalism has thus been contingent on a location within a series of democratic equivalences that has tended to take the form of identity politics. The quest for an identity for nature is, in environmentalism, thus understandable as a product of articulation. Given that the project of many contemporary social movements has been to find and empower a speaking subject that can somehow be an authentic voice of a set of oppressed experiences, the quest for a speaking, natural subject represents a radical move in the direction of democracy: the construction of a voice to represent, in a forum of democratic identities, a distinct but equivalent subject position. The move toward an identity for nature is, in context, a deeply democratic one.

What this putatively democratic project overlooks, of course, is the impossibility of finding a nature to be spoken devoid of human social construction (that would represent the speech of the antagonist!) and unaffected by processes of subjectivation. The quest for an alternative way of reading and living in nature that is not characterized by hierarchical constructions placing humanity over nature may be a useful exercise in the quest toward new constructions of nature, if articulated with new constructions of other social relations. It can never be a presocial nature that speaks in a democratic forum, however. The nature that we may find in ecological searches for a subject is always a construction of that Other from the point at which we appear to ourselves as natural or natured, not nature itself; finding the subject of environmentalism is always a project of language, of the Symbolic order, of creating images of likeness in the context of a structure that emphasizes certain elements defining similarity. What we may find in our quest is a permanently social product apprehended through a certain filter defining some elements as representing nature to ourselves—the trace of the impossible subject as a particular subject position. This is not to say that the rest of the world does not exist except as a human construct. It does suggest that members of the human species cannot know nature except through, and in the context of, specifically human social and natural relations. Not only is it the case that what counts as nature changes drastically across different cultures and historical periods, nor is it only the case that nature tells us nothing about itself except through the particular(ly) human language through which we listen to it; rather, it is also the case that nature as a realm to know or represent is already the product of a particular understanding of it, an opposition to the artificial, the human social, the virtual. In other words, nature cannot be represented in human language in a way that does not distort its being-in-itself.

It is this problem of representation that shows the limits of identity politics themselves, not just for environmentalism but for democratic politics more broadly. It is not just the natural subject that cannot be apprehended through the taking up of a subject position, an identification in the realm of the Symbolic. The subject is the point of failure of subjectivation; identity is impossible, as is a speech that claims to represent it. Thus, the trip through the Lacanian subject is potentially very relevant for ecology; it highlights a political problem already present in the fact that the quest for a democratic environmental subject position to fit an alliance of identities cannot be realized. This impossibility is highlighted in—even if it is not unique to—environmentalism, and it calls into question the promise of the project for those struggles with which it is articulated.

Although the radical potential of environmentalism can be achieved only through its articulation with other democratic struggles, the process of articulation itself shows the limits of contemporary versions of social movement politics. Speaking as animals or speaking as nature is a project grounded in notions of democracy and liberation, but its fundamental impossibility suggests the necessity of alternative configurations. The seeds of an alternative political form, one that includes a notion of subjectivity markedly similar to the Lacanian version outlined above, are already present in ecological struggles and contain the potential to transform social movement struggles toward a more progressive articulation.

Culture, Nature, and the Limits of the Social

Žižek suggests that the main achievement of Laclau and Mouffe's political vision, the construction of a radical politics based on the articulation of democratic subject positions rather than on an a priori empirical subject, "is that, perhaps for the first time, it articulates the contours of a political project based on . . . an ethics of confrontation with an impossible, traumatic kernel not covered by any *ideal* (of the unbroken communication, of the invention of the self)."[24] Such a project was not, of course, theorized from thin air; it was born of the incapacity of Marxism, with its emphasis on a clear class protagonist realizing its objective interests, to represent contemporary social conflict.

In many ways, ecological politics have also responded to the limitations of the Marxist subject, both through criticisms of Marx's location of the class subject in a notion of nature as a "necessity to be overcome" and through more general explorations of the constructions of nature implicit in various political projects oriented toward human liberation. Ecofeminism is a particularly good example of this process, highlighting as it does both the need for feminism in environmental politics and the need for a consideration of nature in feminism. Environmentalism has clearly developed through its location in other political forms and has become more radical as a result; it has always, however, existed in a somewhat uneasy relationship to these other forms because of its emphasis on the limits of human action in the world. As social movements have moved toward transformations of human life in the world, environmentalism has suggested that there are always nonhuman actors involved in this process and thus that there are limits to the social.[25]

The idea of limits frequently is invoked in a rather crude way: limits to growth, limited numbers of resources, limits to pollution beyond which irreparable damage will occur, etc. Such limits are seen as produced by nature; they are biological lines beyond which the social cannot go if nature is to survive. Clearly, this notion is problematic: it assumes a particular idea of nature—nature as balanced, nature as an objective presence—that Will Wright, among others, suggests is more the product of scientific desire for technical coherence than it is the presence of the natural world.[26] The idea of an objective nature perpetuates a problematic opposition between nature and culture, nature as a realm of reality for technical knowledge to measure; it also fails to point out that limits are a social product, a question of tolerance levels conditioned by particular human, power-laden constructions of what nature is supposed to be like.

At the same time, however, environmentalist politics have a more radical conception of limits: the idea of nature as a horizon produced through the social. William Irwin Thompson suggests that the idea of an objective existence of nature is seriously questionable, based as it is on the very historically specific idea that nature is what is left over when the human subject is subtracted. In an interview for a 1990 Canadian Broadcasting Corporation (CBC) *Ideas* program, he describes a view that suggests nature as an arbitrary threshold rather than a positive presence:

> Let me give you Lynn Margulis' example of what is nature. She said all the environmentalists come to Boston and they look at Boston harbour and say it's dead and it's polluted and it's unnatural. And she says no, I see all my friends out there—meaning all her bacteria that she studies—and they're chewing the tires and they're frolicking in the oil slick. And you have a whole sense that it is an arrogant consumer's 19th century aristocratic image of nature that [the environmentalists are] talking about. So nature is a fiction. I think the only precise way you can define it is there is no such thing as nature. Nature is the horizon of culture, and whatever you are in, in whatever human activity, you will always have a horizon.[27]

Despite the common tendency to characterize nature as a positive presence, there remains a moment even within this very discourse that subverts its positivization. Because of the very lack of a speaking subject to give voice to a set of positive experiences, environmentalism has been characterized by an agenda of searching for ways to construct a natural subject rather than one of assuming that the subject exists in some completed form in the present. This search actually draws attention to the limits of subjectivity—the point at which nature is achieved is always beyond the grasp of social identity, partly as a result of these particular constructions of what nature is in the first place. For example, in the wilderness view, nature exists by subtraction; if nature is the point where the social ends, then it cannot possibly be represented through the social as a positivity. The quest for natural identity is always marked by the failure of the social. Thus, the limits implicit in environmentalism are not biological, but social: the failed quest for identity shows, in a dramatic way, the impossibility of the project of completed identification, of the completed social, itself.

There always remains a fundamental core of nature that resists subjectivation; this problem is implicit in all ecological politics, and is explicit in more contemporary views that question the possibility of the positivity of nature. Neil Evernden, for example, writes that "Nature" (with a capital "N") is also a mode of concealment, a cloak of abstractions which obscures the discomforting wildness that defies our paranoid urge to delineate the boundaries of Being . . . [yet] even a rigorous nomenclature may not constitute a permanent constraint."[28] Any language of nature is destined to fail, and this failure requires recognition of a moment of nature that overflows any attempt to capture its positivity.

It is this process of questioning the positivity of nature that underscores the radical potential of ecology. If nature is impossible, then, as Thompson has noted, ecology is the study of what lies within our horizons, the study of the construction of nature as a social process, the temporary representation of the impossible Other as it marks human activity. Ecology is thus primarily oriented toward the recognition of antagonism, the impossibility of self-constitution (or, in other language, of naming), rather than toward the recognition of a clear and transparent enemy; the antagonistic force shows itself within the realm of human activity, within the social, and shows by extension that limits mark every identity.

Stated differently, ecology has us reexamine the subject of politics; it calls into question, in an urgent and profound way, the possibility of full human self-constitution as a political project. It shifts the basis of politics away from a quest for a speaking subject, a bearer of revolutionary consciousness, toward an understanding that this subject cannot possibly exist and that social change is based on this impossibility, an inherent self-limit. This recognition means that political actors cannot rely on a speaking subject to produce a new truth, be it a truth of nature or one emanating from any particular set of experiences, but must instead shoulder the responsibility for constituting a society that validates plurality as permanently unfixed and that recognizes ambiguity. This idea is reflected in Laclau and Mouffe's conception of radical democracy. In Mouffe's words,

> What we need is a hegemony of democratic values, and this requires a multiplication of democratic practices, institutionalizing them into ever more diverse social relations, so that a multiplicity of subject-positions can be formed through a democratic matrix. . . . Such a hegemony will never be complete, and anyway, it is not desirable for a society to be ruled by a single democratic logic. Relationships of authority and power cannot completely disappear, and it is important to abandon the myth of a transparent society, reconciled with itself, for that kind of fantasy leads to totalitarianism. A project of radical and plural democracy, on the contrary, requires the existence of multiplicity, of plurality, and of conflict, and sees them as the *raison d'être* of politics.[29]

This notion of a proliferation of democratic struggles is embedded in ecology's implicit recognition of the impossibility of the subject: if every identity is in itself inherently blocked, then the environmental subject is only temporarily captured through its location in a contingent chain of subject positions. While ecology is created and radicalized through its location in a series of democratic discourses, the inclusion of nature in transformative struggle highlights the fact that it is democracy, not identity, that forges the links in the chain. No identity is fixed; each is only temporarily captured through its construction within a signifying chain. It is the chain itself, not some solid organic convergence, that defines the transformative potential of any politics.

Thus, articulation is not simply useful; it defines the potential of each element in the chain. The creation of any form of solidarity rests upon the strengthening of a chain of struggles not through the recognition of a privileged revolutionary subject but through the solidification of equivalences among struggles. Ecology highlights this necessity. Struggles "for" nature must be, ultimately, radically democratic, as there is no other way of struggling "as" nature; instead, we produce nature through the process of articulation itself. While increasingly, transformative social movements are moving in the direction of coalition, more profoundly understanding the interconnectedness of democratic struggles and the impossibility of the construction of a speaking "I" to represent revolutionary consciousness, in no other movement is this necessity so starkly displayed. And the growing inclusion of environmental issues within other social movements shows that just as ecology cannot exist without democracy, so too must democracy include ecology.[30]

Perhaps even more profoundly, the inclusion of ecology in chains of democratic equivalence points to the ways in which the misrecognition of identity, as discussed in chapter 2, might become increasingly visible. Calling nature into question shows the problems of invoking nature as the referent for any identity. If nature is not a priori, then its invocation as a moment of origin, its discursive use as a metaphor for order, is called into serious question. It becomes apparent that nature tells us nothing directly and that social ideas of nature have been used to give order and legitimacy to visions of the ideal world. With the disentangling of ideas of nature from ideas of order or origin, it becomes more difficult to point to some tangible presocial domain in which identity can exist outside of mutable political and social relations.

But what of ecofeminism? Is its analysis so irrevocably grounded in misrecognition, standpoint epistemologies and identity politics, so strongly committed to a transparent speaking nature, that it cannot be recalled from the edge of the democratic cliff? It is obviously my opinion that this is not the case. Despite many ecofeminists' tendency toward the use of natural identity as a ground for epistemological privilege and political legitimacy, there have been—especially in recent works—many attempts to critique and transcend the theoretical and political inadequacy of identity politics. In the end, most ecofeminists' desire for democracy is fundamentally more important than their desire for identity, and this promise can be rescued from the inevitable limits of identity politics. Put even more forcefully, there has always been in ecofeminism a tacit recognition of the limits of identity, and even of the problems with standpoint epistemologies, because of the uncertain and problematic nature that lies at the heart of ecofeminists' desired speech.

Lori Gruen writes toward an ecofeminist moral epistemology with precisely this understanding in mind, so I will end this section with her gesture toward ecofeminism's radical democratic promise. Gruen begins from the fundamental understanding that nonhuman nature cannot speak for itself in human language, but this does not dampen her desire to include nature in democratic conversations. She thus writes, pragmatically, that "actual experiences of the nonhuman world will create better knowledge of nature and can only help us make more informed judgements about our relation to it."[31] But here is the most important part: not only does she refuse to privilege a single, best voice for nature, she recognizes that people's relations to nature are embedded in good, bad, and contradictory experiences. Not only does she include the possibility that there are nonexperiential episte-mologies of nature that might have some value in democratic conversa-tions, but she refuses the idea that the truth of nature can be discovered by way of a quest for identity at all. And best of all, she argues that democrat-ic speech must proceed with a sort of humility that requires a recognition of the limits of standpoint truth claims:

> The inclusion of nature in normative epistemic communities not only al-lows for a wider set of experiences from which to draw in generating value claims, but also provides important opportunities for reconstituting our-selves. This type of inclusive community forces everyone in it to reassess their relationship to each other and the natural world. This reassessment is facilitated by the practice of "methodological humility," a method of deep respect for differences. Methodological humility requires that one operate under the assumption that there may be some concept or event that cannot be immediately understood. . . . It is enhanced if it is practised not only with people, but with nature as a whole.[32]

PART II

The Quest

for a Radical

Democratic

Politics

5

Cyborgs and Queers:

Ecofeminism and the Politics of Coalition

[Ecofeminist] struggle must not be fractured by the unnecessary divisions of reform vs. revolution, personal change vs. political struggle, ideological purity vs. well-meaning confusion, or the sustainability of the planet vs. the livelihood of workers. What matters is that we build "bridges of power" reaching out to each other and moving toward a common dream.

Mary Mellor, "Building a New Vision"

In light of the splits that have taken place within the ecology and feminist movements, I would argue against calls for coherence . . . [and] cite eco-feminism as an example of a coalitional practice that has combated eco-logical destruction and masculinist domination without (yet) succumbing to the totalizing impulses of hegemonic politics.

Lee Quinby, Anti-Apocalypse

It is my contention that one of the most pressing questions faced by eco-feminists and other democratically inspired political actors surrounds is-sues of coalition and affinity. In ecological politics, it is only through some sort of a coalitional move—a desire to speak with and of but not for the Other—that nature can be spoken in a democratic forum, given that its presence cannot be grasped through the taking up of a natural identity (indeed, given that nature actually shows a moment of disjuncture between subject position and subject, thus offering a route into the questioning of the possibility of identity itself). More broadly, coalition has come to represent the struggles of connection in which new social movements are seen to transcend the kinds of sectarianism and parochialism that have come to be associated with identity politics. It is in the process of finding common ground for discussion (or, to use other language, creating "chains of equivalence") that apparently narrow interests may be linked together conversationally in a broader agenda of democratic transformation.

But this process of linkage and articulation, as Laclau and Mouffe note, has the effect of temporarily fixing the identities of the actors thus made equivalent. In the context of a feminist politics (eco- or otherwise) that seeks to challenge and disrupt the social categories through which women (among others) have been represented and arrested—as is the challenge, for example, of feminist postmodernism—coalitional politics would seem to have the unintended effect of undermining the possibility of transgression. Even if chains of equivalence are not produced out of natural convergence or inner necessity, in order for a politics of shared position to last beyond the fleeting moment of its production, something has to be made solid from the surrounding air. Despite the unnaturalness of chains of equivalence, they are not arbitrary, and the nodal points producing them are part of the potentially reified system of signifiers that feminist postmodernists, among others, seek to challenge.

Tensions between coalition (the possibility of a collective politics beyond any given identity category) and transgression (the desire to subvert dominant identity categories) are part of contemporary social movements' democratic desire and trajectory. While both of these directions can be understood as taking identity politics away from a singular focus on a singular identity, the former by showing the limits of identification and the latter by demanding the location of identification in the context of multiple possibilities and multiple antagonisms, they pull politics in opposite directions, as it were. Transgression suggests an inward-looking focus on disrupting the possibility of a given identity; equivalence suggests an outward-looking focus on connection with other identities through at least a temporary halting of the play of identificatory possibilities. Although these two projects exist in tension, I think they are not necessarily mutually exclusive.

Specifically, there is in recent ecofeminist literature an attempt to pro-

duce a version of political appearance for concerns around gender and nature that is explicitly critical of both essentialism and the limits of the
charge of antiessentialism. In such texts, elements of an ecofeminist orientation toward a transgressive or ironic parody of its own subject position
are readily apparent. In the context of ecofeminism's founding on a moment of coalition between feminist and ecological politics (in which one
can argue that each distinct position bars the full appearance of the other,
producing an ironic claim to representation) and in the context of its
growing recognition of the nonsolidity of nature itself, the tensions between equivalence and antagonism so productive to a radical democratic
vision find a good example in ecofeminism, but only if ecofeminism resists
the desire toward the reinscription of a solid identity. This ironic position-
ality, while not the be-all and end-all of politics (ecofeminist or otherwise), suggests a starting point for a revivified understanding of articulation that does not rest on halting the play of signification but instead sees
signification itself as a political site.

Coalition, or Creating Chains of Equivalence

I begin with a rather contentious statement: coalition inhabits post-
Marxist political discourse in much the same way as the revolutionary class
did in some older Marxist rhetorics (or at least in 1990s retrospective
views of them). Indeed, it has in many ways replaced this class subject as
an idealized form of political comprehensiveness and solidarity. In older
rhetorics, solidarity was seen to come about as the result of recognition of
shared interest, even shared identity, in relation to an objective location in
capitalist relations of production; given that this location was the site of
the singular conflict that would spawn revolutionary activity, class became
the site for the recognition of objective solidarity.

   Coalition, while similarly privileging relations of solidarity, reflects a
contemporary denial of the transformational primacy of any single social
location. Given that no one set of objective interests encompasses the totality of social conflicts in need of transformation, the process of making
connections among a variety of antagonisms becomes crucial to a politics
that maintains some commitment to comprehensiveness or, in Laclau and
Mouffe's terms, a hegemony of democratic values. Coalition here is seen to
reflect both a respect for the particular and a continued desire for a universal politics. Perhaps even more importantly, coalition is able to speak to
the proliferation of identities associated with new social movements, to

signal the possibility and desirability of site-specific alliances, and to both respect and engender the production of identities in and for particular political struggles, even as it continues a desire for a politics that transcends any specificity.

Coalition is thus to be understood as a political response to fragmentation in light of a continued desire for something beyond the self-limiting social movement. In one reading, coalition represents the tying together of a range of identities produced in late-twentieth-century rearticulations of capital. To Carl Boggs, for example, coalition is the process of identifying the ways in which a variety of actors share an apparently objective interest in transforming the mode of production. While different actors find themselves differently situated in capitalist relations of production, and thus faced with particular struggles and interests, coalition holds out the potential of recognizing a common interest in challenging capital and thus of linking these diverse struggles together.[1]

In Laclau and Mouffe's radical democratic reading, however, no such objective interests are in place through which to cement a shared politics; chains of equivalence are not a product of the recognition of shared objective interests but result from the retrospective ability of a nodal point to produce shared meaning among a variety of different political spaces, a shared understanding of position in a democratic chain. Clearly, this shared meaning is not simply an ephemeral production of political rhetoric; the ability of a nodal point to temporarily fix a sense of shared direction among a variety of struggles stems from its engagement with existing antagonisms. But these antagonisms are neither objective nor fixed; they are fluid, contextual, relational, and permanently partial. The nodal point does not spring from thin air, but neither is it determined by any natural convergence of issues or positions. Indeed, a vital moment in coalitional political rhetoric is its ability to construct connections among struggles that may be not only diverse, but opposed to one another in many respects. Coalition here represents "a transient island in a sea of antagonisms"; the island may emerge above sea level as a result of volcanic social eruptions, but its eventual topography is the product of active political construction.[2]

An example might clarify my meaning. In Canada (as elsewhere), there exists a dominant rhetoric that explicitly pits workers against environmentalists. In conflicts over the preservation of old-growth forests, like the ongoing controversy in Clayoquot Sound, loggers are perceived by some wilderness advocates from Greenpeace, the Sierra Club, and the Western

Canada Wilderness Committee as embodying precisely the attitudes and practices that are the source of the problem; they are seen as narrow and self-interested in the constructions of wilderness advocates who see themselves as embodying ecological values and respect for the needs of future generations and other species. From the apparently opposite perspective, some loggers—like many employees of MacMillan Bloedel—view environmentalists as urban meddlers and spaced-out hippies more interested in the welfare of marbled murrelets than in the health and livelihood of logging communities; to some forest workers, environmentalists are the source of the problem and embody a very narrow and partial self-interest at the expense of the general good that loggers see themselves as representing.[3]

This conflict exemplifies what Laclau and Mouffe call antagonism: the presence of the Other is seen to prevent the full constitution of the self, expressed here through two opposing discourses as to what is to count as the common good in contrast to parochial and partial interest. The task for the coalitionally minded (as many on both sides of the Clayoquot controversy are coming to be) is to produce a discursive term that allows for the rearticulation of these subject positions as allied rather than antagonistic. Where Boggs might argue that loggers and environmentalists need simply to recognize their shared opposition to capital (as producing both alienated labor and ecological devastation, for example), it is not at all clear that either position can be reduced to a question of false consciousness, that capital is the ultimate cause of the bifurcation or of the problem itself, or that the constellation of cultural, political, gendered, racialized, and environmental discourses at play in Clayoquot Sound are usefully or effectively rounded up by this analytic move.

Chains of equivalence are, as this example suggests, discursive productions of democratic commonality that rely on the ability of an intervening term to create relational meaning among a variety of constructed constituencies that may be not only diverse but antagonistic in many respects. These chains are forged from social relations but are not determined by them. In the absence of objective interests, the processes through which a radically democratic politics negotiates between antagonism and equivalence becomes crucial. Given a desire for a politics beyond the particular, such coalitional processes are vital, but they are always already traversed by the fact of their existence in a sea of antagonisms. Their character is thus transient and temporary, the product of particular discursive attachments rather than natural or inevitable convergences; in addition, who is an antagonist and who is an ally become subject to question.

As soon as one begins to question the solidity of identity or to argue that identity politics are a particular constructed political form rather than a true representation of collectivity or political being, chains of equivalence become even more problematic, and even more important. Specifically, a particular dynamic emerges: in contemporary social movement struggles, identity has played an important role in creating equivalential political forms through the identification of an antagonist, yet the emergent understanding of the impossibility of identity itself—including the identity of the antagonist—signals the limits of this version of equivalence and the need to think elsewhere.

As I argued earlier, identity politics have tended to rely on the foundational fantasy of presociality; for an identity to be understood as politically legitimate, its origins have needed to appear as outside the realm in which the identity is taken up politically. I would add here that these identity politics have coalesced into a chain of equivalence through this fantasy: it is the identity of the antagonist that has acted as nodal point. Specifically, the fantasy of identity is implicated in a particular chain of equivalence that names its antagonist as the white-heterosexual-male-capitalist-speciesist, and from a common recognition of this subject position as antagonist has sprung a wide variety of actors who claim their identity as solid in their difference from that hyphenated antagonist. It is the projected antagonist, then, that has allowed for the creation of a chain of equivalential identity politics that share a fantasy of presociality and wholeness, an origin beyond the influence of the antagonist (who also becomes understood as solid and prefabricated).

Whether or not political movements recognize or care about the impossibility of identity, it is quite clear that antagonism is appearing within the apparently solid categories upon which this chain of equivalence has rested and that the particular identities bound up in it are no longer comfortably inhabited. (Indeed, it is in the gradual disintegration of the unity of these categories that hyphenated identities have been created, a last-ditch attempt to stitch together some kind of identity-based quilt). What is becoming apparent in many different places is that the Other of these categories is within, not simply outside; the antagonist is appearing anarchically within the women's movement, within environmental politics, within antiracist strategies, and can no longer be safely identified as inhabiting particular social spaces or categorized bodies elsewhere.

To understand the antagonist within is not only to engage in a process of recognizing the appearance of spaces between once allied or apparently allied actors, but also to question the solidity of the identification through which any actor appears politically. What was safely outside lurks within; what was the preserve of the inside may appear without. As the boundary between an objectively defined "us" and an objectively defined "them" becomes riddled with holes, the possibility of new affinities appears alongside the creation of new antagonisms, the result being that identities themselves become highly suspect as guarantors of solid(ar)ity. In other words, to understand politics as currently subject to proliferating antagonisms and shifting affinities is to question the possibility of reliance on identity as a political myth, including the coalitional possibilities emanating from it. If the terrain of identity is no longer safe, then on what grounds may political affinities proceed? What myth of union can replace solidity?

The demise of the myth of solid identity has not gone unremarked in the political world; indeed, far from lamenting the fragmentation of identity characterizing the death of the unitary subject, numerous commentators have wrestled with the political potential of the disjuncture between politics and identity in search of a new political myth to guide radical struggles. One of the most interesting terrains for this inquiry is the one frequently circumscribed by the label *feminist postmodernism*. While departing in many respects from the Lacanian position outlined earlier, feminist postmodernism likewise responds to the apparent and perhaps increasing impossibility of the fully identified, fully whole subject of politics—here, women.[4]

Donna Haraway describes the feminist rejection of the myth of identity this way:

> It has become difficult to name one's feminism by a single adjective—or even to insist in every circumstance upon the noun. Consciousness of exclusion through naming is acute. Identities seem contradictory, partial, and strategic. With the hard-won recognition of their social and historical constitution, gender, race, and class cannot provide the basis for a belief in "essential" unity. There is nothing about being "female" that naturally binds women.[5]

The story goes something like this: although we think that once the category women was taken to hold some substantive truth about those who possessed/were possessed by the the label/state, now the collective noun seems fictive, even oppressive. What coherent list of attributes does it describe that is not part of the patriarchal narratives through which it was constructed? What unique standpoint does it reveal that is not produced in, because of, and through destructive social and political relations that consign women to an unwilling, undesired specificity? In short, what epistemic and ontological coherence does the category hold that is not the site of the problem itself?

These questions are neither flippant nor academic. For feminism, the reliance on the category "women" signals a problematic support for a gendered solidity that is the product of power-laden discursive "Othering" and often smacks of a blindness to the process of social construction.[6] The solidity of the identity "women"—even, or perhaps *especially*, if pluralized— functions politically by concealing the mode of its construction. Given that in patriarchal discourse the construction is the site of the problem, then that solidity must be rejected.

Such a realization did not, of course, occur in a political vacuum. Writes Haraway, "white women discovered (that is, were dragged kicking and screaming to notice) the non-innocence of the category. That consciousness changes the geography of all previous categories; it denatures them as heat denatures a fragile protein."[7] Specifically, it was through the fragmentation of the category "women"—through the struggles of "women of color," working-class women, and lesbians inscribing and defending their hyphens—that its eventual demise at the hands of the postmoderns was heralded. "Women" no longer worked to describe concrete struggles; what, then, did it work to do?

If the answer is to constrain—and to many, this was the visceral response—then what was signaled as a new political project was some sort of flagrant transgression of the category, the category itself being seen as implicated in the discursive conditions of oppression. And, in my understanding of the story, this is precisely what happened: feminism became a site for the politicized disruption of the identity category "women," for the critical interrogation of epistemic and ontological claims to unity, for the embracing of heteroglossia, transgression, and partiality. The cultivation of heteroglossia is, in this view, a political act in and of itself, but exists in tension with other elements of feminism. As Judith Butler writes,

> Within feminist debate, an increasing problem has been to reconcile the apparent need to formulate a politics which assumes the category "women" with the demand, often politically articulated, to problematize the category, interrogate its incoherence, its internal dissonance, its constitutive exclusions.[8]

Antagonism, Equivalence, Cyborgs, and Queers

If problematizing the categorical stability of "women" is seen as a crucial political act for feminism, how does this transgressive politics fit with coalition-building? Based as they are on a model of interest convergence or affinity construction, coalitional politics would seem to point to a process in which interests/identities need to become at least partially fixed so that equivalence may be produced or recognized: we need to see something solid and recognizable in the Other that connects with the solidity the Other sees in us. However much one may underscore the transience of the equivalential construction, the recognition of the thing that is shared would seem to require a momentary halt in the endless sliding of signifers. If transgression and disruption are the political forms that best express feminist rebellion against the destructive/productive category "women," then how can this project possibly be reconciled with the strategic need to be or represent women—at least in the view of the others with whom coalition is to be practiced—for the purposes of struggle?

In my view, the answer is to be found in the development of an ironic political attachment that highlights the substantive emptiness of the very term that is being produced in articulation. As one can never stand outside the Symbolic order (for example, the category "women" in its discursive/productive effects) in order to claim a "pure" representation unmarked by the categorical relations of oppression and domination, one is left with the possibility of an internal categorical parody based on the inevitable disjuncture between subject (Real) and subject position (Symbolic). Or, as Drucilla Cornell writes,

> the answer lies in the fact that there is always a gap between these [political] constructions and the lives of actual women. . . . Feminism functions within this gap, the space necessarily left open between the constructions and our actual lives as "sexed" creatures.[9]

Relying on the Lacanian gap between language and unsymbolized reality, Cornell argues that the Symbolic construction of woman is always subject to the slippage of meaning; the question becomes one of developing a political form that does not halt but rather takes up this ambiguity, as it is in ambiguity that one can highlight the perpetual inability of categories to represent. Although coalition as a political form already gestures in the direction of this gap—no single identity can fill the revolutionary position—it is important from Cornell's view to note that no coalition can capture the Real and that democratization requires an act of barring the

ability of any position to claim to represent coherence. And barring requires ambiguity: by inhabiting an intentional space between the actual
lives of women and fantastic (phallic?) representations of the category,
feminism enacts a form of mimetic identification to challenge the hegemony of the Symbolic to represent the lives of actual women. This form of
mimetic disruption relies on the inevitable incoherence of the representation itself; it does not solve the paradox between transgression and identification but rather works within it to highlight the failure of the Symbolic
to capture reality. "Miming," writes Cornell, "not only implies mirroring
but as enactment it is also a parody of what it mirrors. Miming *always* carries within it a moment of parody of what it mirrors."[10]

This is not a strategy confined to a privileged performative elite. On a
daily basis, most political actors are aware, on some level and with some discomfort, of the space between "reality" and representation. For example, the
common question of who gets to speak for women is tied (again, at some
level and with some discomfort) to an understanding that no speech will
capture the category in its entirety. Who ends up getting to speak is frequently a question resolved by deliberations over who will, in a sense, give
the best performance: whose position in political space best produces the
discursive needs of the utterance, whose character or style best responds to
the demands of the space itself. (This is not to suggest that performance is
purely strategic, only to suggest that it is already there.) My agenda is thus
not to sidestep the discomforting concerns over representation that spawn
the question of who speaks but to include more overtly in feminist politics
the idea that any speech is performative and plays in Cornell's gap. The political point is to recognize and work with the gap rather than to attempt to
fill it, as would be the tendency of identity politics.

This broadly performative view of politics does not suggest a stance in
which the political actor can somehow transcend the identificatory practices constituting her subject position(s) in the world only to be forced to
invoke them temporarily for the express strategic purposes of politics.
Instead, it relies on the inevitable failure of these practices to represent the
subject; the point is not to forget the gap in order to do politics but to
widen it as a political act (and as part of a larger project), thereby exposing
the internal limit of representation. A process of intentional distancing
from the apparent truth of the category does not mean that the category
cannot be invoked; it does insist that some parodic practice be inserted
into the invocation in order to highlight its malaise.

In this view, coalitional politics are not additive processes in which
solid and positive social positions come to appear as naturally allied.

Instead, the antagonism within each articulated subject position must come to be exposed through a discursive process of mirroring. The hyphens between subject positions in a chain of equivalence come to look more like bars through them, as, for example, the internal limits of the category "women" are reflected through the insertion of the category "black." The failure of the former to reach self-completion is a product, in part, of the inability of the term to capture the full meaning of the latter, and vice versa. Thus from this view, coalitional politics may represent a process by which the construction of contingency highlights the incompleteness of any position captured in or animated through the articulation.

The difference between this view of articulation and the view more broadly associated with identity politics is one of irony. Put simply, coalition itself must be understood as a performative construction; given that no number of hyphens can specify fully a subject or political position, the gap between reality and even the most comprehensive Symbolic articulation of subject positions is still there to be played in. The recognition of the partiality of the subject position through the ironic taking-up of a place in a chain of equivalences signals a relation to affinity in which there can be no perfect correspondence between raw reality and political language. Thus, the will to construct the most complete chain of equivalences—as a way of filling the gaps in the inevitable incompleteness of the coalition—is displaced by a recognition of the contingency of the affinity itself and the particular position within it. In this understanding, coalitional politics may come to highlight the gaps rather than hide their traces.

In many respects, this view of coalition echoes Haraway's understandings of situated knowledges and the privilege of partial perspective. The point of a coalitional politics is not an ability to claim to have "got it right" through some perfect enumeration of subject positions (which becomes a view from nowhere, in her terms) but a process by which each position in the chain comes to recognize its profound partiality, its inevitable contingency on all of the others, in order to foster an open and noninnocent view of the discursively produced self and the discursively produced affinities that flow from and around it.[11] To Haraway, the metaphor most appropriate to this view of the political self is the cyborg, a creature that thrives on its lack of closure, on its resistance to any form of categorical symbolization. "Cyborg feminists have to argue that 'we' do not want any more natural matrix of unity and that no construction is whole";[12] the process of affinity-building, then, has to do with the creation of a mode of political attachment that privileges the inevitable partiality of any position in a chain of alliances and that allows the process of alliance-building itself to highlight the gaps in the identities in question. In the cyborg view of affinity, the subject position is offered up to others with the express purpose of experiencing its failure; the thing that is shared is not an experience of completion in the halting of the slide of signification, but the experience of radical contingency itself.

It is certainly the case that part of the point of this experience is the disruption itself; as I will argue in chapter 8, for ecofeminism in particular the recognition of the limits of representation is part of a politics that includes an ethical relation to the Real. But it is also the case that the experience of radical contingency produces a movement toward affinity within the realm of representation itself; the cyborg, for example, demonstrates the imbrication of all subject positions within a discursive web that is not fully revealed in any single position within it. Affinities may never be perfect, but they are what we have in terms of representation; irony isn't just about disruption, but about making clear this fact of equivalential and partial production.

To Judith Butler, the mode of political attachment most suited to this sort of discursive production involves a specifically parodic repetition of the compulsory categories of contemporary social existence.[13] Drawing from an analysis of the relations between discursive heteronormativity and bipolar and dimorphous sex and gender, Butler argues that there is no space that is out of (or liberated from) categorical relations of power and identity and that it is thus crucial (especially but not only for a politics hoping to create spaces for queers) to parody the practices of identity and appearance on which heterosexuality, sex, and gender rely. To "queer" the subject through public appearance—a form of drag—is, more broadly, to destabilize the assumed expressiveness of any performance of identity and to highlight the performative qualities of the identity itself, revealing precisely the constitutive limit of the subject position. Performativity, she writes,

> describes [a] relation of being implicated in that which one opposes, [a] turning of power against itself to produce alternative modalities of power, to establish a kind of political contestation that is not a "pure" opposition, a "transcendence" of contemporary relations of power, but a difficult labor of forging a future from resources inevitably impure.[14]

For many gay men and lesbians, practices of drag are a crucial element in both political and personal life, as they mark a breathing space in which elements of nonheterosexualized representation are made possible through the strategic use of farce, ridicule, and/or irony. Rather than claim a new identity (which is, of course, always formed from within the discourses of heteronormativity), drag offers the possibility of subversion. While not arguing that drag is an essentially subversive practice and while not limiting queer (or other) politics to the practice of drag, Butler points to the need for an ironic attachment to the categories of identity and public appearance of the kind that some practices of drag produce: the careful use of mimetic repetition to show the arbitrariness of the signs through which the category is "normally" performed. In the context of a coalitional desire, ironic repetition suggests a form of affinity in which the identity of each constituent group is queered (made strange) through the insertion of the others. In the constitution of equivalence, each category is opened up to the possibility of the influence of the others; rather than move toward a stance of completion, an ironic position of affinity would open each category up to the potential subversion of all the others, thus perpetually keeping the conversation open.[15]

The point is not by theoretical sleight of hand to do away with the tensions between antagonism and equivalence, to suggest somehow that antagonism is illusory, or to argue that there are not real places where affinity finds itself blocked by apparently intractable differences of interest. It is not to reduce questions of equivalence and coalition to questions of identificatory mimicry and subversion. Rather, the point is to argue that one of the most promising elements of coalitional politics—their ability to open up different subject positions to the possibility of influence by others—depends on displacement of the solidity of identity and its replacement with an orientation to contingency. This stance of partiality, in my view, requires a mode of political attachment in which transgression is embraced, not strategically put aside; as the category "women" is displaced from its Symbolic place by the insertion of hyphens, the openness produced by this displacement can only be sustained if the "discovered" subject position is shown to be just as fictive. Thus, irony seems to be a promising tactic; an intentional performance of coalition potentially widens the sphere of disruption and fosters continued and ongoing inclusion. The coalition is no more pure than its constituent elements, but its field of potential disruption is both internally and externally wider.[16] And while disruption is, as subsequent chapters will demonstrate, neither the only goal of ecofeminist politics nor the only mode of political appearance appropriate to democratic or ecological concerns, it seems the case that more promising versions of affinity can proceed from this view of political subjectivation than was the case with identity politics.

Ecofeminism, Antiessentialism, and Performativity

Having spent the first four chapters critiquing ecofeminism's reliance on identity to produce and represent connections between feminist and ecological politics, I approach the project of re-reading ecofeminism for its potentially transgressive promise with some trepidation. Ecofeminism has, at a number of different stages in its development, constructed an ontological woman/nature connection to legitimize its existence as a movement distinct from both feminism and ecology, but this linkage has produced a series of chains against which a number of recent ecofeminist authors are currently rebelling. I will not invoke the language of paradigm shifts to describe the movement in ecofeminism away from identity and toward a more transgressive stance, but I will certainly say that the languages of social constructivism and anti-essentialism have had a strong and positive effect on ecofeminist political theory.

As I described earlier, one of ecofeminism's inheritances from cultural feminism was essentialism; at the very least, it seemed politically necessary to show some underlying coherence to the category woman in order to explain the relationship between the degradation of women and the exploitation of nature. Like cultural feminism, early ecofeminism relied on a notion of woman's essential difference from man in order to highlight the ways in which a woman's standpoint on nature could produce less exploitative, more nurturant, and more harmonious human relations with nonhuman (and human) nature. But the ecofeminist category "woman" was, as in other feminisms, problematic: it was challenged by a variety of differently situated women because of its Western and white, middle-class, and (eventually) heterosexual bias and because of its overtones of biological determinism.

As a variety of different ecofeminisms arose from these critiques to attest to the continued viability of the movement's primary analysis, that of the interrelationships between the exploitation of nature and the degradation of women, two general themes became apparent. First, women were a rather more diverse lot than first theorized; second, any common experience of women as women was the result of social construction, not biology. While it is possible to argue that these two threads were there all along, as I discussed in chapter 3, this new ecofeminist understanding emerged as dominant at about the time of the publication of Greta Gaard's 1993 anthology, *Ecofeminism: Women, Animals, Nature.*[17]

While these understandings are still far from consensual, and while much of the critical discussion had already taken place in myriad other places long before 1993, the primary assumptions of diversity and social construction within Gaard's collection signalled an important move: the recognition of the need to investigate the category "women" and to analyze ways of making connections between feminism and ecology that respected both the internal multiplicity and the socially produced character of femininity. The essays in this text included a specifically interrogative foray into the cultural limits of past and present ecofeminist representations of women and nature—Huey-li Li's essay "A Cross-Cultural Critique of Ecofeminism"—as well as a general displacement of the primacy of philosophical, theological, and psychological discourses by other authors' interesting moves into natural history and cultural studies. In short, at the same time as the range of narratives present in ecofeminist discussion was widened beyond the taxonomic representations of ecofeminism I reproduced in chapter 3, the elements of founding collectivity were such that essentialism could become a topic of conversation.

The proliferation of viewpoints in Gaard's text did not displace all of the essentialist tendencies of the movement, even within the anthology itself. Indeed, the only article in the anthology to defend ecofeminism explicitly against the charge of essentialism, Janis Birkeland's "Ecofeminism: Linking Theory and Practice," conflated essentialism with biological determinism and ended up producing an account of ecofeminism that others have rightly characterized as sociologically essentialist. (More on this in an upcoming section.) What was perhaps more important than proliferation itself was the text's potential for demonstrating the perpetual instability of the category "women," the dangers involved in its invocation as politically monolithic, and, as a final result, the limits of a politics based on identity. Specifically, the process of interrogating a monolithic reading of "women" and the inclusion of a broader range of kinds of ecofeminist narrative destabilized the anthology's ability to find in the term "women" a content-filled subject position: there were simply too many differences to represent, and it seemed less important to be unified than to be critical and multivocal. Although some writers continued to argue abstractly for the coherence of the category in the face of differences, it became extremely difficult for ecofeminists—in Gaard's text and subsequently—to reconcile the abstract attributes of this "women" with the kinds of struggles that came to be described as part of ecofeminist politics, globally or locally. This gap is thus the first hint of the possibility of performative affinity.

The gap between the lives of actual women and ecofeminist representations of the category produced, in a few places within the collection, an interesting questioning of the use of the category to refer to anything stable at all. If the women/nature connection is not given in nature but in patriarchal relations, and if these relations are seen as a source of the problem, then the unquestioning inhabitation of the category is no longer possible. Indeed, what was once a question of how the category was oppressed was sometimes transformed into a question of how the category was constructed. The construction, it seems, came to be understood as a key element in the politics of domination and part of the point for ecofeminism was then to show the limits and constraints of the representation itself. As Gaard wrote, "one task of ecofeminists has been to expose . . . dualisms and the ways in which feminizing nature and naturalizing or animalizing women has served as justification for the domination of women, animals, and the earth";[18] the gap between women's lives and the dualistically produced category "women" is here made an explicit part of the political location of ecofeminism.

The gap between representation and reality highlighted in that brief quotation indicates both a broader and deeper skepticism toward the ability of women to act as a totalizing referent and the possibility of a challenge to the power relations through which the representations of women and nature are seen to correspond naturally. The need to take apart the solidity of the category "women" is thus underscored. If the next logical step for ecofeminists is into the gap to perform some form of mimetic parody, then it is true that few have taken it, preferring instead to claim social construction and proceed anyway, content to live with the incoherence of the category but not exploring the political possibilities of incoherence itself. Lee Quinby's long-standing insistence on the necessity of ecofeminist political multiplicity and Karen Warren's more general call for a principled epistemological diversity are exceptions to this trend, but a recent article by Elizabeth Carlassare even more carefully questions the use of the category "women," heralding the specific possibility of parody.

Carlassare's work represents a sophisticated response to the charges of essentialism leveled at cultural ecofeminism by many socialists and socialist/social ecofeminists. Her desire in the article is to situate cultural ecofeminist claims to a notion of essential womanhood in the context of a distinct political stance and to locate socialist/social ecofeminist claims to social construction as themselves tied to potentially essentialist positions. Drawing from the work of Diana Fuss,[19] her argument produces a notion of ecofeminist "strategic essentialism," thereby untying political claims to represent women from ontological claims around any essential nature constituting the category.

She begins her article with a strong commendation of ecofeminism's internal diversity, suggesting that it "derives its cohesion not from a unified epistemological standpoint, but more from the shared desire of its proponents to foster resistance to formations of domination for the sake of human liberation and planetary survival."[20] This starting point suggests that ecofeminism cannot be seen to represent a coherent subject position but rather acts as an umbrella term to produce an overtly political connection among a range of viewpoints. Within this framework claims of essentialism or antiessentialism represent different political positions in the web of ecofeminist possibilities rather than warring statements in the search for truth about women's nature.

In her story, cultural ecofeminism's apparently essentialist claims to a notion of women's innate connection to nature have been strongly rejected by social/ist ecofeminists, who see "ideas such as woman as nurturer, woman as caretaker, and woman as closer to nature [as] oppress[ing] women, limit[ing] their sphere of activity, and squelch[ing] their potency as social and cultural agents."[21] A self-identified social ecofeminist herself, Carlassare chooses to ask why cultural ecofeminists like Susan Griffin would rely on these representations and whether they are not better understood as politically useful resistances to patriarchal narratives. She suggests that Griffin's *Woman and Nature* (usually condemned along with Mary Daly's *Gyn/Ecology* as archetypal essentialist ecofeminism) is actually "asserting women's essentalized gender characteristics while at the same time acknowledging the construction of woman's essence within a particular social, cultural, and historical context."[22] In other words, she sees this textual production of essence as a conscious political strategy, thus opening the space for an interrogative reading of the "woman equals nature" logic.

She then asks social/ist ecofeminists, "What is going on when texts such as these are labeled 'essentialist' and dismissed as regressive?"[23] Pointing to the "poetic allusive" narrative strategies of Griffin's text (and Daly's), she argues that claims about Griffin's inherent essentialism by the likes of Janet Biehl privilege certain modes of academic writing. In response to Biehl's critique of ecofeminism's "incoherence," Carlassare suggests that Biehl's desire for an ecofeminism "untainted" by claims potentially read as essentialist ironically suggests a desire for a strongly unified epistemological position, thus producing precisely the desire for an essential unity that Biehl's claims purportedly reject. The critique of essentialism, Carlassare claims, ends up privileging a particular materialist way of knowing, and thus is guilty of shutting down the epistemic diversity that the rejection of essentialism is supposed to produce. Indeed, as she notes,

Social/ist ecofeminists recognize that "woman" is a mobile construction that rests on spatially and temporally variable social relations, and they deny that there is any immutable eternal essence that defines women. Social/ist ecofeminists often work, however, with a historically continuous, simple, essentalized notion of "woman" despite their recognition that "woman" is a construction, a mutable representation with a history.[24]

Given the potential constructionism apparent in some purportedly essentialist positions and the underlying essentialism of some purportedly social constructivist positions—in other words, the slippage across them despite original intentions—Carlassare asserts that the category "women" cannot be asserted without essentialism in some form. Her conclusion is that the category "women" must be understood as a politically strategic invocation that is used variably within different ecofeminist productions of its source and meaning. Useful as this argument is for its transcendence of social/cultural ecofeminist arguments over essence, what Carlassare fails to address is the fact that strategic essentialism is never simply strategic but contains within it the potential to create a perception of essence despite the supposedly ironic nature of the stance. The question of performative subversion remains unaddressed in her work; her "unity in diversity" argument for strategic essentialism rests on the assumption of a political need to be seen as representing a common identity even if none of the participants actually believes in its existence. Thus, while she rejects the need for coherence and heralds ecofeminism's potentially subversive multiplicity, her validation of essentialist claims under the rubric of strategy misses the key point of performative parody.[25]

It requires only a small step, however, to take Carlassare's argument into the realm of performativity: she has already argued that "woman" is a socially situated category, ripe for deconstruction as part of an ecofeminist politics, and that the desirable stance with which to utilize the category "woman" is an ironic one. Both of these are significant moves; she has taken ecofeminism into a self-critical place in which any and all claims to social construction must be examined for their own essentializing possibilities, thus making antiessentialism part of the self-defined agenda of an ecofeminist politics. Importantly, she has also pointed to the fact of diversity as underscoring the perpetual incoherence of the category women; given her overt rejection of totalizing narratives (she is strongly allied with Quinby, whom I have mentioned repeatedly, on this point), her agenda of unity in diversity implies a strong rejection of any claim to have "got the identity right."

Carlassare's is an ecofeminist vision born of a shared political desire rather than a shared epistemological or ontological position.[26] While she never names it as such, I would call this political desire a radical democratic one. Implicit in her call for diversity and respect for a variety of different modes of political appearance is a version of coalition based on a politically produced affinity, a shared orientation to resisting a patriarchal master narrative rather than producing a new matriarchal one. In other words, Carlassare suggests an ecofeminism that is primarily oriented to showing the ongoing impossibility of the category "women" by inviting critical interrogations of its apparently solid Symbolic presence. If one adds a moment of overt irony to this vision, one ends up with a politics that clearly resembles the type of performative affinity I outlined earlier.

In the next section, I would like to argue that this ecofeminist performative affinity relies on the insertion of a strongly parodic understanding of nature into its discourses. Carlassare's argument has opened the door to the realization that discussions of women's connections to nature are not necessarily essentialist any more than claims to social construction are necessarily antiessentialist in an ecofeminist political strategy.[27] The next step, it seems, is to argue for a nature that does not reproduce the totalizing claims to identity that have tended to plague many ecofeminist discussions.

Ecofeminism and the Destabilization of Nature

As I noted in chapter 3, one response to the apparent incoherence (or, more accurately, the obvious internal diversity) of the category "women" was to reemphasize nature as the term tying together a variety of distinct women's relations; where the category "women" failed to achieve coherence, the category "nature" could be invoked to allow ecofeminism the sense of identity permanence apparently necessary to draw together a coherent articulation of oppositional positions. If "women" isn't (and women aren't) internally coherent, then we can at least achieve a temporary sense of common interest in relation to environmental degradation. As described earlier, this coherence is illusory—nature cannot be a human identity unproblematically—and ironically draws ecofeminism back into the woman/nature connective trap through the reassertion of concrete convergences of supposedly feminine (even if socially constructed) actions in/toward a stable nature. Thus, the suggestion of the nonsolidity of nature itself in some ecofeminist writing is a particularly promising gesture toward performative affinity. Although it is true that there has been throughout ecofeminism's history a lingering doubt about our ability to represent nature fully (to which I will return in chapter 8), what is interesting about the recent move to overtly disrupt representations of nature is the recognition of the need to move away from a view of nature's solid appearance and toward a more anarchic and democratic construction. The insertion of a radically unstable nature into a story about women's relations to natural environments also destabilizes the coherence of the category "women."

The idea of nature as something other than an inert, determined, and determinable realm apart from human culture has been explored in a variety of ways in recent literatures. Chaos theory and other so-called postmodern sciences have, for example, been influential in displacing the idea that nature (nonhuman or human) is governed by a series of constant laws that humans can discover through the rigorous application of so-called scientific method. In another vein, social ecologists have argued for some time that nature is a potential or inherent "realm of freedom" in which biological potentiality does not inevitably produce any given outcome, in human life or elsewhere; evolution is always, at least in part, a matter of choice. This view understands humanity as part of nature but, unlike sociobiology, destabilizes the idea of nature as a determined or deterministic realm.[28]

For ecofeminists, perhaps the most influential source of destabilizing nature narratives and representations comes from conversations between environmentalism and so-called postmodern cultural studies. In their investigations of the presence and meaning of nature (human and nonhuman) in late capitalist cultural landscapes, authors such as William Cronon and N. Katherine Hayles call into profound question not only the stability and equilibrium of nature as both representation and physical presence but the multiple and often contradictory relations between and among humans and nonhumans revealed and produced in these representations.[29] Going beyond the familiar narratives of modernity, separation, and dualism, Cronon and other so-called postmoderns argue that both contemporary and historical human/nonhuman relations cannot be adequately understood through a linear narrative of culture's domination over a passive and victimized nature. Nature and culture are both far more complex than this narrative allows, and part of that complexity lies in the multiple interactions between different natures and different cultures.

It is thus to Donna Haraway—one of the most recognized advocates of such a position—that Stacy Alaimo turns for guidance for a feminist environmentalist take on the indeterminacy of nature.[30] Alaimo's article involves an interesting comparison of ecofeminist and cyborg approaches to the development of an environmental feminism that is overtly critical of deterministic notions of nature or women. Indeed, she begins with a question inspired by Laclau and Mouffe: If the positions "women" and "nature" have no predetermined meaning, then how can one assess the political value of two vastly different visions of their articulation, the one (ecofeminism) focused on building women and nature as coherent and connected actors and the other (Haraway) focused on destabilizing both? While I think, for reasons that will become apparent below, that the two projects are not as opposed as they seem, I also think her questions lead in some promising directions in terms of the value of an artifactual and unpredictable nature for ecofeminist politics.

Alaimo begins with the suggestion that ecofeminism "makes sense" in a particular (U.S., contemporary) context; "like radical feminism," she writes, it "seeks to overturn . . . hierarchies by reversing the valences of the terms," by recovering, for example, Mother Earth imagery in the service of radical change or by blurring the boundaries between women and animals to show their alliance in resistance to patriarchal oppression.[31] She goes on to show, however, just how easily this project is articulated with profoundly regressive political aims. For example, in the 1990 American Broadcasting Company's Earth Day Special, Bette Midler as a hospitalized Mother Nature is "saved by capitalist consumers and good housekeepers," thus supporting both continued capitalist growth and the notion that environmental problem-solving is just another domestic chore to be assigned to women (who are also to be blamed for irresponsible domestic activity if things go wrong).

In particular, Alaimo takes aim at Susan Griffin's *Woman and Nature*; unlike Carlassare, she is not willing to be satisfied with the potential strategy of its essentialism (although she agrees with the possibility of this interpretation), but rather criticizes it for the particular ways in which a connection between women and nonhuman animals is produced. Not only does Griffin's text rely on a naïve epistemological correspondence between women and animals (e.g., the idea that any human can really imagine what it's like to be a horse), but its particular blurring of boundaries between women and nature occurs under very monolithic ideas of "womanhood" and "victimhood"; to Alaimo this blurring "supports the historically ingrained position of women and animals as Other to a male subject, roles that easily fit misogynist narratives of oppression."[32]

What is interesting in Alaimo's article is that she is engaged in the political potential of the blurring itself; her concern is not the possibility that women will be associated with animals or other nonhuman actors but, rather, the kinds of discourse in which that association is produced.[33]

Thus, she explores other constructions of human/animal continuity, including animal rights advocates' construction of nonhuman animals as rights-bearing individuals, in particular the Whale Adoption Project's construction of whales as individuals with personalities.[34] Despite the problematic power relations involved, including the projection of human traits onto animals, "whale-tail portraits discourage the domination of nature by representing animal-human affinity and kinship."[35]

While recognizing the political significance of such moments of affinity production within ecofeminism, Alaimo is determined that the nature that gets spoken through them is not the reified, victimized, epistemically transparent and passive entity of Griffin's text. It is here that she suggests the particular import of Haraway's strategy for disrupting human/nature boundaries. For Haraway, nature is an active, unpredictable, and ungendered trickster she terms Coyote whose agency allows it to defy the totalization of human representation. Although nature is active, it is also artifactual: made, constructed, changing, and not "out there" as Other to human culture. In other words, nature is "made, but not entirely by humans; it is a co-construction among humans and non-humans."[36]

What is crucial to note here is that the displacement of the idea of nature as a passive victim of the social is tied to the displacement of nature as a solid ground to naturalize human activity. Nature is an agent (or, perhaps more accurately, a series of agents), not a deterministic force, a crude biological limit upon human activity, or even a realm out of which the social emerges in all of its constructivist glory. Nature is always already an artifact, but, as Alaimo writes,

> artifactualism recognizes the agency of nature without personifying it into a mirror of human actions. [Thus,] destabilizing the grounds of appropriation and domination by emphasizing the agency of nature and . . . breaking down the borders between subjects and objects, nature and culture, is an immense project, but one potentially rewarding for environmental feminism.[37]

This re-creation of nature away from reductionist and determinist understandings is intentionally and intensely transgressive. Nature and culture are not opposed as object and subject; nature is not a realm of necessity to culture's realm of freedom in which crude and slavish cyclical repetition can be easily counterposed to human creativity; ties to nature are not a question of determination or inevitability. If nature is thus understood as an active and unpredictable character, it is difficult not only to justify its exploitation as Other, as passive and inert resource for human activity, but to justify the dualistic terms through which a certain segment of

humanity has progressively come to understand itself as separate from nature. As Haraway's cyborg also shows, it is not possible to rely on a dualism
between organism and technology.

Connections to nature here lose their deterministic overtones; indeed,
biological determinism itself is shown to be a particular, historically specific understanding of nature. The phrase "biology is destiny" only makes
sense in the context of a series of assumptions about the inevitability of
natural processes; thus, destabilizing contemporary ideas of nature opens
the way for a whole realm of human/nature affinities that have been generally rejected precisely because of this sense of inevitability. Indeed, given
the apparent solidity of certain identity categories (in ecofeminism and
elsewhere) despite the general rejection of their biological grounding, it is
possible to argue that social categories are far more deterministic than the
nature that has historically been invoked to justify them.

Clearly, what I am suggesting involves a radical displacement of contemporary wisdom. For ecofeminism to move beyond the reified identity
categories of "women" and "nature" that have plagued it, it is insufficient to
claim social construction and proceed anyway. As Carlassare argues, there
is no inevitable relationship between social constructivism and antiessentialism. What Alaimo's work adds to the political equation is that it is possible to create affinities between humans and nature that do not involve
statements of biological determination so long as nature is carefully re-
inscribed as an active agent in its and our artifactuality. That this is a difficult task is quite clear: discourses of biological determinism are alive and
well. But it is not sufficient to claim that everything is social any more than
it is to suggest that this claim produces infinite flexibility. A more appropriate response is to engage with the culture/nature dualism itself, to argue
that continuity with nature does not consign humans to necessitarian repetition, and to use this blurring as a way of shaking up the apparent solidity
of the social categories produced through their apparent connection to
nature.

Alaimo is more skeptical about this leap. According to her, one of the
greatest strengths of Haraway's Coyote is its lack of gender; where she
sees Griffin's empathically constructed nature as part of a reified femininity, the strength of Coyote as a metaphor is precisely its failure to identify/
be identified with women. As she writes, "the articulation of woman-
native-animal-other is so deeply entrenched that any attempt to rearticu-
late those terms into a feminist conversation seems extremely difficult."[38]
While I would certainly agree about the depth of this entrenchment, it
does not follow that the only way we can shake up gender is by pretending

to be outside the discursive relations through which the connection was produced. While Alaimo acknowledges that "abandoning a female connection with nature leaves the whole discursive field untouched,"[39] she also argues that any affinity must be grounded in a political understanding of the separate recognition of women and nature as active agents.

Enthusiastic as I am about a coalitional politics that promotes the agency of the actors involved, I feel that Alaimo stops short of the most radical point of the argument to which she alludes: the gap between the agency of women and nature as real actors and the Symbolic representations in and against which they struggle. Playing in this gap is not only about creating new ideas of women and nature (which are, in my framework, always already inadequate) but about active engagement with the old ones to *disrupt* notions of gender solidity, natural necessity, and reified identity in order to reveal their impossibility. In other words, Alaimo does not acknowledge the parodic possibilities of a performative woman/nature affinity. Given that it is not enough to claim social construction, and given that nature is to appear as an allied actor in ecofeminist struggle, it seems crucial to show that the affinity is not based just on separate agencies but on shared performative possibilities. Again, this performativity does not summarize the political, but it is, in my view, a step in the right direction for ecofeminists and others.

Ecofeminism, Antagonism, and Equivalence

The story that I have told in the preceding pages concerns ecofeminism's growing awareness that neither "women" nor "nature" is stable, that each is preceded and crosscut by a long chain of contingent representational fictions, and that these fictions are the target of necessary deconstruction. While by no means an inevitable outcome of the recent predominance of social constructivist language in ecofeminist discussions, the recognition of the categories' perpetual incoherence is at least incipient in this recent movement. In my view, this recognition suggests the potential of ecofeminism to negotiate between antagonism and equivalence and to produce the kind of politics of performative affinity that I believe to be crucial.

Ecofeminism was founded on a specific coalitional gesture. If I might give that gesture a particular spin, women and nature are located in a series of narratives that connect them in some way as equivalently positioned products of certain narratives and practices of domination and oppression. It is from this position of constructed connection that ecofeminism can produce a politics of performative affinity. Rather than deny any continuity between women and nature (as has been the tendency in many feminisms, including those ecofeminisms that argue that the woman/nature connection is to be completely rejected as a totalized patriarchal falsehood), a performative affinity between women and nature allows for the possibility of each to disrupt the other. To take ecofeminism beyond the essentializing identity that has tended to result from this connection, it is necessary to insert a more critical and ironic stance. If the understanding of women and nature as socially created (but not socially determined) and mutable categories is taken to a politics in which these representations are constantly challenged (through parody for example), then the woman/nature affinity becomes a statement in which the one set of constructions is constantly held up to the other to show each's contingent, fictitious character.

From Carlassare, we can take the suggestion that "women" is a category embedded in complex and changing historical relations; we can also produce a refusal to take it up in any way that is not aware of its essentializing potential. From Alaimo, we can take the critical rejection of a stable and passive nature to the task of interrogating its effects on the production of human life as part of nature, including human subjectivity; we can also produce a political stance that destabilizes the ability of nature to produce anything approximating genuine coherence. From the convergences of these two arguments, I assert that ecofeminism's productions of affinity between women and nature can be read as potentially destabilizing both through the performance of one impossible representation against the other.

As I noted earlier, the recent proliferation of ecofeminisms should be seen as a response to the inability of the category "women" to produce coherence. If the next step is to suggest that relations to nature form the term providing the commonality among diverse positions, then the category "women" is necessarily produced as one that only achieves the appearance of coherence through the insertion of another term. "Common interest" in relation to nature is not the same thing as "common nature"; "women" achieves a temporary permanence only insofar as a particular series of practices in relation to nature can be seen to be relatively coherent, given nature itself. If this nature coherence is then called into question, both through the recognition of diversity in these supposedly women's relations and through the assertion that nature is an unpredictable and active agent rather than the passive recipient of the female gaze, then its ability to (re)produce women's solidity is also displaced.

The ecofeminist assertion that women and nature are somehow connected can then become a statement of joint subversion; in resistance to but located within hegemonic narratives, the idea of women's naturalness can be taken up as a performative subversion of the solidity of both. If women are connected through statements of women's biological essence to a nature that is radically unstable, then embracing nature means embracing the failure of women as a coherent identity. If nature is connected through feminization to a category "women" that is not coherent, then the gendering of nature calls attention to its own irrepresentability. What seems necessary in this potential production of destabilizing affinity is the explicit parody of the one against the other.

Interestingly, this kind of stance would seem to advocate embracing the woman/nature connection in some respects; rather than denying any and all associations in a perpetually failed quest to produce an account of the purely social character of women's lives (or of nature itself), it would seem to say, the affinity must be one which the Symbolic connection is shown to be impossible from within. Only by studying and repeating the language through which the connection is made can the subversive performance work. The embrace, however, must be a very careful one lest it lapse into the kind of biological determinism that produces both human and nonhuman actors as solidified, as not disrupted, by the connection. As many ecofeminist texts have shown, the political move to parody the woman/nature connection through its mimetic repetition is a politically risky one (i.e., as Butler suggests, not all drag is subversive); it is extremely easy to lapse into a form of performance that would rebuild the proverbial master's house rather than use his tools to resist it by building something else (however undefined that something else might be).

While bringing together women and nature in a distinctly political project has always been on the agenda of ecofeminism, it is only through a sense of the poor fit of any categorical affinity that this political coproduction can lead toward the performance of one against the other. This is why Haraway's Coyote and cyborg are such important metaphors; their performance of animal and machine against human does not allow for a comfortable inhabitation of any of them. The gap between the category "women in nature" and the real lives of the women and nonhuman actors involved in it is the space in which this kind of critical performance can be fostered; embracing impossibility, playing in the gap, is thus the political safeguard against reproducing the woman/nature connection too seriously. This is also why Butler's call to queer gender and sex and sexuality must be taken seriously; parody makes strange the normative relations of gender—and here nature—about which many people have been made to feel far too comfortable. At the same time that ecofeminism must remember and recognize the lives and bodies and natures of those queers whose very lives challenge heteronormative ideals—whose lives, as Gaard shows, have been degraded and demeaned by normative categories of nature and gender[40]— it must also take the act of queering to an array of performative spaces.

An interesting example of such a performance is a poster on my office wall that resembles a *Time* magazine cover. It pictures a young, hip woman (ultra-trendy hairdo, sunglasses) wearing a flesh-colored body cast over her torso. (The model, Matuschka, is actually the creator of the artwork.) Implanted in the right breast of the body cast is a clock. In the same type as that of the magazine, the caption reads "TIME for prevention." The campaign, about the relationship between organochlorines and breast cancer (and about getting *Time* magazine to honor its commitment to use unbleached stock), deprivileges dominant discourses about genetic and lifestyle "causes" of breast cancer at the same time that it inserts the question of environmental health into public discourse; the side caption reads "cancer has been linked to chlorine in the environment."

In my view, this poster plays beautifully with the woman/nature connection in the context of a campaign that could easily be read as arguing that women and nature (especially mothers, as exemplified by the breast) are invaded by men and their nasty toxins. Matuschka *wears* her body; it is both obviously female and obviously artifactual: the body is her body, but not quite. (Indeed, given that we know the model is also the artist, we know that she made the body she wears.) The clock, too, is part of that body that is neither purely social nor purely natural. Thus, the woman/ nature that is being disrupted by the clock (the cancer is equally artifactual) is not pure and is definitely not an Earth Mother. But the disruption of nature occurs through the specificity of gender, and gender is parodied through the blatant production of an artifactual nature. The cancer is not the evil technology of male culture writing itself on a natural, gendered body; that very body is an artifactual co-production of nature and technology, and the cancer is a very deadly part of the same complex.

In addition, the representation is a parody of the "great person" covers that typify *Time*; her eyes covered by sunglasses, her hands behind her back, the model's body and her breast are the center of attention, not her face. Thus an individualizing reading is also deprivileged; the poster is a call for a form of affinity made possible by a gendered embodiment; the specifically female association of breast cancer (men are, of course, also susceptible to it) is not formed around a heterosexual maternal breast, however, but around a queer and a cyborg one. Thus, I would argue, a very ironic "women" is produced: we are made, but not entirely by humans, so the articulation of gender and nature must also be seen to be made. We act politically for women and nature from a strong position of their mutually revealed impurity.

The final point of the poster, and of this chapter, is that all of this is accomplished in a political campaign that is about something else. Matuschka's overt purpose is to call attention to the seriousness of the links between environmental degradation and breast cancer and *Time's* corporate complicity in it. But in her quest for a politics, she does not rely on essentialism, and actually magnificently subverts its possibility. Disruption is not the only point of politics (Matuschka's, coalitional, ecofeminist, or otherwise), but the two projects can indeed go hand in hand (hand in prosthesis?). En route to an ecological future, en route to democracy, disruption is part of the process; it also enhances the possibility of moving toward either.

6

Ecofeminism, Universality, and Particularity

Women are the revolutionary bearers of [the] antidualistic potential in the world today. In addition to the enormous impact of feminism on Western civilization, women have been at the forefront of every historical and political movement to reclaim the earth. A principle of reconciliation, with an organic practice of nonoppositional opposition, provides the basis for an ecofeminist politics. The laboratory of nonoppositional opposition is the actions taken by women around the world, women who do not necessarily call themselves feminists.

Ynestra King, "Feminism and Ecology"

Why isn't ecofeminist philosophy meaningful to working-class and poor people in the United States [and Canada]? Why haven't ecofeminists taken on the issue of environmental racism . . . ? Precisely whom, in short, does ecofeminism purport to empower?

Carol Stabile, "'A Garden Inclosed Is My Sister'"

The tension between antagonism and equivalence is framed both by issues of identification and its transgression and by the contemporary significance of coalition as a political form. On the one hand, identity groups—

women, "people of color," queers, workers, and the like—are engaged in a process of categorical interrogation in which the discursive processes that render solid political categories are subject to important questioning. On the other hand, there remains a need for politics to encourage the process of articulation, the formation of a version of a collective beyond any individual constituency. Both are possible; it is not the case that the dissolution of the old organic dualisms upon which collective identity rested spells the death of the political, but rather that new collective chimerical actors are created in the spaces freed in the mutative process. In ecofeminism, a multitude of cyborgs and queers inhabits the tension between antagonism and equivalence, creating an odd collection of potentially subversive cousins.

But the problem of the collective in ecofeminism needs to be approached in a different way as well—specifically, through an examination of the ways in which ecofeminism claims or doesn't claim to be a movement oriented to universal political issues and not just particular transformations related to specific identities and their production and representation. This is the tension underscoring coalition as a vital political form: although there is, among radical social movements, widespread skepticism about the ability of any group to claim to embody or represent a universal (or even universalizing) transformative standpoint, there remains a desire for democratic politics to tie together the experiences and voices of particular groups in order to present an alternative vision that is not only counterhegemonic but at least potentially hegemonic. Thus, the call for political universality coexists with a desire for the epistemic privilege of particularity; it is in the tension between them that democratic values emerge in recognition of the space between reality and representation.

This chapter begins with a discussion of the ways in which the processes of so-called environmental globalization have created a renewed call for a universal politics. One could argue that "the universal" has never really left the Left, but it seems particularly the case that in our current global environmental crisis there is a need not only for affinity but for a form of global consciousness that transcends the irrevocably particular interests in relation to nature that are theorized as the cause of the crisis. At the same time, especially in recent (post–Rio Summit) writings on environmental politics, there is the sense that the tension between the global and the local is in need of some serious consideration in the wake of the recognition that not all people share the same interests in relation to nature. There are thus very auspicious radical democratic contours to this discussion: the universal and the particular exist in some tension.

Ecofeminism has taken up these imperatives toward globalization in a number of fruitful ways. The inclusion of the voices of women from the South has served to tear apart some of the Western assumptions upon which its earlier analyses rested, and it has also directed ecofeminist attention more strongly toward the global relations of capital in which gendered struggles over nature are located. In so doing, it has produced the desire for a universal vision to represent these specific struggles at the same time as it also seeks to preserve that specificity for its own sake. It has thus respected the promise of the tension between universality and particularity in many ways. Unfortunately, the imperative toward a universal standpoint has inscribed a new inflection of identity politics in some ecofeminist works; against the promise of partiality, the authors of these works have taken up a space in the gap between reality and representation that badly universalizes the experiences of certain peoples.

This chapter concludes with a discussion of how a hegemonic desire for universality can be retrieved from a mistaken emphasis on its ontological possibility, a different way of thinking about the promise of partiality. It is my view that ecofeminism is currently engaging with the limits of the possibility of a standpoint, and it is in the recognition of this limit that it can play an important role in producing a strong version of universality oriented to hegemony rather than ontology. Thus, where chapter 5 suggested the possibilities of an ironic strategy, this chapter suggests that an orientation to universality as a horizon is another way of respecting the gap between reality and representation.

Environmental Globalization and the Resurrection of the Universal

If the 1987 World Commission on Environment and Development (WCED) Report *Our Common Future* was not enough to irrevocably tie the word *global* to the phrase *environmental crisis*—and hence to crisis response—then the 1992 United Nations eco-expo at Rio (also known as the Earth Summit) performed this discursive task admirably. In the legitimating presence of thousands of environmental nongovernmental organization (NGO) participants, 117 heads of state were seen by millions of television viewers worldwide to commit, however partially, to global cooperation to save the planet. A spectacle entirely made possible by global communication technologies and overflowing with the powerful rhetorics of "one earth" and "international partnership," Rio was truly a celebratory festival of eco-globalism.

As numerous commentators have pointed out, of course, the dominant version of eco-globalism producing and produced by the Earth Summit is also a thinly veiled excuse for a profoundly invasive and inequitable international eco-managerialism. However imperfect, the UN Action Agenda 21, with its focus on so-called sustainable development, is clearly intended as a way for countries of the North to better hold countries of the South as environmental hostages to particular global economic agendas.[1] Frederick Buttel and Peter Taylor write that internationally constructed alarm over a global environmental crisis was

> integral in constructing a portrait of global change in which it was stressed that communities, regions, and nations were impotent to deal with these problems on their own—hence the need to override "politics-as-usual" and urgently to erect a new global regulatory order with the moral imperative to address these profound threats to human survival and biospheric integrity.[2]

Even among those Rio critics most vocally opposed to this regulatory agenda, however, there remains an imperative to speak of the global when referring to things environmental. One indication of this is the careful discussion of the difference between globalization from above and globalization from below found in the works of Vandana Shiva, Wolfgang Sachs, and many others. In this distinction, the locally devastating regulatory globalism of multistate negotiation and the profoundly exploitative international division of labor associated with the expansion of multinational capital are carefully divorced from a vision of a global network of empowered, sustainable communities, locally based and culturally specific but internationally connected.

But the term producing the rhetorical need to differentiate "from above" and "from below"—globalization—remains significantly unchallenged in this discussion. Globalization, it appears, is an uncontestable empirical fact to which any significant ecological response must pay close attention if it is going to be useful. Some commentators support this statement by pointing out the apparently obvious "global-ness" of environmental problems such as ozone depletion and global warming; others use arguments from nature to point to the dissolution of the relevance of national or other human boundaries. "The major problems we face today," write Charlene Spretnak and Fritjof Capra, for example, "are *global in nature*."[3] Or, to quote Karen Litfin, a paradigm shift toward a global ecological vision, "would arise from the structural contradiction between the Earth as an integrated system and the nation-state system based on the principles of sovereignty and territorial exclusivity."[4]

In either case, environmental problems are constructed as inherently global and the planet itself becomes the object of attention. Despite the rejection of global ecological regulation—an agenda that stems from a similar construction of global nature—there is still, in these discourses of "one planet," a moral imperative toward some form of global ecological sensibility. In order for the local environmental struggle to carry legitimacy, its interlocutor must be, in some respect, the globe, lest the movement come to bear the dreaded stamp of NIMBYism[5] (Not In My Back Yard) or other unenvironmental parochial interest.

Often engaging with these accounts of transnational nature but in a rather more critical vein, many authors focus on the increasing global reach of capital to highlight the importance of a global perspective on social and environmental change. Rather than focus on nature as the moment founding the need for a view beyond the local, these authors argue that capitalism is (or is becoming) a global system and that it has produced the environmental, social, and economic relations in which a distinctly global solidarity is both possible and necessary. While this chapter will not consider in significant detail the large literature on capitalist accumulative processes and their effects on the ecosphere (e.g., as discussed in the journal *Capitalism, Nature, Socialism*), it is useful to outline some of these arguments so that the relationship between globalization and the call for a universal politics may be understood.

One of the most apocalyptic articles on the globalization of capital—bearing the warning "accumulate and die, or change"—is by Michael Clow. Following from James O'Connor's analysis of the "second contradiction of capital,"[6] Clow argues that "the drive of global capitalism in the West and South, and in whatever form it emerges from the changes in Eastern Europe, will lead in the *normal course of capitalist development* to ecological exhaustion, probably around the middle of the 21st century."[7] By virtue of its inherent drive toward accumulation, capitalism not only destroys whatever nonexploitative productive relations to nature it happens to find along the way but spells the imminent death of humanity as a result of its inherently gluttonous practices of resource extraction and waste production.

To Clow, minor tinkering (including the Brundtland Report's call for sustainable development[8]) is clearly insufficient. What is necessary is a complete reorganization of the global socioeconomic system: "Such social changes, which must be initiated in this generation if they are to head off ecological exhaustion, amount to nothing less than a magnitude of change similar to that which took us from feudalism to competitive industrial capitalism."[9] Clearly, to Clow, any political movement capable of initiating these rapid changes must be global in scale; fortunately for his argument, he believes "that workers, small independent producers, and ordinary people in general share a real material interest in reorganizing the economy towards a smaller, more stable, and production-for-use economy that can fit within the limits of the biosphere's capacity to sustain it."[10]

In Clow's understanding, globalism is simply a fact of tendencies internal to capitalism. Accumulation pushes the destructive frontiers of the market ever outward, halted only when faced with apparently natural limits. Resistances to capital (which are the only real solution to environmental crisis, in his view), thus must occur on the same scale and must strike at the level of the problem: production itself. Given the crisis, therefore, the appropriate response is to recognize a globally articulated solidarity of interests. What we have in his vision is a global-ecological working class; in good dialectical-materialist fashion, the crisis engendered by the second contradiction will succeed in uniting a diverse array of interests where the first contradiction apparently has failed to do so.

Less deterministically, Carl Boggs argues that the ecological crisis of capitalism is engendering "broad, militant, and often violent local struggles around material demands, empowerment, and ecological decay in a context where neither large corporations nor large governments can adequately respond to the pressures."[11] Unlike Clow, he is not particularly confident that the forces of history will inevitably lead to global class solidarity; rather, he argues that the contemporary fragmentation of politics— including what he calls the "depoliticizing effects of localism"—is something that needs to be carefully overcome in the quest for a global social movement capable of challenging global capital. While he recognizes the uneven and disparate contours of what many have called global civil society,[12] he remains adamant that change must be planned at the global level.

Boggs argues that the global scale of capitalism has created the conditions in which local, regional, and even national bodies (especially nation-states) are no longer potent political actors. Given that currently existing international organizations (the International Monetary Fund, the World Bank) are at least in part the source of the problem, the only solution appears to lie in the creation of a new global consciousness built out of the articulation of local democratic interests with a common environmental agenda. He writes that an international merger of social movements

> will require a new type of international discourse, at once ecological and
> democratic, forged through popular struggles in dozens of countries. In
> Samir Amin's words: "A humane and progressive response to the problems
> of the contemporary world implies the construction of a popular interna-
> tionalism that can engender a genuinely universalist value system."[13]

This kind of call for a new international consciousness is present in a variety of political projects aimed at the transformation of global capital and its environmental devastation. Clow notwithstanding, most authors seem to suggest that local interests need to be tied together (i.e., do not "naturally" converge) through some sort of common critique of the crisis or through some sort of production of the local interest through a discourse of global solidarity. The desire to preserve the local stems, in Boggs's case, from a certain resignation to the nature of contemporary social movements; other writers, such as Vandana Shiva, regard struggles of specificity with a kinder eye, arguing that it is from the deeply felt realm of the particular that mobilization will occur and in which struggles will be played out. But throughout, there is still a strong sense that the scale of the problem forces a solution of similar dimensions.

Such a position is apparent in Daniel Faber and James O'Connor's critique of the U.S. environmental movement; local victories (e.g., effective resistance to toxic waste facility siting) tend only to displace the problem elsewhere (i.e., where there is less regulation or resistance). "By not designing a comprehensive political and economic strategy to combat the processes of capitalist restructuring and to develop radical alternatives to capitalism," they write, "the environmental and labor movements have failed to halt the growing environmental and health crises of the 1980's–90's."[14] It is also apparent in the transformation of NIMBY to NIABY (Not In Anybody's Back Yard) or NOPE (Not on the Planet Ever), which has been one of the discursive mainstays of the environmental justice movement. Here it is quite clear that some intervention needs to be made to transform struggles of specificity, however valuable, into struggles of connection; the intervention may not be the production of a uniform global interest, but it must take the local discourse outside of itself. The phrase in diversity seems to require the preceding term unity.

In the context of the widespread rejection of state-centered internationalism, this kind of political project is often phrased in terms of the development of a new kind of global citizenship. It is in the notion of a global democratic community fostered by new communications technologies, by mass travel, by common interests in the development of global commons that both specificity and universalism are seen to potentially coincide. The problem for this citizenship, it seems, is to foster the sentiment or practice that one is both a member of specific groups (bioregions, sexes, classes) and a member of what Richard Falk calls a "One-World Community." What is needed to produce this sense of community is the intervention of a term to transform the isolated local interest into the systematically contextualized local interest:

> The gropings of global civil society encourage a human rights and democracy orientation toward global citizenship—the world as delightfully heterogeneous, yet inclusive of all creation in an overarching frame of community sentiment, premised on the biological and normative capacity of the human species to organize its collective life on the foundations of nonviolence, equity, and sustainability.[15]

Globalization, Universality, and Particularity

If I were to step back and paint a broad picture of this discursive constellation, it would illustrate the ways in which globalization represents the imperative toward a political universal in a context where the local is held up as the site of the deepest possible democratic practice. Against those global visions compelling us toward a homogeneous state- or market-dominated world system, globalization from below holds the promise of a locally based diverse democratic politics articulated through common resistance to a common antagonist—capital. But here, unlike older visions of international worker solidarity or global sisterhood, the relations of the particular are privileged. Any given site of struggle is not simply an obvious manifestation of a single logic of domination, thus subject to a predestined mode of political practice; rather, conditions and resistances are specific, and it is toward the empowerment of local communities to define and defend their particular interests that global politics are to be oriented.

There is one final image to be added to this picture: in many ecological discourses, the local is seen not only as the most democratic site but as the most ecologically sound level of production, consumption, and deliberation. Critics of globalization such as Shiva rightly point out that the construction of environmental problems as inherently global tends to wrest control of their resolution from local communities; the global, as it appears in the United Nations Commission on Environment and Development (UNCED), is really the globalized local of Western capitalist interests. Indeed, she writes, "The *roots* of the ecological crisis at the institutional level lie in the alienation of the rights of local communities to actively participate in environmental decisions."[16]

The project resulting from this critique, the empowerment of local resistance, sets up local practices of nature as necessarily benign and cultural diversity as equivalent to biological diversity in the good book of environmental politics. "The reversal of ecological decline," writes Shiva, "involves strengthening local rights. *Every* local community equipped with rights and obligations constitutes a new *global* order of ecological care."[17] The globalized local thus becomes the eco-democratic rhetoric tying together a proliferation of otherwise unconnected struggles; the defense of diversity is itself the political project.

To phrase this constellation in Laclau and Mouffe's radical democratic terms, the intervention of a universal, acting as a desired nodal point, is designed to retroactively construct a variety of local struggles into a global chain of equivalences. Each term in the construction of alliance comes to be influenced by the signification of all of the others; each term develops meaning outside of its specificity because of its location in a relational web of meaning.[18] In the construction of globalization from below, if capital is the common antagonist (and the operations of antagonism and equivalence should be noted here), then a variety of different interests can form specific but, from a retrospective view, seemingly naturally connected resistances to it.

More precisely, the local struggle comes to embody the universal itself: it has been transformed from "the pursuit of local self-interest" into part of "the democratization of the global."[19] Each struggle is thus impregnated with the meaning and desire of all the others in the chain; in the political anthology of grassroots struggles, resisting deforestation in Northern India becomes equivalent to reclaiming indigenous plant lore in Zimbabwe, Hispanic community self-development in the Lower East Side of Manhattan, protecting indigenous hunting practices in Nitassinan, and struggling to preserve old growth forests on the North American West Coast. It is not that these disparate struggles have nothing to learn from one another, or that there is no such thing as global capital; it is, rather, that the way in which each becomes an instance of the so-called globalization of the local serves as a form of retrospective symbolic overdetermination.

As Laclau and Mouffe note, the discursive process by which the meaning of each element in a chain of equivalences alters and is altered by the presence of the others lies at the heart of a hegemonic radical democratic politics. The call for globalization from below is thus not inherently problematic; symbolic overdetermination is part of the process through which collective meanings and identities are formed. The problem, rather, lies in the all-too-easy slippage from the universal as a desire to the universal as an already achieved state, as I will discuss below. The democratic-hegemonic project lies, rather, in the constitution of the universal as a horizon. Indeed, Clow, Boggs, Falk, Shiva, and Faber and O'Connor all point in some way to globalization from below as a political frontier not yet achieved. Laclau would go one step further: the universal is "a symbol of a missing fullness," a state not possibly achieved.[20] The crucial point to take from Laclau is that, in a democratic context, the universal is both politically necessary and politically unattainable. It carries the weight of the common good but is always derived from particular identities and interests; the processes by which the universal is constituted defines the movement of radical democracy.

On the one hand, we cannot say that the universal overrides the needs of particular communities. In fact, universality is always a fictitious representation of an impossible wholeness: its construction is always based on some particular representation, and new voices continually challenge just how common that representation is. On the other hand, we also cannot say that the particular exists apart from some notion of the whole. As Laclau explains, social and political life are not simply a proliferation of absolute differences. Rather, specificity and particular group identities are the result of historical enunciation, referred politically to some idea of the universal (e.g., quality of life, liberty, equality, autonomy, self-determination, or even sustainability). The universal and the particular are thus contingent (unbridgeable) moments in an ongoing democratic process. As Laclau writes, "If democracy *is* possible, it is because the universal does not have any necessary body, any necessary content. Instead, different groups compete to give their particular aims a temporary function of universal representation."[21]

In this context, it is important to understand the desire for globalization from below as a hegemonic desire. As desire, globalization speaks of articulatory practices, of the quest toward a form of solidarity in resistance, of an orientation to coalition in which the achievement of true universality beckons from the future yet can never be achieved. This always-future universality functions politically to orient challenges to the apparently illegitimate universality of capitalist productive relations and state-centered eco-globalism and the very particular interests they represent. In the terms of Shiva's analysis, the status quo of eco-managerialism poses itself as global where it is, in fact, a globalized local; in place of global management, the localized global seeks to challenge the legitimacy of the relations in which the part stands for the whole, offering up for the future a more genuine construction of universal interests in which the local becomes the primary and truer global term.

Thus, globalization works in eco-democratic discourse as a political horizon. By exposing the particularity of the interests that currently stand for the universal (we could read this to be Western capitalism, including its unquestioning valuation of the market), globalization from below seeks to challenge the legitimacy of these interests to produce a version of the global to represent the particular interests of the peoples, cultures, and ecosystems it encounters in its expansive practices. In its place, the perpetual desire of globalization from below offers an unfillable universality in which local interests come to temporarily inhabit the privileged realm of the global. It is thus through explicitly challenging the current hegemonic universal and offering no particular singular contents in its place save the future desire for globalized locals that the radical democratic potential of the project is produced. Universality itself is not rejected; indeed, it is the term producing the legitimacy of the local as embodiment of the general interest. Rather, the orientation of political desire toward a truer universal widens the sphere of practices caught up in the democratic project; the particular becomes (re)constituted as an element of a larger political process.

As I suggested earlier, however, there is the possibility of slippage in this project between the universal as an unattainable future horizon and the universal as an embodied represented existence. Where the former does not allow any specific content to embody the whole, the latter suggests that the genuine universal is already attained in the practice of the particular. It is this tension—between the universal as challenge and the universal as standpoint—that I would like to take to ecofeminism. In essence, ecofeminism has found itself caught between its position as a particular project in a broader orientation to future globalization and its self-representation as embodying the universal future in its practices of resistance.

Ecofeminism and Globalization

As the two quotations beginning this chapter portray, ecofeminism has something of an identity crisis. Influenced as it has been by the imperative to create a global environmental politics, ecofeminism has been stretched in the direction of casting a wider and wider net to include more and more positions in its theoretical and political conversations. At the same time, however, ecofeminism claims to emanate from a very particular standpoint, that of some women sometimes, and defends that particularity through its attachment to a democratic politics of resistance. Thus, ecofeminism has developed a very ambivalent understanding of its claims to universality; it is this ambivalence that spawns the possibility of its being, simultaneously, everything to everyone and nothing to anyone.

Clearly, this ambivalence must be viewed in context. Most obviously, there has been a problem of marginalization: ecofeminism has not always been taken seriously by other green movements. Feminist issues have often been considered peripheral to the "real" problems of pollution, preservation, planning, and even population. As a result, ecofeminism has concentrated largely on developing a women's perspective on ecological issues to both supplement and critique this narrow, androcentric environmental agenda. The Women's Action Agenda 21, for example, was created as a necessary counterpart to the 1992 Rio Action Agenda. It represents a detailed (if contested) articulation of this women's perspective and acts as both a complement to and a strong criticism of the official statements of the Rio Summit.[22]

While it is fair to say that ecofeminism provides a much-needed social analysis of environmental problems, its status as a green politics remains unclear. Specifically, the question is whether ecofeminism is articulating a particular view that needs to be incorporated as one voice among many into a broader democratic movement or whether it is providing a universal, a new analysis to replace other environmentalisms, a better framework of interpretation that does not fall prey to hitherto partial or impotent green perspectives.

Although one may justifiably reject either/or solutions to this question, it is also insufficient to say simply that ecofeminism must be both/and,[23] for part of the very problem of marginalization confronting ecofeminism surrounds the ways in which universality and particularity are understood in ecological discourse. As long as greens are able to say that the real issues of environmentalism concern pollution, preservation, and the like, ecofeminism will be considered particular in relation to these universal problems. There may be a unique women's perspective on pollution that needs to be taken into consideration in the formulation of a given policy or strategy, but the central problem will be seen as a human one. In calling this formulation into question, ecofeminists are faced with a question: Is their perspective a particular one and therefore really only one voice among many, or is it genuinely more inclusive of a variety of voices and therefore a better universal to represent the subtleties of the problem?

Nowhere is this question better illustrated than in ecofeminism's attempts to become a genuinely global politics. In the works of Maria Mies, Vandana Shiva, Bina Agarwal, and Joni Seager, to name but a few, it is quite clear that ecofeminism is attempting to come to terms with some of its Western centric limitations and to theorize more explicitly the role of global capital in both the domination of women and the exploitation of nature. By including the specific struggles and needs of women from the

South, ecofeminism seeks to more effectively speak to women's lives worldwide; as its scope expands, however, the call for a diversity of ecofeminist perspectives becomes all the louder.

Maria Mies and Vandana Shiva's *Ecofeminism* is one of the most sustained ecofeminist attempts to deal with the diversity of international feminist/ecological struggles against globalizing capitalist relations.[24] Throughout the individual articles that compose this loosely collaborative text—there is no single, overarching narrative, but rather a series of particular cases that culminates in a final chapter on grassroots mobilization—they argue that women in *both* the so-called South and North bear the destructive brunt of capitalist productive and reproductive relations, including the environmental degradation that these relations produce, albeit in a variety of different ways. Women, they argue, are the primary objects of increasingly intrusive medical and genetic technologies. In the North, women's bodies are a new frontier for invasive new reproductive technologies, while in the South, women's fertility is being controlled by racist population control strategies. Women's productive and reproductive lives are degraded by structural adjustment policies, by economic development projects aimed at erasing biological and cultural diversity in favor of export-oriented monoculture and by the ecological havoc wreaked by toxic waste disposal, deforestation, and nuclear proliferation. In the South, women are impoverished and disenfranchised by "catch-up" development strategies; in the North, they are increasingly policed and regulated by state intervention into private life. And among women and other marginalized peoples in both the South and North, the mounting effects of ecological crisis are felt most specifically, deeply, and fatally.

Yet while the individual sites of patriarchal-capitalist destruction that Mies and Shiva examine are diverse—from Bhopal and Chernobyl to eugenics and intellectual colonization—they believe that it is through the adoption of a subsistence or survival perspective that local grassroots struggles for change may find a common ground in which to plant resistance to capitalist economic and political agendas. Specifically, they argue that ecofeminism must reject a capitalist version of "the good life" based on high technology, mass consumerism, and unrestrained economic growth in favor of locally based, life-affirming, culturally diverse, and self-reliant productive and reproductive communities. These subsistence forms, they argue, engender new relations among people and between people and nonhuman nature. And, not coincidentally, the social and ecological knowledges that give rise to this survival perspective are to be found in many women's experiences of the world, which are precisely those experiences most trammelled by the global march of capital.

What Mies and Shiva produce is, in a sense, an ecofeminist chain of equivalences. They begin with a careful account of the differences that situate the specific sites they describe (and themselves as politicized authors within them)—North/South tensions, racial, economic and cultural specificities—and then rely on the cases themselves to tell the story rather than bringing each example back to a central narrative structure. They offer specific sites in which women's lives and bodies are being colonized through particular manifestations of capitalist productivism, commodity fetishism, accumulation, and state intervention. At the same time, they make a strong case that local knowledges and resistances are globally interwoven; the connections are the product of a shared set of experiences of capitalist colonization that transcends local conditions even as it is articulated with them.

It is not until the very last chapter, not insignificantly titled "The Need for a New Vision," that the cases come to be treated as articulated examples showing the need for a broader movement. This new vision is thus attached to retrospectively orient our reading of the situation toward the necessity of globalization from below; in rejection of what capitalism offers as a universal, a collection of local economic and cultural sites collected around the common theme of subsistence forms the new horizon of sustainable universality toward which ecological politics should be oriented.

The problem in Mies and Shiva's argument arises in their suggestion that some women (and, in their reading, a few men) already embody the kind of ecologically benign, inherently egalitarian and sustainable lifeform that gives rise to the desired universal consciousness. Immediately before describing in some detail the precise character of their universal subsistence perspective, they write that

> These women and men's concept of what constitutes a "good life" of "freedom" is different, as is their concept of economics, politics, and culture. Their utopia may not yet be clearly spelt out explicitly, but its components are already being tested in everyday practice[,] it is a potentially *concrete utopia*.[25]

Thus, they argue that the new universal is already embodied in the particular, that the kinds of economic, political, epistemological, ethical, ecological, and gender relations that will save the world are not desired of the world but somewhere present in it. Most notably, their subsistence perspective relies on the rather shaky premise that the forms of (re)productive activity in which women engage—at least, prior to capitalist invasion—hold a key to the development of nonalienated, meaningful work for women and men in respect for natural limits. Even as they acknowledge that men may share in this understanding, it is not at all clear that women as a collective entity share (or have ever shared) so fundamental an experience as to crystallize world resistance. It is also not clear that subsistence activities, gendered or otherwise, are as inherently emancipatory as Mies and Shiva seem to think; their claim in this regard ironically seems to rest on a very particular set of women's experiences.

In its treatment of the tensions between universality and particularity, Mies and Shiva's text makes some excellent democratic moves. Where it fails, however, is its indication that ecofeminist practice is embodied in the lives of some women and that this practice is itself the desired universal toward which all eco-democratic projects should be oriented. There is no question in Mies and Shiva's minds that their subsistence perspective might not be the most relevant, or even effective, mode of political/economic/reproductive/ecological activity for all people in all anticapitalist struggles. Ecofeminism, in this version of its global relevance, becomes an unproblematic, existent universal; there is no tension between its desire and its practice, no gap between the particular and the universal.[26] In my view, it is not the hegemonic desire that is the problem. Rather, the attempt to construct a singular subject position through which the universal can be viewed strikes me as a failed response to the productive tensions between universality and particularity outlined earlier as the promise of globalization from below.

Ecofeminism, Universality, and Particularity

Universality and particularity, as I have suggested throughout this chapter, are political terms that connote both rhetorical postures and ontological fictions. In Laclau's formulation, it is the ability of a particular interest to appear universal (through the denial of its particularity and the erasure of its own history of becoming) that gives it political weight. But this process of erasure is both precarious and awkward. If part of the point of politics is to destabilize the possibility of erasure, to call into question the relations by which an identity appears solid, then how can we imagine an ecofeminist political claim toward the universal that does not end up reifying the particular as Mies and Shiva's work eventually does?

As noted in chapter 3, social ecofeminist Val Plumwood relies on the argument that neither a "feminism of uncritical equality" nor a "feminism of uncritical reversal" produces an adequate standpoint from which to formulate an ecofeminist vision. In the former, the quest toward equality reinforces a masculinist definition of the good life as women seek a greater piece of the androcentrically valued pie; in the latter, the quest toward difference also reinforces androcentric dualism as women seek a version of the good life that is specifically opposed to these values. Both leave intact the structures of dualism, the fact of androcentric bias in the social creation of value and meaning. It is in Plumwood's rejection of both alternatives and her call for a new political form that we can find the beginnings of a call to universality that might not reify the particular as embodying the universal, but only if one rejects the ontological claims she attaches to it.

To Plumwood, the third wave of feminism that she calls for represents a process of questioning dualistic categories themselves. Rather than being content with the representational status quo, both women and men need actively to take on the deconstruction of dualisms themselves, revealing their fictive qualities and the androcentric interests in which they are located. Women are not nature; men are not culture:

> In this alternative, women are not seen as purely part of nature any more than men are; both men and women are both part of nature and culture. Both men and women can stand with nature and work for breaking down the dualistic construction of culture.[27]

In other words, what Plumwood suggests is an ecofeminist stance that challenges not only the adequacy of existing representations of gender and nature but their legitimacy to represent the universal. What she tries to do is disrupt patriarchal conceptions of value, patriarchal discourses constructing women and nature. Throughout her analysis of dualism, she tries to shake up a series of widely held hegemonic discourses: that what is associated with masculinity and humanity is good, and that what is associated by default with femininity and nature is bad. She tries to break the association of masculinity with humanity, showing that hierarchical conceptions of value—dualisms—are not natural or inherent but are part of a specifically patriarchal worldview. This worldview is based on the experiences and interests of men; it is part of the operations of power in which men are the center of definitions of humanity, worth, and what is supposedly good in the world.

Discourses of rationality, transcendence, mind over body, reason over emotion, and conquering nature or biology are seen, in this worldview, not just as obviously valuable but as characteristics of humanity that all people should try to approximate, characteristics of value by which all things and processes are to be judged. Of course, there is at the same time a moment in this discourse that suggests that not all people, not all living things, can approximate these ideals. These are the Others, those who are defined as less than human, less than perfect—those who by definition are construed as less able to embody and further these so-called human projects.

As Plumwood has shown, what we have here is an apparent contradiction. These characteristics are supposed to be universal, yet they are clearly produced through exclusion. Only by defining a series of opposed lesser Others are these projects of rationality and transcendence possible. Only by saying "this is not good" is it possible to arrive at a definition of what *is* good; this process would seem to necessarily entail a delineation of us and them, the construction not just of dualism but of hierarchical dualism, giving specific content to the opposed poles of good and bad. So the patriarchal universal is produced here though devaluation of the Other, who becomes, in a sense, the repository of the bad, the mirror reflection of the good, not just different but, because of difference, inferior.

Thus, what Plumwood does is show just how particular this so-called universal is. Her ecofeminism challenges its hegemony. It shows, quite forcefully, that what currently passes as good, what currently passes as human, is based on a very specific experiencing of the world. It does so by stressing that this universal is produced through a logic of exclusion as it operates in hierarchical power relations, a logic that is both particularly oppressive for women and nature and generally destructive for the world.

As Plumwood emphasizes, ecofeminism understands itself as forming a new, more truthful politics for the contingent liberations of women and nature. Both uncritical equality and uncritical difference leave the patriarchal universal intact, the former by failing to question its notions of value and humanity and the latter by simply reversing the categories of value defined in and by patriarchal dualisms. So the third wave, ecofeminism, would challenge the dualisms themselves. In a telling passage, she writes that

> an approach critical of dualism would . . . insist that women must be treated as fully human and as fully part of culture as men, but that both sexes must challenge this dualized conception of human identity and develop an alternative culture which fully recognizes *human* identity as continuous with, not alien from, nature.[28]

This is ecofeminism's moment of promise: it maintains a commitment to the redefinition of the universal by accepting an abstract notion of universality to redefine male/female and human/nature relations. Plumwood does not stop at showing particularity, however, or even at inviting a new democratic conversation toward a new horizon. As was the case with Mies and Shiva's analysis, her ecofeminism proclaims itself to already embody a new universal. Through this type of argument, ecofeminism advocates a standpoint that somehow represents the particular experiences of women in relation to nature while also embodying Otherness itself. In this move, ontology becomes politics; by listening to the voices of women and nature, or even the voices of women as representatives of and speakers for nature, we can arrive at a better universal that truly represents these Others. Men and women will both participate in challenging culture, writes Plumwood, but

> in doing so they will come from different historical places and have different things to contribute to the process. Because of their placement in the sphere of nature and exclusion from an oppositional culture, what women have to contribute to this process may be especially significant.[29]

True to its globalizing desire, ecofeminism would have us replace a destructive universal with a new, better one. In ecofeminism, the form of this replacement involves drawing from the experiences of women in nature to find an alternative and leaves much to be desired. This new universal is not seen as a new hegemony, a new configuration of power that may be better than the old one. It is seen as a necessary, existing truth, a truth that emanates from ontological difference, from women's apparently unique experiences of nature. In Ynestra King's words, "Acting on our own consciousness of our own needs, we act in the interests of all."[30] By getting in touch with the oppressed aspects of life, the Other-ness, the part of life excluded in the patriarchal universal, we can transform the world for the benefit of all. We may do so through a quest to be equals in the world of culture, but a strong moment of difference remains; it is women's difference, not women's equality, that produces our ability to know better, our ability to transform, and our ability to have a more integrative universal at our disposal through our experiences.

But this movement toward the enunciation of ontological difference is not necessary nor is it omnipresent. While it is certainly the case that ecofeminism remains plagued by the ontological problems of the earlier feminisms that it has chosen to identify as its ancestors,[31] it is not the case that ecofeminism needs to forever remain hopelessly mired in them. Plumwood's and Mies and Shiva's texts themselves take ecofeminism well beyond some of the narrative limitations I described in chapter 3. If the remaining problem, as viewed through the lens taken up in this chapter, is seen as the collapse of the universal into the particular (or perhaps the expansion of the particular to fill the gap of the universal), then it becomes possible to suggest ways in which ecofeminism can avoid this problem and contribute more effectively to a democratic project.

A recent article by Martha McMahon critiquing neoclassical constructions of "economic man" illustrates this potential extremely well. In this work, McMahon's intention is to offer an ecofeminist account of the ways in which hegemonic forms of economic thought not only exclude but systematically exploit women, nature and others.[32] While this analysis is echoed in other ecofeminist writings on the ways in which women and nature provide invisible subsidies to capitalist development,[33] McMahon's explicit focus is on pointing out the actual embodiment and partiality of an identity that is, in the main, unproblematically understood to be true, universal, and desirable. In fact, McMahon underlines the ways in which the assumption of universality itself is part of the problem; women, nature, and others are scrutinized and found wanting through an idealized notion of individuality and reciprocity at the same time that their associated modes of being and doing are absolutely crucial to (if invisible in) the operations of the market.

What particularly distinguishes McMahon's work is its explicit refusal to posit an essential feminized or naturalized Other who exists as the template of an alternative way of acting in the world. She proposes the limits of the universality of economic man as a model of selfhood and leaves open the resulting conceptual space for a political conversation about other ways of being a self in the world. In addition, she is careful to write of the process of self-construction as a narrative and contextualized process, to thus destabilize the presumed universality of any identity at the same time that she produces a powerful critique of the hegemonic political operations of economic man as a partial identity. She argues that

> the model of "economic man" as a separate, autonomous, detached, competitive and primarily self-interested individual is anti-feminist, anti-ecological, and oppressive of those who are "other" than economic man. Yet . . . while this notion of the individual is falsely universalizing, it is also locally and partially true. It is the partiality of its truth that makes neoclassical economics such a powerful intellectual and political tool.[34]

McMahon's ecofeminism proposes what she calls a *"ground up* approach to addressing environmental degradation,"[35] a project that bears a strong relationship to the discourse of globalization from below I outlined earlier. The strong democratic moment of the project of globalization from below lies in its simultaneous critique of global capital (although there are other potential starting points for this process) and movement toward the per- petually future production of a new universal to quilt together a variety of local conflicts. It is those moments, such as those I have discussed earlier, when ecofeminism claims to be free of the need for a future orientation that it loses its place as an element in a broader articulation of struggles; in its understanding as of itself as complete, it shies away from the responsi- bility of democracy.

But in moments such as McMahon's article, ecofeminism is clearly founded on a democratic desire: it invites conversation, encourages the con- struction of divergent perspectives on nature, and welcomes the progressive inclusion of a wider variety of voices into its debates without suggesting that this articulation ever really embodies a revolutionary standpoint.[36] As an analytic current, the desire of ecofeminism is clearly to expand the process of democratic questioning; by problematizing an expanding terrain of social relations, and by making the relations between gender and nature explicitly political (as I will discuss in the next chapter), ecofeminists want to continue the interrogative process even as they may, sometimes, shut it down in their invocations of embodied utopia or standpoint.

It is precisely this interrogative potential that Lee Quinby points to as one of the most promising elements of ecofeminism. In her view—and, oddly, in the view of Janet Biehl, who rejects ecofeminism for this very rea- son—ecofeminism is a viable movement because it does not, for all its at- tempts to do so, offer a single narrative of liberation. Rather, it has inspired analysts and activists working in multiple sites to produce the kind of gen- dered questions that make for locally grounded analyses of social relations to nature. As Quinby writes,

> A rejection of programmatic coherence does not mean that ecofemi- nism . . . lack[s] direction or cohesion. On the contrary, in turning attention to the ways that domination of the land, labor, and women intersect, eco- feminism underscores the need for coalitions that are both aware of gender hierarchy and respectful of the earth. If other terms and different politics emerge from that questioning and that struggle, then we can strive to place them in the service of new local actions, new creative energies, and new coalitions that preclude apocalyptic constraints on freedom.[37]

What Quinby recognizes is the importance of openness to ecofeminism: its promise, and indeed its practice in many areas, is to offer analytic and political tools by which new chains of equivalence may be constructed for the future. In this process, ecofeminism would lose its privilege as the cen- tral term (or the embodied universal) in the articulation, but by drawing attention to the specific intersections of gender and nature it would open up a fertile ground for political cultivation.

In Plumwood's analysis, there are possibilities for an ecofeminist orientation to universality that does not end up reinscribing women's particular relations to nature as ontologically based or inherently utopian. She is quite explicit that there is no essential relation between women and nature producing the desired ecofeminist standpoint; even as she feels politically compelled to reproduce the need for a standpoint to ground her claim for feminine specificity, she implies its historical contingency and partiality, its current production according to male narratives of mastery and domination. In other words, the identities she eventually claims as configuring distinct standpoints on nature are revealed as traces of a distorting social logic; part of her political vision is to uncover the tracks through which the categories are produced. (Indeed, the whole book is oriented toward dismantling the master's dualistic house.)

Plumwood wavers on the need to invoke the category "women" as the ground for a feminist third wave; at some points in her text, she argues for investigating the profoundly incoherent status of the identity, where at others she resolidifies it to mark the distinctiveness of her standpoint.[38] But where Mies and Shiva's narrative begins with openness and ends with closure, Plumwood's does the reverse. Indeed, her final chapter deviates significantly from her earlier standpoint arguments about the relative difference of women's experiences in nature. In this chapter, her orientation is clearly to the future production of an ecological identity and not to its current embodiment in the lives of women. Her project necessarily "implies creating a democratic culture beyond dualism, encoding colonised relationships and finding a mutual, ethical basis for enriching coexistence with earth others."[39]

It is, then, possible to read this transcendence of dualism as a perpetually incomplete desire (like Quinby's and McMahon's). Given that women and men and nature are socially produced through problematic dualisms, it is not possible to take up a view outside them in order to forge better relations to nature somehow uncontaminated by them. It is only through deconstructing the dualisms themselves that a future harmony can be reached; the master subject, however, should not be reproduced. Given that Plumwood's future culture beyond dualism is a specifically democratic one, there is the implicit suggestion that no harmony can ever be reached without a constant process of negotiation. It is not too much of an extension, I think, to argue that the feminist standpoint she occasionally advocates is impossible; it is a horizon of desire rather than an existing place and is thus amenable to the open universality that globalization from below (universalization from below?) suggests. If it is democracy that beckons from the horizon, then it seems that nobody is ever going to "get it right."

Indeed, in a number of places in the text, Plumwood alludes to the need for ecofeminism to be allied with other struggles of liberation; all share an interest in dismantling "the dualisms which have characterised western culture,"[40] but none, it would follow, has direct access to a better alternative. If women already have a privileged access to these better relations to nature, then why engage in any kind of affiliational process? Plumwood's effort to deconstruct the patriarchal universal[41] is not necessarily—even in her own account—followed by a strong claim to a liberatory standpoint. Given the places where she is oriented to a future democracy capable of producing the relations to nature she desires, and given her gesture to a version of alliance quilted through a common resistance to dualism, it is quite possible to see in her work the ground of a hegemonic rather than ontological universality.

Like Mies and Shiva's globalization from below, Plumwood's third wave can be seen as part of a radical democratic universality *if* openness and futurity replace embodiment and standpoint. In ecofeminism, as in other movements coming to terms with the call toward a universal in the face of globalization, democratic promise involves developing a political stance that is not sure of its solidity and that is thus dependent on a constant process of reinclusion as a move toward a future universal. While the solidity of identity beckons, its production and interrogation according to an always-future achievement allows for a profoundly democratic engagement. As an interrogative politics that calls into question the possibility of any universality that does not include attention to specific relations of gender and nature or as an antidualistic or anticapitalist politics that calls into question the adequacy of the relations that currently pass as universal, ecofeminism contains an enormous democratic promise; by orienting itself toward a universal desire and simultaneously refusing its embodiment, ecofeminism can deepen precisely that promise.

There are practical, concrete instances of this promising universal desire. I mentioned earlier a document called the Women's Action Agenda 21 (WAA 21) written by NGO activists in part to show the inadequacies of the Action Agenda 21, the official document under negotiation at the Rio Summit. In the condensed version widely circulated by the Taskforce on the Churches and Corporate Responsibility, the document is prefaced by the following statement:

The World Women's Congress Action Agenda 21 . . . is a compilation of the work, ideas, and values of 1500 women from around the world, North and South, East and West. It represents the essence of four days of expert testimony, jury panels, and workshop discussions that are distilled in this document. While it does not necessarily represent the views of each and every individual who participated in the process, it is meant as a challenge to women and men to work together to create a safe and sustainable future.[42]

According to Rosi Braidotti, Ewa Charkiewicz, Sabine Häusler, and Saskia Wieringa, the UNCED preparatory process indicated that "an increasingly transformative view on women, the environment and sustainable development entered the UN system"; the WAA 21 document represented a "major breakthrough because for the first time ever women across political/ geographical, class, race, professional and institutional divides came up with a critique of development and a collective position on the environmental crisis, arrived at in a participatory and democratic process."[43] But these authors are also cautious about certain tendencies in the UN process, especially the "masked tendency to emphasize commonalities between women, resulting in an implicitly essentialist position—women as closer to nature than men—as the basis for a collective position."[44] Indeed, for some participants, even the process leading up to the creation of the WAA 21 was deeply problematic for these reasons.

This commentary shows an interesting tension in the UNCED process, and in ecofeminist politics more generally: coalitions oriented toward proposing an alternative universal run the risk of essentializing the position of particularity from which the writing occurs. This tension is certainly present in the WAA 21 and the discussions that created it; speaking as "women" almost requires the invocation of some common essence, and it is true that the WAA 21 does not engage in the sort of destabilizing or ironic ecofeminist "drag" I outlined in chapter 5. But, as Braidotti et al. note, part of the document's essentialism is explicitly strategic: "Arguing that women have a special connection to the environment has undeniably had the effect of forcefully bringing out their right to be heard by other actors involved in the debate."[45]

I would like to argue that the WAA 21 document offers, despite its moments of strategic essentialism and problematic creation,[46] a strong example of a universalizing politics that does not claim an embodied and stable alternative and thus leaves open multiple and useful spaces for future conversation. The excerpted WAA 21 document itself begins with a preamble titled "Towards a Healthy Planet" that outlines the embeddedness of all human beings in "the web of life" and then speaks of women as coming together through a common desire "to voice our concern for the health of our living planet." It describes the fact that the document is produced from conversation (specifically at the conference in Miami where the document was composed) and then produces a version of the conference's authority:

> We speak on behalf of those who cannot be with us, the millions of women who experience daily the violence of environmental degradation, poverty, and the exploitation of their work and bodies . . . [due to] so-called "free-market ideology" and wrong concepts of "economic growth."[47]

The preamble mentions, but does not claim to speak for, "rainforest dwellers, island peoples, and inhabitants of fragile arid zones"; it also speaks of a "we" that is "deeply troubled" by economic inequality between North and South, child poverty, militarism, and a lack of human rights (including basic needs) and that is committed "to the empowerment of women" at the conference itself and elsewhere. This commitment is demonstrated through the construction of a long list of interrelated action demands, beginning with "democratic rights, diversity, and solidarity" and also including issues around environmental ethics and accountability, militarism and violence, foreign debt and trade, biodiversity and biotechnology, nuclear power and alternative energy, science and technology transfer, and the composition of the UN itself.

While the content of these action demands is clearly important (as with Matuschka's poster, it is in the quest for something else that we find a particular democratic promise), it is the document itself that I would like to examine as a call to democratic universality. First, the whole point of the document was to challenge the UN's representation of globalization; against the agendas of states and multinational corporations,[48] a global collection of concerned women came together to suggest an alternative, one based primarily on an active resistance to the increasing global reach of capital. The collective is oriented toward a healthy planet; the universal good calls from the future, and no one knowledge or position is ever held out as its embodiment (including the document itself). Still, the interests collected pose themselves as universalizing, as speaking to/of "people" and "human beings" and not to/of any particular group.

Second, the document was presented (and presented itself) as the product of debate and discussion, including (apparently to a limited extent) dissent; the fact that the common political agenda was accepted in the face of differences of interest and opinion suggested the possibility of diverse interests temporarily representing themselves as part of the common struggle but with no claims to a totalizing we. Indeed, the "we" invoked in the text is never solid; it shifts between women as a whole and the particular women who happened to be at the conference. It also shifts between a "we" that acts on its own behalf and one that reaches out a hand of concern to other struggles not primarily collected around a "women's" issue.

Third, the "actions" *begin* with democracy; the ability of local people to voice their specific concerns, organize freely, and be taken seriously is positioned as a prerequisite to action on any other specific issue. Interestingly, a version of global citizenship is also present; the democracy section begins with the phrase "recognizing that Nature is not limited by national sovereignty or boundaries," thus globalizing the need for democracy. At the same time, however, the demands that follow in the rest of the document are clearly locally specific; for example, indigenous people are mentioned specifically, as are toxic disposal (which particularly affects poor communities and nations) and bovine growth hormone (which particularly affects consumers and farmers in countries with a large commercial dairy industry).

In other words, the WAA 21 represents an agenda of globalization from below. Constructed for (and against) an altogether different global vision, it calls for a universality based on the recognition of diversity, the political centrality of democracy, and the need to take local needs and struggles into account. Its feminist content is abundantly clear, as is its ecological concern, but in no way is the voice that speaks this concern seen to embody an ideal feminist/ecological position in and of itself. Its will is "towards" a version of planetary health that can only be produced democratically; it thus represents a future universal that creates the call for global citizenship.

It is possible now to see more clearly how performativity and universalism may be part of the same project (although not, of course, without tension). Insofar as universalism involves an orientation toward a future form of democratic conversation, it marks the fact that there is no identity currently able to produce it. And insofar as the imputed stability of identity categories is one of the barriers to the development of this future orientation, performative destabilization may be one route through which the necessity of future conversation is highlighted. Likewise, universalism's orientation toward the future suggests a space in which questions about the current shape of any identity may be asked. Transgression and parody imply the interrogative: "If I am not this, then what am I?" The answer, like the universal, perpetually beckons from the future and invites a democratic conversation about the possibilities.

7

Ecofeminism, Public and Private Life

Many women's ecological sense has been sharpened by the *historical* fact that they are both mothers and intellectually trained workers. Their political consciousness thus resists the split between private and public spheres of responsibility and the denial of concrete feeling for organisational efficacy which deforms conventional politics.

> Ariel Salleh, "From Feminism to Ecology"

Anne Cameron [suggests] that: "Every decision a person makes in her life is a personal, political, and spiritual decision." . . . From such a relativizing perspective, it becomes difficult to make crucial distinctions between levels of political action and commitment which often results in a fragmented, micropolitical vision of the problem at hand.

> Carole Stabile, "'A Garden Inclosed Is My Sister'"

The tensions between antagonism/equivalence and between universality/particularity involve modes of political speech appropriate to a radical democratic politics; in a sense, both tensions are born from questions about representation, about the ability of any political form to stand in for a cacophony of experiences, interests, and desires. In these tensions, the centrality of diversity to political speech is abundantly clear; where equivalence and universality represent a move toward a hegemonic politics, one capable of collecting diversity and representing or producing solidarity, the totalizing and suturing potential of these moves is constantly disrupted by the appearance of difference, the impossibility of achieving a singular standpoint around which to organize resistances. Thus, for a radically democratic political speech, openness to the perpetual appearance of new constitutions of plurality is a founding moment.

But it must be remembered that diversity is not simply an enumeration of existing subject positions. Radical democracy involves a desire for the cultivation of plurality, an ongoing skepticism about the ability of any political representation to represent. In my view, this desire is a specifically political one; if part of the point of a radical democratic politics is to come to terms with, and act from, the lack of correspondence between subject and political subject position, then there is a specificity to the political that needs to be investigated. What is it about radical democracy that prevents the comfortable inhabitation of subject positions? How is it possible to imagine a political sphere in which the gap is kept open as part of the preservation of democracy? Perhaps most importantly, what is "the political" in a radical democratic politics?

This chapter departs slightly from the overt engagement with Laclau and Mouffe apparent in chapters 5 and 6. While it is clear that the tension I will describe between public and private spheres can be understood as formed according to the logic of impossibility (i.e., the gap between Real and Symbolic, subject and subject position, reality and language), I find in the works of Hannah Arendt a particularly apt description of a democratic politics that respects—indeed, privileges—uncertainty. Although Mouffe treats similar issues in her many discussions of radical democratic citizenship,[1] I choose to place Arendt at the center of the theoretical constellation of this chapter because of her explicit call to defend political life against the incursions of administrative and bureaucratic logics. This defense is particularly important in environmental—including ecofeminist—political struggles.

There is, to be sure, a point at which Arendt's and Laclau and Mouffe's arguments (and mine thus far) are diametrically opposed, and I wade into Arendt's world and worldliness with some fear. Where Arendt, for reasons that will become apparent below, is hostile to the idea that subject positions carry political validity and thinks they should be erased upon entry into the polis, Laclau and Mouffe see them as the basis of politics. For that reason, the version of Arendt's thought that I use here is significantly tinged with modifications by her feminist critics, for whom (like Laclau and Mouffe) one cannot ever escape from private identity. Hence, the tension. But Arendt's notion of politics as a realm of the performative construction of the self is, in many respects, quite consonant with the vision I have thus far outlined; politics is the realm where identities should be questioned, and even if they cannot be left behind at the door when one enters the polis, they will not be the same when one leaves it. Even if daily life requires most of us to live with something less than performative attachments to our subject positions, Arendt's suggestion of the specificity of the political offers a crucial space in which that kind of challenge is cultivated.

The Demise of Environmental Politics

On April 5 of 1994, a headline in the *Globe and Mail* caught my attention: "Environmentalists Not Seen as Force in Next Ontario Election."[2] This prophecy proved distressingly true in the 1995 provincial campaign itself: despite the demise of the Ontario Waste Management Corporation, which left the province with no policy on hazardous waste whatsoever; despite Progressive Conservative Mike Harris's commitment to gut the Planning Act, which would reopen every possible door for suburban sprawl; and despite then–New Democratic Party (NDP) leader Bob Rae's former environmental commitment (demonstrated by an arrest over Temagami clearcutting while he was still leader of the opposition) and then-Liberal leader Lyn McLeod's former status as Minister of Natural Resources in the previous Peterson government, the observer of the campaign would have concluded that there was no environment about which to be concerned. Planning Act aside, the Conservatives were elected without an environmental platform.[3]

In 1994, what really caught my attention was the article's suggestion that public political interest in environmental issues had declined dramatically since the last Ontario provincial election. In 1995, I was disappointed to see that even the anti-Harris protest on the lawns of the Provincial Legislature designed to highlight the flaws and injustices in his agenda failed to note his complete lack of concern over things environmental.[4] The protest was a parody of the Tory swearing-in ceremony with which it coincided; for each "real" minister, a "community" minister stood up to state an alternative agenda (plus one or two extras, including a minister of gay and lesbian issues). There was no community minister of the environment.

While I would be the last person to argue that electoral campaigns (or the legislature's lawn) are the only, or best, sites for the politicization of environmental issues, I found this trend disturbing. A recent Angus Reid poll confirmed my distress. In 1989, when asked what was the most important issue facing the country, 33 percent of Canadians polled replied that the environment was. In 1990, the figure fell to 24 percent; in 1991, to 17 percent; in 1992, to 7 percent; in 1993, to only 4 percent, and the trend continues marginally downward.[5] While it is increasingly true that people thought environmental issues are important, such issues were not at the top of the political list of priorities.

As the *Globe* article suggested, "The strength of the environmental movement has been sapped in the recession." While the poll shows that many people are still concerned about environmental issues (to the extent that 21 percent of respondents claim they are "environmental activists," whatever that may mean to Angus Reid), the economy is clearly foremost in the minds of most Canadians. Said Colin Isaacs, "With jobs at the head of the public's concerns, the message that many do not want to hear is that the solution to environmental problems is to shut down industry, ban logging, and stop the development of mines."[6] Add that widespread if inaccurate perception to the fact that many environmental groups' financial support has also dwindled in the recession and we end up with a situation where environmental issues are, apparently, neither raised nor particularly appreciated when they are.

At the same time, however, the Angus Reid poll suggests that a clear majority of Canadians say they are engaged in green activities, that they would pay more, even in these recessionary times, for so-called environmentally friendly products, and that they would support stiffer penalties against polluters. One in three say they would support a ten-cent deposit on all aluminum cans and a total ban on logging of old-growth forests. Indeed, an environmental store in my neighborhood seems to be doing extremely well selling hemp clothing (expensive), key chains made from computer boards (as if there weren't already enough key chains in the world), and organic chocolate made with Oregon raspberries (so much for bioregionalism). So why is it, in this context of such apparently widespread concern, that the political voices of environmental movements in Ontario are, to quote the *Globe*, a "whimper"?

Important though the recession may be (and although 1998 may be witnessing a certain resurgence of environmental concern due to strange weather), it does not explain this apparent contradiction. What we need to look at as well is the status of environmental issues as public political issues. Here, I would argue that the environment has been generally depoliticized. Specifically, it is in the move by which environmental concern can be relatively unproblematically expressed in such actions as recycling, paying deposits on aluminum cans, buying cute little green keychains, and condemning polluters and forestry practices to Angus Reid pollsters that we see the demise of the environment as a site of genuinely political contestation.

There are, of course, significant exceptions like Clayoquot Sound, which was considered sufficiently political to mobilize over eight hundred people to get arrested in the summer of 1993 and thousands of forestry workers and supporters to engage in counterprotests. In general, however, there seems to be a relationship between the ways in which environmental issues have become routinized, bureaucratized, and individualized and the ways in which they have become de-politicized. As Tim Luke notes, for example, environmental issues have become much more respectable now that corporations have painted their reputations green. Twenty years ago, "any serious personal interest in the environment often was seen as the definitive mark of radical extremism"; now environmentalism has become a much more mainstream concern, to the point where "major corporations now feel moved to proclaim how much 'every day is Earth Day.'"[7]

It is certainly true that state and corporate green rhetorics have had the effect of narrowing the possibilities for a more radical outlook. In addition, as Brian Tokar writes of the United States in particular, the perception of a decline in environmental concern "is substantially tied to the increasing political submission of the leading national environmental groups."[8] But it also seems that many environmental groups—especially, but not entirely, those in the mainstream—have themselves participated in the process of depoliticization. As Laurie Adkin notes, despite the wide variety of positions apparent in Canadian environmental movements, some of which are strongly oriented to revealing and acting upon the specifically political aspects of systemic environmental problems, all too few groups are willing or able to resist dominant ecocapitalist "technocratic and market-oriented" discourses.[9]

I would like to argue that the relative absence in much environmentalism of a clear idea of "the political" itself is also a large part of this problem. Specifically, much contemporary environmental concern is all too easily seduced by trends toward private, often bureaucratic, solutions. Where environmental issues contain the possibility of constituting and mobilizing diverse publics and do so, as in the case of environmental justice, this potential is seldom fulfilled because the political is not located as a central element in most environmental struggles, as if saving the earth were a task that overrides the importance of democratization. (Indeed, some environmental groups and currents, notably some deep ecologists, have made it very clear indeed that saving the earth is a chief priority and that democracy can wait.) In the absence of an overt agenda of politicization, it is not surprising that environmental issues are all too often placed behind a corporate, technocratic, and fundamentally conservative screen or held aloft as a purely mystical and emotional quest. Thus, it is the status of *politics* with which I am primarily concerned.

Politics in Arendt's Age of "the Social"

One key to Arendt's understanding of public life is her much debated conception of the *vita activa*, the three fundamental aspects of the human condition: labor, work, and action. Labor, to Arendt, "is the activity which corresponds to the biological process of the human body"; it involves the production and reproduction of life itself, the basic needs of members of a species embarked on a mortal journey from birth to death. Work, in contrast, "is the activity which corresponds to the unnaturalness of human existence"; it "provides an 'artificial' world of things, distinctly different from all natural surroundings . . . [and] meant to outlast and transcend them all."[10] In Arendt's view, both of these activities are necessary to human existence, labor by securing life itself and work by providing human permanence beyond ephemeral biological growth and decay.[11]

But to Arendt, it is action that most fully captures human potential; action is the capacity for speech and deed, the ability to bring into being new beginnings, the unpredictable transcendence of both necessitarian labor and instrumental work, the production of distinctiveness. "Action," she writes, is "the only activity that goes on directly between men without the intermediary of things or matter"; it "corresponds to the human condition of plurality, the fact than men, not Man, live on the earth and inhabit the world."[12] Thus, unlike labor and work, action is necessarily collective; its essence is human plurality, simultaneous equality and diversity, and the fact that "we are all the same, that is, human, in such a way that nobody is ever the same as anyone else who ever lived, lives, or will live."[13] Action is also necessarily uncertain; unlike biological processes—to Arendt, the epitome of necessity and inevitability—action can never be sure of its result, and hence her emphasis on its ability to bring the new into being.[14]

To Arendt, the realization of the human plurality and beginning that lies at the heart of action occurs when people gather together to appear publicly, to voice their views in the presence of others. In other words, action requires a public realm. By *public,* Arendt means two things: first, that "everything that appears in public can be seen and heard by everybody and has the widest possible publicity" and, second, that this appearance concerns "the world itself, in so far as it is common to all of us and distinguished from our privately owned place in it."[15] These characteristics of the public realm are crucial; publicity requires openness and commonality requires the production of a world beyond private interests. It is only when citizens are able to appear freely and equally in the presence of multiple others and to leave behind the chains of identities and interests grounded in private life that action becomes possible; it is only through action that human beings produce their individuality in commonality; thus, a public realm is essential to the human condition.

Arendt's understanding of the public realm was importantly born out of a profound concern for its demise. Specifically, she understood that, from the seventeenth century on, social life has increasingly come to close the spaces available for politics. If I might borrow Seyla Benhabib's description,

> The same historical process which brought forth the modern constitutional state also brought forth "society," that realm of social interaction which interposes itself between the "household," on the one hand, and the political state on the other. . . . Arendt sees in this process the occluding of the "political" by the "social" and the transformation of the public space of politics into a pseudospace of interaction in which individuals no longer "act" but "merely behave" as economic producers, consumers and urban city-dwellers.[16]

In other words, to Arendt, the expansion of the activities and mentalities of labor and work into so-called "political" discussion combined with the increasing bureaucratization of state activities threatens the very possibility of publicness. The spaces available for human beings to transcend private interests—not to mention the necessity and instrumentalism grounded in them—are narrowing as issues from the private realm come increasingly to dominate what putative political spaces may be open to us. The common world is lost to us, as we have "ceased to think of ourselves as, potentially, something more than just reproducers, producers, laborers, role-players, or fragile psyches."[17] Writes Arendt,

> The public realm, as the common world, gathers us together and yet prevents our falling over each other, so to speak. What makes mass society so difficult to bear is not the number of people involved, at least not primarily, but the fact that the world between them has lost its power to gather them together, to relate, and to separate them. The weirdness of this situation resembles a spiritualistic seance where a number of people gathered around a table might suddenly, through some magic trick, see the table vanish from their midst, so that two persons sitting opposite one another were no

longer separated but also would be entirely unrelated to each other by anything tangible.[18]

To Arendt, then, the public is that space in which we reach our highest
human potential; it is where we live among each other, producing a common world and producing ourselves diversely within it. Its demise at the
hands of the expansion of private life through the rise of the social into
places where it should not be is thus to be resisted.

Feminism and Arendt on the Public, the Private, and Beyond

It is, of course, precisely the clarity with which Arendt draws the distinction between public and private life that causes feminists so much alarm
and which makes an ecofeminist reading of Arendt a risky venture. (It is
also this clear distinction that signals her differences from Laclau and
Mouffe.) While some, such as Mary O'Brien, dismiss Arendt completely
for her valuation of action over reproduction—O'Brien claims that the former is an inherently "masculine" activity possible solely because of its
degradation of the latter[19]—others are more concerned with the ways in
which Arendt's notion of politics rejects the appearance of issues from the
private sphere. While they believe Arendt's work on the specificity of action has much to offer feminist politics, feminists will almost inevitably
challenge her public/private distinction.

Drucilla Cornell and Nancy Fraser are two of many theorists who engage with Arendt's notions of action and publicity.[20] Cornell's argument
concerns Arendt's assumptions that action requires a relation among equals
and that such equality requires the careful distinction between freedom
and necessity. "Arendt insists that for the realm of freedom to exist, the
realm of necessity must be conquered. But she also assumes that conquering must take place in the private realm, in the household, if it is not to
contaminate the realm of freedom."[21] For women to achieve the equality
necessary to participate in action, it is clear that a variety of social changes
are necessary; to Arendt, however, the struggles to achieve these changes
in the private realm are, by definition, not political.

If the feminist phrase "the personal is political" has any consensual
meaning, it would seem to be that the privacy and idiosyncrasy that have
historically been attached to women's concerns must be challenged; so-
called women's issues need to appear publicly, to be discussed as issues of
the common good, if significant changes are to occur and if politics are to
lose their aura of quintessential masculinity. Arendt's vision would seem to

delegitimate this politicizing process; indeed, the appearance of issues such as rape or employment equity (or breast cancer or household toxins) into the putatively public realm would signify, to Arendt, a demise of politics.

In response, Cornell, while celebrating Arendt's defense of democracy, argues that the division she draws between action and necessity is too rigidly gendered; democracy, based as it is on an agonal male fantasy (Cornell invokes Lacan here), would require that space be made for specifically feminine virtues and dialogical processes. Both political and social changes are necessary, and the line between the two cannot be so clearly carved. Writes Cornell, "To change the world in the name of democracy, we need not only to change the rights of man to include the social rights of women, we also need to challenge the masculinization of the rhetoric of the ideal of politics itself."[22]

In a slightly different vein, Fraser argues that Arendt's defense of the political relies on the assumption that the realm of necessity is not subject to discursive contestation. In her own work on need interpretation, Fraser argues that contemporary tensions around the welfare state inscribe fundamental struggles over the power to interpret what is a need, to whom, and in what circumstances. Thus, Fraser argues, needs are not inevitable: they are interpretive constructs configured by precisely the uncertainty and commonality that Arendt claims is missing from the social.

> The emergence of needs from the "private" into the social is a generally positive development, since such needs thereby lose their illusory aura of naturalness as their interpretations become subject to critique and contestation. I, therefore, suppose that this represents the (possible) flourishing of politics rather than the (necessary) death of politics.[23]

What these arguments suggest to me is that there is a specificity to politics worth struggling for although there cannot be a clear line drawn around its appropriate contents. In the context of what must be seen as an erosion of the political at the hands of interest group administration and through backroom deals between multinational corporations and nation-states, creating or protecting spaces in which action is possible would seem to be vital. But the notion of "the common," in any feminist vision, must be subject to question; what is private and what is public is a line drawn in the sand, not cast in stone. As Benhabib writes, "The struggle to make something 'public' is a struggle for justice—thus, the process can never be complete: there can be no agenda to predefine the topic of public conversation."[24] There can be no inherent content to politics because politics itself is the process through which the common is contested and constituted; thus, to predefine an appropriate realm of discussion closes off the possibility of action itself.

In this context, the personal must always be seen to be potentially political, but that is not to suggest that it is always already political. While we must certainly interrogate the arrangements by which public and private life are constituted, that does not mean that they should be the same thing. Following Arendt, I agree that there is a need to argue for distinctions among moments of human life and, more particularly, that action is a specific human good to be promoted. Or, in Fraser's words, "When everything is political, the sense and specificity of the political recedes, giving rise to . . . [a particular] inflection of the expression *le retrait du politique*: the retreat or withdrawal of the political."[25]

If the desired specificity of politics cannot rely on a constative division between action and necessity, then on what grounds can we argue for action as part of a strong feminist public? In my view, such a politics relies on a *character* of conversation, the outlines of which I think are already present in Arendt's own work. Specifically, she insists that the common world of action is a space constructed beyond any interest or identity formed in private. Indeed, action is characterized by its ability to transcend the inevitability or predictability of any other human activity; it is unique in that it is a new beginning, a collective intervention where the outcome is not known in advance and where the actor is undetermined. In other words, this public realm is performative; indeed, Arendt herself uses the word *performance* to describe the speech process by which the actor reveals her unique personal identity in relation to the common world.[26] Moving away from what they are—identities inscribed in the private realm of labor and the economic realm of work—individuals appearing in public reveal who they are, thus constituting themselves as individuals in relation to the shared world of public life.

In this agonal moment of Arendt's public, it is important to note that she considered the human self fundamentally multiple; this is apparent not only in her tripartite *vita activa* but in her understanding of the process of thinking, as she understood humans to be engaged in a two-in-one conversation with the self. While this multiple self differs significantly from the multiple subject of feminist postmodernism, it is still the case that, for Arendt, in private life the self is fragmented and conflictual. Only through performative appearance in public, in the presence of others, does it attain identity, a sense of who it is as distinct from the constraints of what one might call the identities of private life. As Bonnie Honig writes,

For the sake of "who" it might become, [the self] risks the dangers of the radically contingent public realm where anything might happen, where the consequences of action are "boundless" and unpredictable, where "not life but the world is at stake." In so doing, it forsakes the comforting security of "what" it is, the roles and features that define (and even determine) it in the private realm.[27]

What we have in this agonal vision is the sense that action is not the public expression of an individual identity but rather the point at which the individual is created as an individual through a performance in the presence of others. Action does not cement the private self but disrupts it in the creation of something entirely new, something that cannot be grounded in or predicted by private life.

It would be a mistake to equate Arendt's performativity with, for example, Butler's drag. For Arendt, the agonal performance is the only moment at which an individual can be said to exist (the rest of the time, she or he is defined by what, not who, she or he is), where for Butler, parodic performance relies on the careful and conscious repetition of precisely the categories through which an individual is defined (the what) in order to disrupt them. Although the differences are important, this performative understanding of political life does resonate with the argument I presented in chapter 5; feminist politics are not about the revelation of a stable and coherent natural identity but about the public constitution of an acting self formed in relation to doing rather than being. The difference between my argument and Arendt's resides in my agreement with the feminist suggestion that we cannot appear only as individuals and that some disruption is necessary in the public realm if Arendt's desire for action/unpredictability is to be realized. That said, however, it is important to note the agreement between us: Arendt's agonal politics is about the creation of a new and unpredictable self (another future orientation) rather than the revelation of an old and predictable one.

The what does not lie behind the who that is created in Arendt's agonal politics. One can juxtapose this noncorrespondence with a more Lacanian understanding that the subject does not lie behind the subject position of the Symbolic (including political appearance). While the differences are large, the similarity is also interesting: the public realm is not about the expression of identities.[28] For Arendt, it is about the creation of a forum in which new possibilities for individuality are produced. While I depart significantly from her understanding of individuality, the point I take from her is the necessary unpredictability of appearance, its lack of a firm foundation. The specificity of Arendt's agon shows the noncorrespondence between social location and political action; it suggests the need for politics as a space to begin, not to suture, identities.

If one maps onto this agon the notion that there can be no a priori definition of the content of political discussion, no inevitable barring of the private, what appears is the sense that public life demands a particular character of conversation. If action produces a particular constitution of self beyond private identities yet issues from the private must be allowed to appear in public (including performative subversion of the private), what we find is a distinction between form and content. The specificity of the political, in this distinction, resides in the demarcation not of appropriate contents but of appropriate forms. As Hannah Pitkin writes, "Perhaps, then, it is not a particular subject-matter, nor a particular class of people, but a particular *attitude* against which the public realm must be guarded."[29]

One advantage of this formal understanding of politics is that it does not respect existing boundaries. The line between state and civil society, for example, is not particularly related to the contingent movement between private and public; the lines between universal and particular and between antagonism and equivalence are also ruptured, paving the way for a radical democratic constitution of the common world. Another advantage resides in our mobilization to resist the erosion of the political at the hands of the bureaucratic and administrative desires of state apparatuses. If politics requires of each of us an orientation to our own and the world's uncertainty, then we cannot be content with the instrumentality of most of what currently passes as politics. Finally, as Honig notes, this kind of agonal political form leads us away from an identity politics based on the assumption of a monolithic self and toward the public contestation of precisely those identities; we are generated anew and must risk the uncertainty involved in the process. This mode of political appearance cultivates a sense of the noncorrespondence between political representation and private identity to the point where it is the latter that is shown to be most fictional.

But the very instability of this public is cause for concern. To some of Arendt's critics, this agonal view is not only based on a very aesthetic understanding of politics[30] and a very individualized notion of appearance, but it also suggests a very privileged pool of participants—people who have the social solidity to appear equally, to be able to create space beyond their private lives of work and labor, and who possess the strength of character necessary to risk the kind of uncertainty that action entails.

While Valerie Burks argues that the creation of what she calls potency and the cultivation of a worldly Arendtian attitude of caring should be a vital part of feminist politics, the charge of elitism cannot go without comment.[31]

Arendt's agonal view of politics is very much concerned with the extraordinary, the cultivation of acts of greatness where people are able to transcend the banality of their private lives. But existing alongside this agonal vision—especially in her later writings—is another, more ordinary political form, what Benhabib has called a discursive public.[32] Here, Arendt's model of public life is not performance but egalitarian participation and communication; she alludes to this public through historical examples of the hope that it "would permit every member of the modern egalitarian society to become a 'participator' in public affairs."[33] In this view, public life is potentially far more commonplace; it appears wherever people join together to speak and act in concert. The emphasis is on the potential geographic dispersion of politics, the fact that (in Benhabib's words) "these diverse topographies [can be] constitute[d] into public spaces [through] the presence of common action coordinated through speech and persuasion."[34] Thus, this kind of public describes aspects of many oppositional movements; it also has us focus our attention more fully on our ability to bring into being, through active intervention into social life, the egalitarian conditions where common speech and action can be facilitated.

As Maurizio Passerin d'Entrèves notes, Arendt never fully resolved the contradictions between the two understandings of publicness.[35] But where he celebrates the discursive over the agonal as inherently more democratic, I would like to suggest that there is a productive tension between the two that should not be resolved: while Arendt's associational view suggests the possible multiplicity of politics, her agonal view suggests the need to cultivate an anti-instrumental and nonidentitarian stance if the public realm is to foster action. In other words, not all political spaces are political. It is this tension that I would like to use to explore ecofeminism.

Ecofeminism and the Rise and Fall of the Political

Interestingly, Arendt did not believe that any and all conversations about nature were cemented in biological inevitability. While she would have been highly skeptical of the politicality of the kind of environmental identity politics I outlined in chapter 4, she saw the potential of ecological issues to produce the kinds of common conversation she saw as requisite to action. As Kerry Whiteside notes, Arendt was intensely critical of the instrumentalism and productivism that many green theorists portray as significant causes of ecological degradation and saw this orientation as emanating from the same dominance of the *animal laborans* that threatens action.[36] While she held that artifice distinguished humans from other animals, and while she would have argued that environmental politics cannot be a question of humans speaking as nature (as it would be a denial of our specific ability to speak and act beyond biological inevitability), she also believed that questions about the direction of human progress in relation to nature were properly political. As she writes in *The Human Condition*,

> there is no reason to doubt our present ability to destroy all organic life on earth. The question is only whether we wish to use our new scientific and technical knowledge in this direction, and this question cannot be decided by scientific means; *it is a political question of the first order* and therefore can hardly be left to the decision of professional scientists or professional politicians.[37]

It is precisely this argument that generated early ecofeminist discussions of why the relations between women and nature were political questions. In one of the earlier self-proclaimed ecofeminist texts, Caldecott and Leland's *Reclaim the Earth*, the agenda of opening once-private realms to political discussion is quite clear. The anthology, immersed in the political analyses of the peace movement, begins with a commentary by Ynestra King on the 1980 conference "Women and Life on Earth" during which the 1980–1981 Women's Pentagon Actions were planned, and is immediately followed by the political manifesto adopted by participants in the actions, the Unity Statement.[38] The unity of this statement is not claimed through a particular experience of femininity; indeed, the manifesto begins with an articulation of the geographic, occupational, familial, and sexual (but, interestingly, not ethnic or racial) diversity of the participants. The unity of the statement is, rather, organized around a common agenda of "making public" decisions surrounding the fate of the earth. Let me offer some relevant passages:

> We have come to mourn and rage and defy the Pentagon because it is the workplace of the imperial power which threatens us all. Every day while we work, study, love, the colonels and generals who are planning our annihilation walk calmly in and out the doors of its five sides.

> The United States has sent "advisors," money, and arms to El Salvador and Guatemala to enable those juntas to massacre their own people.

The very same men, the same legislative committees that offer trillions of dollars to the Pentagon have brutally cut day care, children's lunches, battered women's shelters. The same men have concocted the Family Protection Act which will mandate the strictly patriarchal family and thrust federal authority into our home life.

We are in the hands of men whose power and wealth have separated them from the reality of daily life and from the imagination. We are right to be afraid.[39]

In all of these passages, the "we" that speaks is constituted in relation to a specifically political agenda. The demands surround the illegitimacy of decision making behind closed doors, where the decision makers, elite men whose interests are clearly grounded in the power and wealth of their private lives, continue to practice politics in secret. These politics impact on those of other countries; the sense in the Unity Statement is of their exposure, their revelation in the bright light of public scrutiny. And these politics have a dramatic impact on private life; against the bureaucratic desire to "mandate the patriarchal family" (not to mention the military desire to amass weapons of mass destruction), the Unity Statement argues that decisions on all matters should be democratic, open, and public.

The connection made between women and nature in the Unity Statement concerns the ways in which both are impacted by political decisions of those men whose private interests prevent a full, democratic hearing of others' needs and desires. The document—although it does refer briefly to the need to include women's activities and experiences in future decisions—does not carve out a specific place for a women's perspective in decision making.[40] The emphasis in the document is on the democratization of public life so that other perspectives may be revealed. Specific demands, including "good food, decent housing, communities with clean air and water, good care for our children while we work," health care, education, physical safety, and reproductive freedom, are obviously present; they are included, however, as examples of issues that are not sufficiently publicized or democratized in existing processes of political decision making.[41]

In other words, the Unity Statement is fundamentally political. While this is perhaps inherent to the manifesto as a rhetorical form, this central politicality continues throughout Caldecott and Leland's internationally inclusive text; after the manifesto come discussions of issues as diverse as animal rights, birth technologies, agriculture in Kenya, female infanticide, and urban development. Not all of these articles are political in the above

sense; their collection as enunciations of issue-related particularity, however, is produced not through their inherent connectedness in relation to
women's bodies or experiences, but through their specific place in the political frameworks set out in the Unity Statement. As Caldecott and Leland
write of this articulatory process,

> The very diversity of the contributions to *Reclaim the Earth* shows that this
> tapestry is not one in which we all subside into a uniform vision. Instead,
> women are expanding and evolving in a multiplicity of directions—*a process
> which both takes us further than we have been before and connects us once more with one
> another.*[42]

This last sentence is strongly evocative of Arendt's description of the public sphere as a table that both connects and separates; the affinities among
us are made through the political construction of a common world. That
common world, "a process which takes us further than we have been before," is very much one that rests on the uncertainty of action and not on
the solidity of preexisting identities. To Caldecott and Leland, developing a political connection among women to "reclaim the earth" requires
conversation in uncharted terrain; that is the stated point of the book.
They do not claim to know what directions this conversation will take;
indeed, they acknowledge "a recognition that human life and human culture are only a very small part of a larger ecosystem, stretching into
realms that, even now, it is hard to imagine or understand."[43] Ecofeminism, to Caldecott and Leland, is about challenging current constitutions
of public life so that conversations in the direction of democratic uncertainty can take place.

In another early ecofeminist collection, the 1981 issue of *Heresies* entitled
"Earthkeeping/Earthshaking," similar political constructions are at work.
One of the centerpieces of the issue is an edited transcription of two inter-
views by Celeste Watson, one with Lois Gibbs (then president of the Love
Canal Homeowners' Association) and the other with Pat Smith (an anti-
nuclear activist who lived near Three Mile Island).[44] Significantly, the stories that Watson chose to tell followed the same sort of narrative: "Before
the tragedy, I was a housewife; as a result of my environmental involvement, I am a feminist." In other words, Watson's desire—apart from showing Gibbs's and Smith's incredible efforts—was to show how concern with
the environment (or, more specifically, with its increasing toxicity) opened
up a specifically political realm of gender that was not previously apparent
in the women's everyday lives. While it may have been through the daily
activities of being a wife and mother that Gibbs and Smith developed their

particular concerns for the environmental health of their children and communities, it is quite clear that Watson does not equate these activities with the political. Rather, politics—here, public protest and lobbying—were influential in changing the identities of these women from housewives to environmentalists and feminists. If Watson's narrative is to be believed, the experience of environmental protest politicized these women's experiences of gender. When the personal became political, it was irrevocably changed, and it irrevocably changed them.

I offer these early examples to show that ecofeminism's genesis was in the politicization of the connections between environmentalism and feminism; this politicization was specifically oriented toward a version of democracy in which the identity women was not a solid basis for political appearance. Rather, these examples suggest a process of opening up the gendered self, through environmental concern, to a process of uncertain conversation—in other words, to specifically democratic appearance. While private concerns may be seen as forming some of the basis for politicization, private identities are specifically shown as not capturing political appearance. Thus, while ecofeminism captured the sense in "the personal is political" of opening private life to scrutiny, it did so partly through the cultivation of democratic uncertainty as its raison d'être. Who knew where ecofeminism would go and what new conversations it would produce?

As I argued in chapter 3, where ecofeminism went was, in general, away from politics; many of its early conversations have ceased as ecofeminists have turned their attention away from the political interrogation of gender and toward the articulation of an already existing environmentally friendly gendered experience or consciousness. Indeed, as Stephanie Lahar writes, "in ecofeminist dialogue in the past several years, particularly in debates about environmental ethics and the relation of ecofeminism to feminist spirituality, reference to political praxis has decreased relative to earlier discussions."[45]

According to Joni Seager, "one of the main critiques of ecofeminism is that it can lead to an apolitical ennui—it can be interpreted as undermining the rationale for women to take political action."[46] She argues that ecofeminism's tendency toward biological reductionism is the source of this problem, but I would prefer to locate the movement away from politics in the quest for identity (socially constructed or otherwise) more broadly. If the subject position "women" already embodies or produces the environmental consciousness or practice necessary to reclaim the earth, then there is no longer a need to bring that subject position to the realm of democratic debate, no longer a need to offer up private identity to the uncertainties of public scrutiny, and certainly no longer a need to investigate the relations that have produced private gendered relations as an apparent distortion of the ideal human condition.

In other words, the more ecofeminists are comfortable with women and nature, the less they are likely to offer up the meanings of the terms to public discussion, the less they are likely to focus on the specificity of the political as a realm in which to engage, and the more they are likely to be happy in private activities, confident of their own natural benevolence. As identity politics increased, democratic desire withered. Unlike Seager, I do not suggest that spirituality is the cause of this problem; it is, rather, the turning inward that accompanies *some* spiritual ecofeminism that speaks of the retreat of the political more broadly.

This critique should be placed alongside some of the ideas from Janet Biehl's tirade against ecofeminism.[47] The best part of her critique is that recent ecofeminist work, rather than focusing on opening up more and more areas of social life to specifically political discussion and debate, has chosen instead to expand the notion of the household, the private sphere, to encompass more and more relations. Rather than engage in building a form of political community, a polis in which the voices of women and nature may be heard, says Biehl, ecofeminists would have us think of the world as an *oikos*, with "women's values" as the organizational vanguard. She is particularly critical of spiritual ecofeminism in this regard and suggests that a focus on spirituality leads toward a valorization of the irrational and the atavistic, both antithetical to the supposedly true liberatory values of rationality, participatory democracy, and politics as a realm of freedom.

This analysis rings true in many respects. Time and time again, we are told by ecofeminists that *ecology* has its etymological roots in the Greek *oikos*, household; time and time again we are told by ecofeminists that environmental action is about learning to do domesticity better, to take women's experiences of nurturing, mothering, and healing to the broader realm of environmental and home cleanup and to the construction of home communities that will better fulfill human and nonhuman needs. The argument seems to be that, as public political life has not only excluded consideration of these needs but has been formed according to a political logic that necessarily expels a women's idiom (an argument strongly reminiscent of Mary O'Brien), ecofeminists must turn to the private realm for an inclusive (or potentially inclusive) model of human/nonhuman interaction.

If ecofeminism is about the revaluation of modes of life degraded by dualistic patriarchal relations, then it is not surprising that the private realm comes to be held in high regard as a place for the creation of new relations. About such responses, Biehl argues that

> while these writings are filled with discussions of "oneness," "aliveness," "goddesses," and "interconnections," they provide very little vision of the democratic processes that can keep these new "ecological" values from transforming communities into tyrannies, the way they have developed historically, . . . or keep community life from deteriorating into oppressive parochialisms, as has also been the case historically. Clearly established, distinct face-to-face democratic *institutions* . . . are essential to a liberatory—rather than repressive—community.[48]

Thus, Biehl's vigorous defense of democracy must be located in what she understands as its demise in ecofeminism (she was once an ecofeminist herself). She sees the devaluation of the political as part of a logic in which transformation requires the embracing of the oppressed pole. Indeed, one of the things Biehl most objects to is her sense that many ecofeminists— including the same Ynestra King whose commentary opens *Reclaim the Earth*—not only valorize so-called private relations, but do so by dismissing democracy. For example, King writes that "The Western male bourgeois . . . extracts himself from the realm of the organic to become a public citizen, as if born from the head of Zeus."[49]

What Biehl fails to concede is that King and many others explicitly recognize the necessity of the political; it is not that all ecofeminist activity is to be private, but that issues from the private sphere need to appear publicly in a way that does not distort the relationship of politics to nature. While it is apparent that the private sphere is specifically valued in ecofeminism, especially insofar as it produces concrete experiences of nurturance, it is not the case that most ecofeminists have retreated from a desire for politics. King, for instance, also critiques "cultural feminism's greatest weakness [as] its tendency to make the personal into the political, with its emphasis on personal transformation and empowerment,"[50] and offers activist examples of politicization throughout her article. She isn't rejecting democracy when she speaks of the public citizen divorced from women and nature; she is rejecting the adequacy of existing democracies to represent them.

While doubtless there are ecofeminists who do resemble Biehl's apolitical nemeses, it is far more accurate to view private and public as tensions within ecofeminist thought. Where Arendt's defense of politics against the social can be read as a desire to preserve a particular character of conversation, so too can ecofeminism's critique of politics be read as arguing in favor of a similar conversation. And while ecofeminism's trend toward moving away from publicly challenging women and nature is certainly part of a process of depoliticization, this process is not irreversible. What is necessary is an abandonment of the solidity of private identity, not a rejection of issues that may emerge from private life.

Ecofeminism and the Public/Private Tension

As I have suggested in this and earlier chapters, to the extent that ecofeminists are willing to engage in a radical democratic project, one in which women and nature cannot be comfortably inhabited, they are capable of producing a strongly politicized agenda. Indeed, despite a trend toward a very private understanding of the connections between women and nature in the world as *oikos*, some currents of ecofeminist thought have persisted in taking the early democratic potential of the movement to new places with an explicitly political public sphere clear in their minds. It is to these writers that I would like to turn, both to offer a contemporary ecofeminist example of the kind of political character that emerges from my appropriation of Arendt and to suggest that ecofeminism has within it the potential to repoliticize environmentalism more broadly.

Biehl offers a useful place to start. In much the same vein as Arendt, she argues that it is necessary to make distinctions between personal and political life: "The intimacies that we develop in personal life cannot be carried over *wholesale* into the relations we must establish in a democratic politics."[51] In this sentence she allows that while there is a part of personal life that can be produced for political appearance, democracy necessarily cultivates relations beyond the private sphere. Indeed, she elsewhere echoes both Arendt's call to revitalize a public realm and early ecofeminists' challenges to the privacy in which most environmental decisions are currently made:

> The democratic political realm—as opposed to the statist public realm—is the only realm we have that has the potential to contest both the private interests that are destroying the biosphere and the public hierarchies that attempt to degrade and instrumentalize human beings.[52]

Because Biehl is intensely committed to a broadly Libertarian Municipalist view of institutionalized, face-to-face democracy and because she is also attached to a strong form of discursive public rationality, she tends to underplay the potentially political character of some ecofeminist challenges to the contemporary constitution of politics.[53] For Biehl, the polis has a particular physical structure and a particular idiom; although she does not follow Arendt into the terrain of specifying a particular content, these requirements seem to blind her to the character of politics. Thus, while we can take from her analysis a keen defense of politics in addition to a good argument against private life as a primary metaphor or space for ecofeminism, we must also consider what she has carefully excluded: the ways in which some ecofeminism speaks of challenging the certainties with which the political has been demarcated.

I would like to focus on ecofeminist engagements with animal rights discourse—more specifically, what Josephine Donovan and Carol Adams call the rights-care debate—to illustrate this challenge.[54] There are two primary reasons for this choice: first, the rights discourse that forms one of the centerpieces of these discussions is strongly oriented toward the political. Rather than speak of animal welfare or animal protection, both of which conform to a much more charitable notion of human/animal stewardship, rights discourses challenge human domination of nonhuman animals (through practices of factory farming, vivisection, product testing, research, etc.) in a way that suggests specific engagement with politics. The point of animal rights discourses is, in part, to expand the political realm through the liberal-democratic notion of rights to include nonhuman animal actors as rights bearers.

Second, in the ecofeminist rights-care debates, the tension between public and private life is clearly revealed. Donovan, for example, is very uncomfortable with the language of rights, pointing out the implicit (and sometimes explicit) construction of rights bearers as ideal liberal-democratic, individualized subjects and the resulting "rejection of emotion or sympathy as a legitimate base for ethical theory about animal treatment."[55] In their challenges to this hyperrational liberal individualism, ecofeminists have specified the need for a distinct ethical relationship to animal subjects that emphasizes notions of care, interconnection, and collective responsibility; this stance is seen as a challenge to the contemporary limitations of rights as a political discourse to represent animals. For some ecofeminists, an ethics of care is to be grounded in private experiences of "care for," i.e., as representing Biehl's argument that the household is replacing the polis as the desired sphere of change. But for others, care is strongly political; the question involves how to take this language to specifically democratic sites in order to expand the political to include nonindividualistic human and nonhuman animal subjectivities. In other words, these discussions clearly illustrate the tensions involved in an ecofeminist creation of the particular character of conversation necessary for public life.

One of the starting points for the rights-care debate is Peter Singer's book *Animal Liberation*.[56] In this text, Singer attempts to disrupt popular understandings of animal concern born from a sentimental attachment to cute, furry creatures and to replace them with a fully reasoned argument supporting animal rights. In his view, for animals to become legitimate subjects of ethical or political attention, their welfare needs to be phrased according to so-called rational philosophical principles. "Ethics," he writes, "does not demand that we eliminate personal relationships and partial affections, but it does demand that when we act we assess the moral claims of those affected by our actions independently of our feelings for them."[57]

To Marti Kheel, this divorce of the emotive from the ethical is part of the problem; what is lacking in animal rights discourse "is the open admission that we cannot even begin to talk about [animal relations] unless we admit that we care (or feel something)."[58] To Kheel, caring is a practice grounded in intimate experience; she invokes Carol Gilligan to argue that it is also a specifically feminine experience, which she describes through the feminist object relations argument I outlined in chapter 1. For men, she claims, abstract moral principles such as rights can engender "caring about," a distanced and conceptual framework of rules and justice based on a general application of liberal individualism. For women, practices of nurturance (and, presumably, the experience of soft ego boundaries) engender "caring for," concrete, felt, and embodied, which challenges the very conceptualization of animals and humans as liberal individuals. "Caring for" speaks of the connectedness absent from political philosophy and liberal-democratic practice. For Kheel, the expansion of rights discourse to include animals may be a "necessary tactical device," but it does not and cannot produce genuinely sensitive human/animal relations.[59]

Leaving aside for the moment the essentialism of Kheel's argument, what she seems to desire is a mode of speech and practice in which to produce and express human/animal relations. This speech should not rely on Singer's particular understanding of political or ethical rationality, as his understanding both excludes a wide variety of experiences and idioms and insists on treating animals as anthropomorphic liberal-individual subjects. It seems that this notion of political subjectivity excludes most of what is going on, is irrevocably based on an understanding of desired human agency that most people (and all other animals) do not live up to, and inevitably places animals (and women) as lesser subjects in a male-derived value system. The necessary alternative is the recognition of a different mode of speech, one that can conceivably express women's and animals' needs. An ecofeminist statement delivered at the 1994 Summit for Animals also communicates this sentiment quite clearly and takes the idea of difference to a specifically political milieu. In the context of demands for affirmative action and ecofeminist awareness within the animal rights movement, it includes the request that

> there be recognition that women's styles of thinking and talking may differ from men's. Thus women's voices may be less abstract and more narrative. While some believe these traits to be weaknesses, we ask that other approaches be fully respected and employed in order to strengthen our organization.[60]

Ecofeminism promotes concrete practices of care; this care should be included in animal rights action. In my view, there are two ways of reading such statements. The first is the more obvious: such calls for a women's voice promote an essentialist and generally apolitical understanding of gender and nature in which women's relations to animals are already the grounding of a new (kinder, gentler) form of human/animal relationship and political organization. This understanding almost inevitably leads us to private life as the primary space for transformation; if caring for is the best practice for engendering good relations between humans and animals, then ecofeminists should foster this sort of direct caring experience in organizational work. It is clear that many subscribe to such a view; those who would abandon rights discourse altogether in favor of a vegetarian diet or the development of empathy with laboratory animal suffering would seem to fall squarely in this camp.[61] Josephine Donovan, for example, writes that

> out of a women's relational culture of caring and love, therefore, emerges the basis for a feminist ethic for the treatment of animals. We should not kill, eat, torture, and exploit animals because they do not want to be so treated, and we know that. If we listen, we can hear them.[62]

For others, however, caring for is understood as part of a specifically political project. While similarly grounded in a critique of the version of rationality offered in more mainstream animal rights discourse, it is quite clear that these authors consider caring for a stance or practice that transcends the private sphere. For Deane Curtin, a politicized ethic of care must not be localized; he also does not see it as necessarily gendered.

Caring for may be valuable, and may offer up specific modes of passionate practice, but it cannot possibly replace caring about, as the entities about whom we are to express care appear to us not only in our intimate experiences. He argues that personal practices of caring for generate a broader capacity to care for or about the world, but this awareness must appear politically through a sense of the limits of the intimate. In other words, the capacity to care for has a specifically political appearance; it conflicts, publicly, with other contextual practices of caring for that may be different from our own, but these conflicts occur within a general political framework of caring about. "An ethic of care," he writes, "provides a very important beginning for an ecofeminist ethic, but it runs the risk of having its own aims turned against it unless it is regarded as part of a distinctly feminist political agenda that consciously attempts to expand the circle of caring for."[63] That expansion means the production of care as a distinctly political mode of speech.

In a recent and interesting article about ethics, animals, and suffering, Carol Adams is quite clear that caring is neither a relation of easy identity between women and animals nor a mode of political speech that transparently represents animals' needs and desires in public life.[64] Despite its essentialized positions on both gender and animality (and an unfortunate equation of gendered suffering with pornography), Adams's argument even gestures in the direction of the impossibility of speech as a representation of nature. Adams's care is based on a recognition that humans and animals share suffering, but that an *ethical* position requires an understanding that (a) animal suffering is inherently different from human suffering, and (b) suffering and pain, by nature, defy language and thus interfere with the possibility of a true representation. Her argument therefore includes both the idea that caring challenges rights discourse as a mode of political speech and the idea that caring is not necessarily epistemically transparent to women (or any human). Trying to represent suffering, however, is an explicitly political act for Adams; it involves bringing what she calls the sex-species system to public discussion and subjecting a variety of experiences of suffering to a principled questioning.

In my view, Curtin's and Adams's arguments point toward an ecofeminist challenge to the particular understanding of abstract rationality that characterizes animal rights discourse, but not one that would replace the political project embedded in the expansion of rights with a privatized and individualized caring ethics. Their purpose is to open human/animal relations to specifically political contestation. Rather than dismiss caring as an inherently private act, Curtin argues that its specific politicization has the effect of subjecting a wider variety of human/animal relations to public scrutiny. Rather than allow caring for to remain a practice in which women (or men) can confidently engage in the comfort and security of their own particular relations to animals (most obviously, companion animals), Adams requires that we take our private questioning to a public forum in which other practices of care and suffering can disrupt our own. Implicitly, then, they offer modes of political appearance for animals, even if that appearance is only through human care.[65] Finally Curtin, by not gendering the practice of care (he suggests that feminism requires the extension of care to women, not the location of care in women), implicitly suggests that nobody can be confident that practices of care are natural; they are to be cultivated as part of a contextualized practice of questioning.

I do not mean to suggest that there are no problems with Adams's and Curtin's arguments. The slippage between ethics and politics in their work, for example, suggests that the concern is not with the preservation of public life as a realm in which human/animal relations can be questioned. Curtin's argument would be strengthened with a clearer discussion of the conflicts and benefits that would certainly emerge among differently situated practices of care appearing in the public realm; who knows what care will look like once its cultural constructions are debated in a public forum? Adams's would likewise benefit from a more thorough questioning of the gendered identities from which she understands specific experiences of suffering to emerge, as her sex-species system relies on quite reified notions of gender. And both would gain from a clearer analysis of how the traditions of public discourse they challenge sustain and authorize particular private relations to animals; welfare, protection, and rights are all interested discourses to some extent.[66]

What I want to emphasize with this example is that ecofeminists, in their engagements with animal rights discourse, deal squarely with feminist arguments that surround the status of the political. In challenging the ability of rights discourse to represent animals, they disrupt conventions of political discourse for animals *and* humans by revealing their inherent constructions and exclusions. If the will toward politics is held central, then this disruption can lead to an expansion of public discussion on animals. By insisting that caring for cannot be adequately contained in vegetarianism, empathy, or having interspecies conversations with your cat, what was once dismissed (and is still often constructed) as a private practice can be taken to a specifically political terrain in which a variety of conflicting perspectives can be produced.

Ecofeminism and the (Re)politicization of the Environment

If the political is understood as a particular character of conversation in which private selves and practices are held up for public scrutiny with uncertain results, then it seems that ecofeminism began with a strong notion of politics, lost sight of it when private identities and practices became an existing embodiment of ecofeminist consciousness, and may retrieve it if these private revelations are once again held up to the necessity of contestation and conversation. In many senses, this story also captures ecofeminism's relations to the other facets of radical democracy I have described; it is in its desire for politicality that we also find the possibility of categorical transgression and future universalism. In the public realm, it seems, ecofeminism finds the uncertainty necessary for democratic articulation.

Of course, this narrative must be located in the more general depoliticization of the environment. While ecofeminism's changing relations to democratic politics are certainly influenced by its variable commitment to identity politics, they are also affected by the changing ability of environmental discourse to foster democratic discussion. The less environmentalism produces a diverse articulation of politicized positions, the fewer opportunities there are for ecofeminism to be challenged by them. Thus, the appearance of a literature and movement broadly labeled environmental justice that deals primarily (but not exclusively) with racialized relations to a variety of environments represents not only a powerful political force in its own right, but a challenging renewal of the political potential of ecofeminism.

The environmental justice movement is not all that recent; "communities of color" in the United States and Canada have been organizing around environmental issues since at least the 1980s, and racialized analyses and politics of occupational and community health and safety go back much further. The term *environmental justice,* however, is relatively new,[67] and the recent publication of a number of texts bearing the label suggests a particular form of appearance in the 1990s. Richard Hofrichter's *Toxic Struggles* contains an excellent collection of articles (mostly from and about the United States) on a variety of topics of concern to environmentalists who persist in linking environmental and social justice concerns. Focused primarily on the ways in which differently racialized communities are affected by and respond to issues such as toxic dumping, the anthology also contains articles that specifically deal with the intersections of class, race, and gender in their relations to environmental politics. There are well-known ecofeminists and critics of ecofeminism in this anthology: Ynestra

King, Mary Mellor, Joni Seager. But there are also new voices; in particular, an article by Celene Krauss offers a renewed commitment to the interrogation of gendered relations to nature through a discussion of class.

Krauss's article begins with this sentence: "The past two decades have witnessed the politicization of everyday life, as seen in the emergence of grass-roots protests around the world."[68] Whether or not one agrees with the implications of this statement (that there weren't grassroots protests twenty-one years ago), what is clear is that Krauss's agenda is to show the specific ways in which gendered and class-based struggles around toxic waste change both the women who come to participate in them (an aim reminiscent of the *Heresies* article) and the agenda of environmentalism itself. Indeed, she goes so far as to label struggles around toxic wastes as part of a new environmental movement; central to this new movement is the public interrogation of gender, race, and class. What is most significant in Krauss's article, however, is that she returns very specifically to the political:

> The women's movement took as its central task the reconceptualization of the political itself, critiquing the ideology that separated the public and the private and constructing a new definition of the political, locating it in the everyday world of ordinary people rather than in the world of public policy and public power. In so doing, feminists also helped make visible a new dimension of social change.[69]

In the context of the other articles in the volume (including one entitled "The Promise of Environmental Democracy"), Krauss's work suggests both that the environment remains, for many, a subject of considerable political import and that ecofeminism remains potentially relevant to environmental politicization. To Krauss, that potential resides in the phrase "the personal is political"; women, concerned about the obviously disastrous effects of existing environmental policy, need to bring their personal concerns—over health, over pollution—to the public realm in a way that shows them to be issues of common concern, only resolvable through a collective and democratic process.[70] In other words, Krauss argues for a repoliticization of the environment: against contemporary public policy processes, the production of personal concerns for the public realm requires that they be shaped according to an explicitly democratic agenda.

In my view, this kind of narrative has always been one of ecofeminism's greatest potential contributions to environmentalism. By suggesting the limitations of contemporary top-down political arrangements, by arguing that the personal may be political, and by insisting that realms of life previously hidden away be exposed to debate, ecofeminists have suggested that the administrative and bureaucratic logics of the state do not capture the political dimensions of environmental problems. It is through the specific problematization of political (including gendered) relations to nature that what currently passes as environmental activity is shown to be problematic, and it is because of the lack of such an analysis that environmentalism is so easily articulated with corporate agendas. In short, in affinity with the environmental justice movement, ecofeminism has within it the potential to reradicalize environmental concerns through a desire for the public contestation of the personal environmental concerns that no number of keychains can represent.

Brian Tokar, in his recent book *Earth for Sale*, insists that grassroots ecological activism contains within it an inherently democratic promise. In the context of a widespread skepticism with mainstream environmentalism's ultimately pro-corporate strategies of accommodation and compromise (which he sees as the cause of the apparent decline of environmental politics in North America) and of an even more widespread valuation of individualism and private well-being, grassroots activism is a way of reclaiming public space and reinvigorating particular traditions of civic life and discussion. He argues that

> an ecological sensibility offers . . . the promise of working cooperatively in
> towns and neighborhoods to rebuild genuine human ties among neighbors,
> while renewing our sense of active engagement with the natural world of
> which we are a part.[71]

Like many commentators on ecofeminism, however, Tokar understands that "ecofeminism has matured largely as a personal sensibility and a philosophical perspective, rather than as a distinct social movement."[72] Even though I can agree with the general sentiment of his analysis and argue that ecofeminism needs to include more fully a desire for politics in the center of its discursive universe, I think also that ecofeminism is a promising route to take—more promising than Tokar allows—for the development of the distinctively grassroots eco-political sensibility for which he calls in his democratic agenda.

Thus, I end with a specific example in this direction. The Stop the Whitewash campaign, part of the activities of the Women and Environments Education and Development (WEED) Foundation in Toronto, was concerned with the effects of organochlorines on the environment and human health. The campaign began with an extremely personal issue: the bleaching of so-called feminine hygiene products and their deleterious health effects on the women who use them. The campaign could have contented itself with getting women to switch to reusable menstrual pads or rubber cups (thus supporting a nice little ecofeminist cottage industry)[73]; it could have focused on getting women to change their consumer behaviors more generally (women are the primary purchasers of most consumer chlorine products); it could have focused solely on getting corporations to stop using bleach for these particular products. While the campaign did all of this, its members also actively participated in the International Joint Commission on Great Lakes Water Quality, lobbied for research into the effects of chlorine on human and nonhuman health more generally (and pointed out the corporate bias in the research that suggests no ill effects), and gave a great deal of public attention to discourses around women's bodies that produce the apparent need for whiter-than-white menstrual products. (Indeed, Stop the Whitewash was eventually transformed into a much larger—and much more obviously political—campaign under the name Women's Networks for Health and the Environment, or WNHE.) All of these spaces and processes were the targets of public opening; all of these spaces and processes linked the interrogation of gender with the interrogation of environmental conditions; none relied on the solidification of a singularly women's environmental position even if all of them linked gender to environment, giving ecological sensibility a distinctly democratic character.

In this case, the personal may indeed be political.

8

The Return of the Real:

Ecofeminism and the "Wild" Side

Fantasy is a paradoxical construction designed to fill the lack in the Other, to conceal the lack splitting the object of identification (ideological discourse) but also to construct the frame enabling us to desire something.
                    Yannis Stavrakakis, "Split Subject and Split Object"

Nature is for me, and I venture for many of us who are planetary foetuses gestating in the amniotic effluvia of terminal industrialism and militarism, one of those impossible things characterized during a talk in 1989 by Gayatri Spivak as that which we cannot not desire.
                    Donna Haraway, "Otherworldly Conversations"

Confronting the [R]eal, humans have two possibilities; either to assume an "ideological" attitude or to recognize lack.
                    Stavrakakis, "Split Subject"

The next morning she sat in the sun chewing her breakfast and shivering because the weather had taken a turn for the worse. The bear lay as usual in the doorway of his byre, staring at her. What does he think? she wondered.

                    Marian Engel, *Bear*

The Real, like the repressed, has been with us all along; first mentioned in chapter 4, it lurks as a limit to language in the democratic tensions outlined throughout Part II: in the gap between reality and representation, on the unreachable horizon of universality, and behind the movement between private and public. It is only fitting that I discuss it directly only in this final chapter: the return of the Real, like the return of the repressed, acts as a final reminder of the unspoken kernel that is both source of and limit to the democratic discourses that circulate around it. That kernel reminds us constantly that we can't "get it right" and thus produces the motion and conversation inherent in the democratic visions I have outlined; it is, thus, lurking in the realm of the limits of democracy itself.

In this work, that unspoken kernel centrally concerns the nature in which ecofeminism claims to work, the nature that is unspeakable in language. By this, I do not mean to suggest that unsymbolized nature is equivalent to the Real, but rather that in ecological discourse the democratic struggle to speak about or for nature always runs up against the part of the Real that is also part of nature. Nature cannot be entirely spoken as a positive presence by anyone; any claim to speak of or for nonhuman nature is, to some extent, a misrepresentation. The perpetual failure of human language to produce an accurate, symbolized nature does not absolve ecofeminist politics from the responsibility of producing alternative conversations about human and nonhuman nature—specifically, democratic discourses in which a variety of different relations to nature are validated and sustained, even if none of them is the whole truth. At the same time, however, this failure of representation also points toward a politics that is cognizant of failure itself: through the failure of human language, other languages may begin to be spoken more loudly. While oppositional (transgressive, universalizing, politicized) ways of knowing nature remain democratically significant for their ability to disrupt dominant constructions of human and nonhuman life and foster new ones, the essential piece that must be added is that there is no articulable nature lying behind them; nature may be speaking, but not in a language that humans can fully understand. And it is precisely this limit to construction that keeps conversation going toward completion but never reaching it. In other words, an inevitable failure of democratic representation must be explicitly included in a radical democratic project if nature is to be represented at all; if the part of nature that is beyond language is to exert an influence on politics, there must be a political recognition of the limits of language to represent nature, which to me means the development of an ethical relation to the Real.

The questions that concern this chapter involve revisiting some of the ideas raised in chapter 4: that natural identity is a fantasy of impossible fullness and unity, and that the best kind of human language around the space of unrepresentable nature is a democratic and politicized one that validates partiality and multiplicity and that can never claim to "get it right." But what about confronting representational failure itself? What place does a posture of embracing the limits of language and representation have in a radical democratic vision that includes nature, not as positive, human-constructed presence but as enigmatic, active Other? How can the recognition of the limits of representation coexist with a desire to include—to represent—more voices more fully?

In this last chapter, I would like to argue that nature often appears in ecofeminism as the failure of representation, as "lack" in Lacanian terms. Specifically, knowledge of the impossibility of fully representing nature has always been present in ecofeminism even though some ecofeminists have tried to avoid the inevitability of this failure by invoking a familiar and feminine face for nature. The production of an accessible, feminine nature—especially through the invocation of maternal and "home" metaphors, as I will argue in this chapter—bespeaks a desire to render nature knowable in democratic and nondominating ways (creating a new language to speak nature), but this desire is always underpinned by a strangeness that permeates even this supposedly immediate and comfortable (and domesticating) representation. Long aware of this ill fit between metaphor and "raw" nature, ecofeminists have also spoken of nature through its unfamiliarity, its Otherness, its enigmatic activity, thus suggesting a politics that implicitly involves the development of an ethical relation to the Otherness of the Other, to nature, to the Real.

An ethics of the Real, in my particular usage throughout this chapter, involves the production of a relation between human and nonhuman nature in which a democratic conversation is simultaneously valorized and recognized as always already incomplete. Thus, there is a double movement: in the search for new metaphoric relations in which nature can appear differently, there also needs to be a point in an ethical relationship at which the ill fit is explicitly recognized, preventing metaphoric closure and opening the need for ongoing conversation. The question, then, surrounds whether and how these metaphoric representations leave open spaces for encounters with the Real and how these encounters shape future representations.

From Bears to Barres

> Once and only once, she experimented with calling [the bear] "Trelawny" [after a companion to Shelley and Byron] but the name did not inspire him and she realised she was wrong: this was no parasitical collector of memoirs, . . . this was an enormous, living creature larger and older and wiser than time, a creature that was for the moment her creature but that another could return to his own world, his own wisdom.[1]

In Marian Engel's superb and perhaps peculiarly Canadian novella *Bear*, Lou, the story's protagonist, finds herself caught between two worlds. Lou is a dedicated archivist, happily engaged in cataloging an eclectic collection of nineteenth-century books bequeathed to the institute she works for by an eccentric, Northern Ontarian landowner. This world, to Lou, is one of human history, glorious and timeless because of its fastidious and dusty detail. During her work, she also becomes intensely involved in an emotionally and erotically complicated relationship with a large male bear who inhabits the isolated island upon which the estate is located. This world, to Lou, represents the sensuous present; it is a world of smell, touch, and bodily presence, of shit, fur, and blood, a world she has lost in her previously urban and "absent" life.

Throughout the novel, Lou recognizes the impossibility of reconciling the two worlds, particularly the impossibility of truly knowing the bear. Despite the obscure bear facts written on pieces of paper tucked into the books she is cataloging (logos, the knowledge of words) and despite her rich but ultimately problematic sexual encounters with the bear (eros, carnal knowledge), she is unable to truly understand the bear. She can neither capture the bear in the life of the mind nor become the bear by abandoning her abstract humanity to the bear's body. The bear, here, is the Other; he cannot be colonized, be made human, any more than Lou can "go wild," can become the bear, much as she tries. The two cannot share a lifeworld, hers or his; they are Others to each other, sharing a mutual unknowing, a sense of the other's irreconcilable difference.

But despite the impossibility of mutual transparency or understanding, Lou and the bear become friends; for Lou, at least, this reconciliation with the Other involves the development of a sense of self-knowledge denied to her in her careful little world of historical detail. She is opened (literally and figuratively) by the bear, and is led to a certain sense of principle (a simplicity in Engel's terms) in her encounters with his mute, intensely physical presence. She becomes reconciled with a part of herself, a part in which she can appear to herself as embodied, as unfinished, as a creature of the sensuous present. She comes to love herself as a visceral being, not as just an archival footnote to someone else's life.

Engel is quite careful to show that we never know what the bear thinks about all of this, or if he thinks about it at all. He simply survives, and returns at the end of the story to his own ursomorphic world. It is Lou whom we are to understand as most affected by the encounter with the Other. Unsticking herself from the bloodsoaked sheets of their failed (not insignificantly) penetrative sexual encounter during which the bear wounded her, Lou noticed that

> she was different. She seemed to have the body of a much younger woman.
> The sedentary fat had gone, leaving the shape of her ribs showing. Slowly,
> she turned and looked over her shoulder in the pier-glass at her back: one
> long, red, congealing weal marked her from shoulder to buttock. I shall
> keep that, she thought. And it is not the mark of Cain.[2]

Lou carries the scar of a traumatic encounter with the Other, an encounter that transgressed the human/nonhuman animal boundary but could not bring either to fit in the other's world. The bear, unnamed and unnameable, appears in Lou's world as a significant and active presence, but this presence is not human, not translatable into human speech. His desires leave noticeable marks on Lou's life and body, but his motives remain forever enigmatic. And it is the very strangeness of his presence, the scar left by the impossibility of the encounter, that causes Lou to change; ultimately, it is not his conversation but his Otherness that propels her to a sense of incomplete selfhood, to a desire to become. His absent language disrupts the fullness of her own. "One morning she got on her hands and knees, and they shared cornflakes and powdered milk and raspberries. Their strange tongues met and she shuddered."[3]

Donna Haraway tells a slightly different story. In her "Otherworldly Conversations," an article organized loosely around the review of three books and the three stories she tells to contextualize her positions on them, she writes that nature is neither "the Other who offers origin, replenishment, and service" nor "text to be read in the codes of mathematics or biomedicine."[4] Instead, she considers nature both topos and tropos, both commonplace and trope, not existing prior to its construction but also an otherworld. She writes that "nature cannot pre-exist its construction, its articulation in heterogeneous social encounters, where all of the actors are not human and all of the humans are not 'us,' however defined."[5] In this passage, one is to understand that nature is neither above nor beneath human narrative; its artifactuality is not, however, a purely human construction any more than are the lives of the humans involved. There are other actors involved, actors whose motives—like the bear, like the Freudian-slip cracks in human self-knowledge—are enigmatic. To argue that these "Other" actors are apart from human discourse is to miss their profound effect on the constitution of human social life; to argue that they can be subsumed into human discourse is to ignore their separate agency, their Other-worldliness, their wildness.

Haraway's nature stories show not only that nature appears in human life as a significant muteness, as an impenetrable wildness, but that in its linguistic difference(s) it is an active agent, not just a site of human othering. There is a space between human and nonhuman animal sociality, but that space is filled with interactions and new, mutant languages. My favorite of her three stories concerns a trip by her household (Haraway, her lover, and Alexander Berkman and Sojourner Truth, their two half-Labrador mutt companions) to obedience training school. One of the dogs "already showed signs of criminality, or at least bore the marks of a shared incoherent relation to authority . . . and the rest of [them] were handling the situation badly."[6] Inserted into moral-legal and property relations in which none of the story's protagonists (human or dog) was particularly comfortable at the best of times, their trip to obedience school was a question of developing together a human/nonhuman conversation about authority.

Training, argues Haraway, involves the development of a relationship between dog and human in which a specific language appears to constitute all actors in the cross-species conversation as moral persons of different sorts.[7] Her concern is that the languages used to represent these relationships—generally, human control over dog—produce "an incoherent and even dangerous relationship that is not conducive to civil peace within or across species."[8] Her experience of training confirmed this representational misshaping; the instructor (Perfection) spoke overtly of her relationship to the dog (Goody-goody) as one of ownership and appropriation even as the two actors were clearly involved in "a complex intercourse of gesture, touch, eye movement, tone of voice and many other modalities."[9] The former completely belied the significance of the latter; "if Perfection had really acted on her explicit words, Goody-goody and she would have achieved nothing."[10]

In her story, Haraway suggests that authoritarian languages of human/ nonhuman interaction, while certainly dangerous in and of themselves, also miss the point. Even in this most banal of situations—training being a common human-generated practice for human/dog relationships—there are complex cross-species languages that cannot be captured in totalizing representations. The drive toward coherent human representations of human/animal conversation is at least partially authoritarian because all such representations fail to represent the language of the animal, because they fail to acknowledge the language produced from human/animal interaction, and because they deny the impact of the nonhuman actor on the human. Human language about nonhuman nature can never be complete; only by acknowledging its limits is the space opened for otherworldly conversations.

As Alan Wittbecker writes, "The earth has innumerable modes of being that are not human modes. Our direct intuitions tell us that the earth is infinitely strange; it is alien, even where gentle and beautiful."[11] I would argue that this strangeness, this moment of the human linguistic unknowability of nature, must be preserved and fostered. Not only is it a moment to engender human humility, but it is a moment to valorize human incompleteness, a limitation of the social, a place where the so-called rational mind has not completely colonized the impulse, the spirit, or the body any more than it has completely domesticated the nonhuman animal. In other terms, this encounter with an ineffable nature signals an encounter with the Real, the unsymbolizable kernel of both human and nonhuman life; as Lou's language failed to touch the bear yet remains forever changed by him, as Alexander's criminal behavior cannot be trained away—or even described—through accountability to human authority, so too does the Symbolic fail to penetrate the Real, yet the Real's presence is constant as trace, as wound, as barre, as question, and cannot be ignored.

Perhaps we might follow Gary Snyder and name this moment *wild*: it is, he writes, "artless, free, spontaneous, unconditioned. Expressive, physical, openly sexual, ecstatic."[12] This wildness should not be confused with wilderness (which is a thoroughly historical and cultural construct); it more closely resembles the Lacanian idea of jouissance, the domain of inexpressible enjoyment that cohabits the Real with the domain of death. It is a part of human and nonhuman existence that defies compartmentalization into specific notions of place or linear time. It is an unrepresentable kernel around which the Symbolic is structured, but which that order can never represent, however much we might desire to tame the Real by doing so. It is, in other terms, discursively impossible, always something other than the language that attempts to domesticate it. This wildness is unspeakable and calls our attention to the limits of human speech itself; it is a barre through language, signaling the impossibility of language to come to full representation. It coexists with and participates in human representation; it actively shapes the discursive life of nature, yet it cannot be reduced to human creation.

This barre through human discourse suggests that there are limits to democracy, parts of life that cannot be immediately opened up to public scrutiny and discussion, because the mere act of discussion constitutes a nature that is always already something other than itself. This barre through human discourse suggests that there is a realm of nature that is not possibly political or politicized; its translation into a public language may be fruitful and even necessary, but translation is really a *constitution* that serves important democratic ends. The translation is not representative of all of the truth of the nature represented. The barre through human discourse suggests the value of a series of relations that are not oriented primarily to the production of capturing discourse, democratic or otherwise.[13]

By saying this, by no means do I abandon my democratic desire; indeed, if the truth of nature is unspeakable, then it is even more important to link struggles over nature with struggles for social justice and to think carefully about the appearance of nature in discourse, as any authorization we might look for in the truth of nature is epistemologically and politically suspect. But by arguing in favor of wildness, I am necessarily led to rethink how experiences of nature might inform a political project. The nature of politics is not, and can never be, a transparent representation of its truth, somehow allowed to emerge or speak through human consciousness. The nature of politics must be spoken by humans who are cognizant of the limits of speech; there must be holes in our understanding, and we must develop an ethical relation to their existence. How, then, can we think of an ecological-political project that respects the limits of speech as a central democratic tenet?

The Real World of Democracy

To consider the place of the Real in ecological politics, one must first turn to its specific place in democratic politics—indeed, to its place at the center of democratic politics. In Claude Lefort's terms, the key difference between monarchic (ancien régime) and democratic social formations involves the place of power. In the former, "power was embodied in the prince, and it therefore gave society a body."[14] While not an unlimited despot, the monarch, "being at once subject to the law and placed above laws, . . . condensed within his body, which was at once mortal and immortal, the principle that generated the social order of the kingdom."[15] The monarch's body represented the unity of the kingdom; the kingdom itself was a body, its unconditional hierarchy reflecting the simultaneous mortality and otherworldliness of the king. "This model," writes Lefort, "reveals the revolutionary and unprecedented feature of democracy. The locus of power becomes an empty place."[16]

In democracy, according to Lefort, "the exercise of power is subject to the procedures of periodic redistributions. It represents the outcome of a controlled contest with permanent rules. . . . Only the mechanisms of the exercise of power are visible, or only the [people], the mere mortals, who hold political authority."[17] The "empty place of power" of democracy is such that it cannot be occupied by a single person or group of people. Because of this, the democratic society organized around it cannot be represented as an organic totality, despite the fact that ideologies attempting to perform this representation emerge within democratic societies as attempts to suture precisely the proliferation of meanings freed up in democracy. With disincorporation, the fundamental basis of the exercise of power is opened to debate and conflict; if no body is the center of power, "democracy is instituted and sustained by the dissolution of the markers of certainty."[18]

Lefort speaks of democracy as a social mode that is resistant to the hardening of ideology;[19] democracy is permeated with a "process of questioning that is implicit in social practice," a foundational lack of certainty to which nobody can answer (through law or knowledge), in contrast to ideology, "which is always dedicated to restoring certainty."[20] Both processes are of democracy, but where ideology seeks to cover the tracks of its own creativity, the democratic space between reality and representation renders this disappearing trick unstable and impermanent.[21] In the absence of the embodiment of power, all law and knowledge circulate around the empty place; nobody has "it" right, nobody has the right to claim the foundational power of the political order, ideological desires to the contrary notwithstanding.

It is, however, from this uncertainty that totalitarianism becomes possible:

> When individuals are increasingly insecure, . . . when power appears to
> have sunk to the level of reality and to be no more than an instrument for
> the promotion of the interests and appetites of vulgar ambition, . . . and
> when at the same time society appears to be fragmented, then we see the
> development of the fantasy of People-as-One, the beginnings of a quest for
> substantial identity [for the social body].[22]

If one can take Lefort's narrative as a warning against totalitarianism, as normative, then it would seem that the difference between democracy and totalitarianism can be marked by the former's continued interruption of the fantasy of totality and substantial identity.[23] It is beyond the scope of this chapter to examine the precise social conditions in which this fantasy is likely to emerge; my point, rather, is to emphasize the centrality of the empty place of power for democratic arrangements and to argue that democratic discourses need to preserve this unembodiable emptiness if they are to avoid the slide into this fantasy. This need for emptiness is precisely why identity politics are, in the final result, problems *for* democracy and not just problems *of* democracy. While they suggest a political form in which division and debate are institutionalized, the fantasy of presocial wholeness that has come to characterize them points to an understanding of power and legitimacy in which, with a bit of effort, we can find the ideal speaker to embody law/truth/power at the center of its constellation, and with that body to contain the entire social body as its reflection. In other words, although democracy creates the conditions in which identity politics emerge, it also contains the spaces in which we can understand them as ideological, as attempts to produce an organic totality that may be antithetical to the openness that produced them.

For democracy, the preservation of emptiness is paramount. This is certainly what Stavrakakis has in mind in his discussion of non-ideological (antitotalitarian) democratic discourse. Stemming from a desire to consider the place of the Real in democratic politics, Stavrakakis argues that a nonideological democratic discourse is centrally concerned with developing "an ethically satisfactory (though not necessarily 'satisfying') position . . . encircling the [R]eal, the lack."[24] While, as is the case with all discourse (language being the realm of the Symbolic), the Real remains veiled and untouched in the nonideological position, the strategy of encircling it rather than bypassing it involves "enacting discursive forms that will attempt to come to terms with . . . the Ethics of the Real":

> The Ethics of the Real calls us to remember . . . the past trauma [of the realization of lack]: "All we have to do is mark repeatedly the trauma as such, in its very 'impossibility,' in its non-integrated horror, by means of some 'empty' symbolic gesture." Of course we cannot touch the [R]eal but we can encircle it again and again, we can touch the tombstone which marks the site of the dead [a characterization of the Real as the empty grave of horror stories].[25]

Like Lefort, Stavrakakis considers ideological discourse an attempt to produce certainty; he sees this ideological desire for certainty as oriented toward the production of a totalized ideal, as a way of avoiding the trauma of the realization of the impossibility of identity, the trauma of the experience of the barre that prevents all subjects from ever being fully represented in language, the trauma of the gap between reality and representation. Rather than engage in a project of fantastic social representation (perhaps an imaginary fantasy of the totalized body or full identity), Stavrakakis argues that democratic subjects need to identify with what Lacan calls the symptom.

To Lacan, the symptom marks a past encounter with the Real, with jouissance, with inexpressible joy or horror. The symptom is a trace of the specific experience of lack; the experience is necessarily repressed in the Symbolic, returned, and given meaning as a symptom in the Symbolic that repressed it. Writes Žižek, "Symptoms are meaningless traces, their meaning is not discovered, excavated from the hidden depth of the past, but constructed retroactively . . . ; the signifying frame . . . gives the symptoms their symbolic place and meaning."[26] The analysis of the symptom involves "bringing about the past, . . . producing the symbolic reality of past, long-forgotten traumatic events."[27] Writes Stavrakakis, "what is foreclosed in the [S]ymbolic returns in the [R]eal of the symptom";[28] though the Symbolic works against the Real by covering the trace of what it has repressed (trauma or jouissance), it is possible to examine the mark of the Real in the Symbolic in the symptom.

Given that my desire in this work is not to engage in debates around Lacan but to show the relevance of some of his thinking to ecofeminism and radical democracy, the point I will emphasize here is that identification with the symptom, as opposed to the fantasy of presocial identity, allows the Real to be retrospectively encircled in the Symbolic in a way that does not produce a fantasy of fullness or completion. If the symptom is a marker of the Real (or a sort of return of the repressed), then an analysis of its shape allows a perception of the contours of the Real—a taste, if you will, of the trauma of lack, of the experience of failing to speak joy or death from a safer futurity. "The subject must identify with the place where the symptom already was"[29]; the Symbolic captures a trace of impossibility and thus points to the constitutive gap at its center. This encirclement, a form of conscious remembrance of or identification with the trace of the Real, suggests the contours of the ethical relation that I wish to promote; while the Real is always with us but never apprehended, an ethical relation to it demands that we pay attention to its leftovers, its traces, its scars.

To Laclau, this lack at the center of subjectivity—and of social and political life—is what is heralded in democratic discourse. It is not only power that is an empty place but, at some point, all content.

> There is . . . an initial split between the empty place of a function which is not necessarily linked to any particular content, and the plurality of the contents which can actualize it. . . . Democracy, in the modern sense, is going to be the institution of a space whose social function has had to emancipate itself from any concrete content. . . . What is at stake is more than mere procedures: it is the institution of signifiers of a social lack resulting from the absence of God as fullness of being.[30]

Thus, democracy is about the perpetual emptiness at its center, and the potential ability of any content to fill it; this is the reason for the constant tension between antagonism and equivalence, the unbridgeable gap between universality and particularity, the failure of any specific content to reside once and for all in public (or private) life. While the struggle to promote specific contents is clearly part of the battleground of democratic politics, certain experiences must be allowed to intrude to reopen the truth of precisely those contents. In order to institute this relation of openness, in order to allow the Real to appear in the Symbolic so that the fantasy of fullness (Stavrakakis's ideological discourse) is negated, democratic discourse must encircle the past place of the Real by identifying with the symptom; encirclement is the ethical act of remembering the Real for democratic politics. If we understand that part of nature inhabits the Real even as other parts are artifactually imbricated in the production of human Symbolic life, then it would seem that particular interactions with nature—those that allow the experience of human humility, lack, and the recognition of wildness, particularly as jouissance—signal the possibility of an ecological ethic that embraces the symptom of that lack and that allows for the appearance of nature in nonideological democratic discourses. In other words, if there are elements of human experience with nonhuman nature's overflowing jouissance that can be understood as traumatic or awesome, as revealing lack, then it is possible to argue that these symptomatic moments can be retrieved into a democratic project as traces of wildness, as failed and now (re)membered encounters with the ineffable, as part of an ethical relation to the Real. These remembrances are part of democracy insofar as they call for openness through the experience of failure; their origins, however, are outside democratic discourse and thus call for a recognition of the limits of democracy *as an act of democracy*. Encircling limits, then, constitutes a foundational move of an ecological democratic ethics of the Real.

As Lou prepared to leave the island of her bear encounters, she cleaned up the house and took a walk to look one last time at the sites of the place in which she had changed so much:

> She went to the river slowly. She felt tender, serene. She remembered evenings of sitting by the fire with the bear's head in her lap. She remembered the night the stars fell on her body and burned and burned. She remembered guilt, and a dream she had had where her mother made her write letters of apology to the Indians for having had to do with a bear, and she remembered the claw that had healed guilt. She felt strong and pure.[31]

In her dreams and in her waking encounters with the bear, Lou had been scarred by nature. Burned by the stars and marked by the bear, her newfound purity evokes the relation to Christ produced through the stigmata of medieval women mystics. As physical signs of a relation to God or nature, these marks can be understood as symptoms, as remembrances of an experience of something beyond the Symbolic. Lou's dream about her mother also suggests this interpretation; the letters of apology mark a relation of prohibition around the Real, but the fact of their prohibition suggests that they have now appeared in discourse and are now no longer impossible.[32] Thus, as the claw marks heal the guilt of the prohibition, they show a retrospective resolution of the appearance of the impossible in the Symbolic.

Haraway's story, in contrast, seems to reveal no trauma; where Lou's extremely sexual jouissance and large resulting scar signal tangible symptoms, the banality of dog training would seem to suggest a relation in which no event marks the traumatic limit of human speech. But Haraway tells a prior story to which the training encounter necessarily refers. In her graduate work in biology in the 1960s she found herself "tremendously moved, intellectually and emotionally, by an ordinary lecture on the enzymes of the electron transport system (ETS)."[33]

> After the lecture, on a walk around town, I felt a surging high. Trees, weeds, dogs, invisible gut parasites, people—we all seemed bound together in the ultra-structural tissues of our being. Far from being alienated by the reductionistic techniques of cell biology, I realized to my partial embarrassment, but mainly pleasure, that I was responding erotically to the connections made possible by the knowledge-producing practices, and their constitutive narratives, of techno-science.[34]

Although I imagine Haraway would look askance at my interpretation, given her insistence on locating her erotic sensation within discourses of techno-science, I find it highly significant that her response to experimental studies of the membranes of mitochondria was a "surging high." This is the kind of experience that many associate with wilderness: a visceral sense of a connection to nature suddenly revealed and fleeting, yet remembered as powerful trace, as loss. While I applaud Haraway's choice to locate her jouissance in such a culturally unlikely series of practices of nature, I find it even more interesting that her representation of that experience as an erotic bond with the tissues of all living organisms suggests a trace of a Real that the discourses of techno-science only accidentally produce. This trace, I would argue, is remembered in her other encounters with the nonlinguistic presence of animals; it permeates her relationship with her dogs, for example, insofar as she remains skeptical of the ability of any totalizing attempt to produce a notion of training that fits unproblematically into human-centered orderings of the relationship.

Particularly for Haraway, it seems that the moment of remembrance is a vital part of an ethical relation to nature. While she is adamant that we not treat nature as Other, as embodiment of difference, and that we pay close attention to what nonhuman actors can tell us about their needs, it is also quite clear that the openness required for this act rests on a recognition of the failure of human language, of the limits of the human Symbolic. This failure, I would argue, is experienced through lack, through an encounter with a nature that overflows our ability to describe it and in which that overflowing signals an inexpressible jouissance or an inexpressible loss that returns later to haunt our future attempts to capture nature fully in the realm of human discourse. In other words, Haraway has produced a symptom of nature; her remembrance of the mitochondria experience has marked her own language with constitutive failure.

These experiences of lack, these reminders of impossibility, can either be bypassed (explained away, ignored) or encircled. For both Lou and Haraway, their attempts at encirclement are of considerable significance. Lou contemplates changing jobs; she is no longer content with herself, with the status quo of her life. Haraway, more politically, contemplates a broader series of changes: her experience of jouissance, her connection to the mitochondria, means she can no longer comfortably inhabit human discourse without the trace memory of its failure. She contemplates what a new human/nonhuman intercourse would look like based on this memory and calls it "criminal conversation." In the shadowy realms of outlaw discourse, she sees a project of speaking differently with nature; speaking differently requires a limit to orderly human language.

The encirclement of lack, the embracing of impossibility, suggests a movement toward identifying with nature as symptom. This is not "identity-talk"; it is a recognition of nature as marking the places where human speech cannot reach, as resisting the tendency of human language to take the ideological stance in which it tries to fully represent the unrepresentable. Identifying with nature as symptom means identifying with the constitutive lack around which discourse circulates. In Stavrakakis's terms, the development of an ethical relation to the Real—paying careful attention to the place where the symptom was—is part of a democratic project. If nature can be said to be a mark of human lack, then nature can appear in democratic discourse; it is the experience of the limit that prevents (eco)ideological totality, that interrupts identitarian fantasy. Thus, an ecological ethics of the Real would suggest encounters with nature that show their existence as symptoms, as marks of human lack. This ethic involves remembering the trauma of the encounter and developing a democratic practice of nature in which this lack can be remembered in the symptom.

There are thus two simultaneous trajectories in this ecological ethic of the Real: one is to articulate liberatory discourses around nature with struggles for social justice as a way of continuing and deepening a democratic and emancipatory project; the other necessary accompaniment to the first is to show the limits of that discursive project as a way of fostering forms of experience that are not readily absorbable by an anthropocentric reliance on speech. Ecological democracy thus seems to require a sense of its linguistic limits; it is not only that we need to speak differently, in a way that fosters the democratic appearance of nature, but that we need to remember the limits of precisely that speech as a way of avoiding an ideological relation to nonhuman nature. An ecological ethic of the Real thus suggests a form of political remembrance of trauma: bringing nature into democratic discourse in a way that opens up the possibility of our remembering our lack.

In many ways, this project bears a striking resemblance to some French feminists' desire for an *écriture féminine*. Following from but intensely critical of Lacan, authors such as Luce Irigaray suggest that the Symbolic realm is constituted around the Law of the Father and that woman's appearance in it as lack signals the impossibility of language to represent woman at all.[35] An *écriture féminine*, a language to represent women (who are unrepresentable in the language of the Father), is thus one that marks phallic language with its own impossibility. It is here, in the production of radical

Otherness, that the contours of a representation of woman may be located.[36] In Patricia Elliot's words,

> It is the conscious production of an otherness, rather than its unconscious
> reproduction that allows women to unveil the mechanisms of their subordi-
> nation. If femininity is but a role, a mask that can be assumed, then it can
> also be disregarded and refused. Woman is not identical to the femininity
> imposed upon her or imputed to her. She is "elsewhere."[37]

For a language of nature, then, what appears from this analysis is a view
that calls our attention to the "elsewhere." In other words, an *écriture naturelle*
would undermine its own ability to represent and would point to the
spaces of Otherness that lie within it. It is my view that ecofeminism has
begun the process of producing such a language, and that it thus offers a
significant example of an ecological ethics of the Real.

Ecofeminist Natures from Domestication to Trauma

Following from this analysis, I would like to argue, ecofeminism presents
us with a paradox. On the one hand, it has attempted to produce democratic discourses of human/nature relations that foster the recognition of
nondominant (and nondominating) experiences of nature. Insofar as ecofeminism has emphasized the political, it has attempted to speak of nature
in a way that allows it to appear as a political actor and thus points to the
need to speak differently about the nonhuman. Despite the importance of
these attempts—and the astuteness of many of them—ecofeminism has,
unfortunately often, offered up a version of nature that signals a quest to
ideological fullness; particularly by representing nature as female and as
home, many ecofeminists have produced a nature that is to appear politically through a specifically familiar women's language.

But skeptical of human constructions of nature that claim to know nature fully, many ecofeminists also recognize nature as symptom, showing
relations between humans and nature that cannot be expressed, relations
that I will call *wild*. In other words, while some ecofeminist discourses fall
into the trap of identitarian fantasy, others reveal human lack and view the
kinds of understandings of human limit that flow from an experience of nature as traumatic encounter with the ineffable. In their gestures toward
wildness as a moment of human/nonhuman life that permeates all linguistic relations, ecofeminists underscore the value of an ecological ethics of
the Real.

Ecofeminist thought places a heavy analytic emphasis on the ways in which dualism works to bifurcate and, in Brian Swimme's words, lobotomize aspects of human experience.[38] To many ecofeminists, this process of alienation of humanity from the natural aspects of itself lies at the basis of humanity's alienation from and domination of nonhuman nature. Thus, the political and philosophical project of ecofeminism is to reconcile what has hitherto been torn asunder, to show the actual integration of what historically has been polarized and hierarchically valued. To heal the wounds between nature and culture, between men and women, between mind and body, between reason and emotion, it is necessary to challenge dominant dualistic traditions of Western thought and to replace them with a more integrated or holistic understanding, one that emphasizes the interconnections among various aspects of human and nonhuman life.

In broad terms, there are at least two routes by which ecofeminism can resolve such problems of alienation and move toward more integrated relations. One emphasizes the ways in which the domination of nature is structured similarly to and intertwined with social oppressions like sexism, racism, classism, and with heterosexism. As Janet Biehl put it before she turned so strongly against ecofeminism,

> The idea of dominating nature stems from the domination of human by human. Only ending all systems of domination makes possible an ecological society, in which all aspects of human nature—including sexuality and the passions as well as rationality—are freed.[39]

In this view, solutions to alienation involve bringing nature into discourse, especially feminist discourse. By producing a nature that is allied with feminism, ecofeminists hope to bring it positively into democratic discussion. By conceptualizing the domination of nature as a hierarchical process of oppression similar to other forms of domination, nature becomes a political problem linked to and interconnected with other forms of oppression. One might call this the moment of equivalence; by showing the similarities among various struggles for social justice, environmentalism becomes articulated with other democratic struggles in ecofeminism. The liberation of nature is only attainable through struggles for social justice, through the application of principles of equality, self-determination, and even subjectivity to nature as a co-conspirator in human activity and as an interdependent actor fully included in the process of democratization.

One of the best statements about the democratic moment in ecofeminism comes from Chaia Heller, who argues for what she calls erotic democracy as a way of capturing the need to include a plurality of human and nonhuman experiences in social struggle. She speaks of the appearance of nature in discourse as part of a process of democratization:

> We must create an "erotic democracy" that decentralizes power and allows for direct, passionate participation in the decisions that determine our lives. We must establish a municipal economy that addresses the needs of all citizens by creating systems that include barter and worker cooperatives. We must rethink technology as a creative art form that can add to the splendor of both the social and natural worlds.[40]

As I have argued throughout, this is a vitally important moment. A proliferation of discourses around nature, a validation of different experiences of nature, is a crucial part of a democratic ecological politics; opening up nature to multiple interpretations means that experiences of nature can be democratized and offers up the possibility of thinking of nature as an actor in the process of co-constructing the world. Clearly, this is what Karen Warren had in mind when she wrote that

> ecofeminist analysis of the sources and solutions to the twin dominations of women and nonhuman nature are structurally multicultural—reflecting the perspectives of local, native, indigenous peoples of both the Northern . . . and the Southern . . . hemispheres—and "pluralistic"—rejecting universalizing, essentializing, "one right answer" approaches to human social and ecological problems.[41]

But making nature familiar through its insertion into discourse carries with it a whole host of problems. Most obviously, many ecofeminists have looked for counterhegemonic truths for nature through the notions of speech mentioned in chapter 4. Insofar as nature requires a representative for political advocacy, some ecofeminists suggest that women, by virtue of their different location vis-à-vis natural processes, are able to speak the truth of nature better than men. The idea of the earth as female, for example (Mother Earth, Sister Volcano, etc.), bears traces of a desire to meld feminist politics with natural experience, as does the conceptualization of ecosystems as home. In both cases, it is clear that nature is produced for political discourse through democratic desire, through a need to signify nature differently in the face of dominant representations of nature as object, but it is also clear that these images are not meant simply as mimetic productions (certainly not as parody), and that they tend to lose their metaphorical qualities in the conflation of representation with essence.

In ecofeminism, discourses of the earth as female are apparently born from a desire to foster respect for nature and to link the reinvention of nature with the reinvention of femininity. Writes Luanne Armstrong, "The current widespread use of [the earth as mother] metaphor reflects an intense personal desire on the part of many North Americans to create a sense of kinship and oneness with the earth."[42] When nature becomes a mother, all of those qualities we associate with human motherhood are invoked to appear in our dealings with the earth (presumably, love, caring, recognition of dependency, intimacy, etc.); the metaphor "personalize[s] the natural world as human and therefore like 'us,'" and thus "'disappear[s]' . . . the separation that . . . has been created between us and the natural world."[43] When nature becomes a sister, a related but different feminization occurs; if we want to downplay the cultural and emotional baggage associated with motherhood, we can count on a more egalitarian sisterly relationship, keeping the sense of family and intimacy and adding solidarity in place of dependency.[44]

While it is useful to consider these representations as metaphoric tools for problematizing dominant representations of nature and opening up future negotiations about the possibility of other experiences, the emphasis on nature as intimately knowable in both of these representations (especially, as Armstrong notes, in the overrepetition of "Earth-Our-Mother") tends to obscure the Otherness of nature, the moment where nature is not female, is not human mother or sister. It also reinforces the idea that struggles for nature by women must be made through some representation of identity—here, identity in the sense of sameness. For nature to appear in feminist politics, it must, in a sense, become a feminist itself, and thereby be known not just as an ally but as a female person whose interests are in fact met completely by feminist politics.

The idea of nature as home (problematized for other reasons in chapter 7) similarly suggests a sense of intimacy between women and nature (although not necessarily, as I will discuss later). Here, nature is not a familiar person but a familiar landscape. Presumably, home imagery is intended to emphasize both safety and intimacy, the possibility of developing long-term family relationships with other species in a well-known terrain and the necessity of not dirtying your own nest. Of course, home is also supposedly the place women know best (even if the private sphere is a disempowered and isolated place), which suggests a particular respect, a particular intimacy, even a particular set of home-loving behaviors. As Summer Fike and Sarah Kerr write, ecofeminists

> agree that we must strengthen our connections to home, and that it must
> be understood as a place of connection—a broadly conceived, grounded,

positive space—which includes the place one feels emotionally connected to, the place where one physically lives, and the community of people and other beings one feels 'at home' with.[45]

In home imagery, we again have the implication that nature must be produced through discourses of similarity if it is to appear politically. For feminists to engage in a politics that includes nature, an idea of female expertise is invoked in the home metaphor. Again, home as a counterhegemonic representation may be useful in some situations, but the domestication of nature apparent in the representation cannot be mistaken for the truth of nature. Not only are these representations profoundly essentialist, but they clearly domesticate nature to the point where it is readily knowable to feminist actors: nature becomes "women's nature," meaning either a nature of women or a nature known intimately by women. In this construction, nature appears in politics without ecofeminists ever really having to consider that there is part of nature that cannot be apprehended in feminist discourse, cannot be known, but must be preserved and respected nonetheless. What I suggest is that these identitarian and familiar representations of nature speak of a quest to ideological fullness. Even more: most of the problems of ecofeminism I have outlined in this work suggest a move by which lack is bypassed and ignored en route to the development of a speech that can be full, a speech that can be seen as already filled by women from their experiences.

But there is another moment, another way of resolving the alienation of humanity from nonhuman nature, that I will tentatively call nonideological. In ecofeminism, it is possible to hold a view that emphasizes the specificity of nature, a moment where it is not fully assimilable into feminist discourses around social justice, a moment where it is revealed as wild and beyond the taming of language. It is this moment that I wish to retrieve alongside the need for open and democratic representations outlined in earlier chapters; beyond sisterhood, beyond home, there are places where nature appears in ecofeminism through its unrepresentability and thereby speak of its democratic presence as symptom in both human and nonhuman life.

It is precisely this sense of wildness as a necessary component to be encircled (if never represented) in ecofeminist discourse that Greta Gaard raises in her recent article, "Ecofeminism and Wilderness."[46] Beginning from a point that is overtly skeptical of any discourse that speaks of women (or queers or "people of color") as closer to nature, she insists that variously situated human groups' alienation from nature is perhaps the most crucial point from which to begin to speak of the wild. As human language always already situates and shapes the identity of nature, it is imperative that ecofeminists recognize that "nature shapes human identity beyond the mere process of physical evolution."[47] What Gaard suggests as a mechanism for understanding and respecting that shaping is not, qua identitarian fantasy, an extension of human subjectivity and language to encompass nature, but a respect for the traces of nature that always appear—however cryptically—in human life. "Suggesting that human embeddedness with and relationship to nature can have such a deep and lasting effect on human physical, cultural, and psychological identity," she writes, "is an absurdity only in the context of Western industrialized culture."[48] And wilderness, despite its very existence as a creation of the logic of Western culture, offers the possibility of seeing this embeddedness differently; the shift in perspective caused by changed attention to details of sight, smell, sound, and even energy and time can condition our sensitivity to the possibility of nonlinguistically determined worlds.

One might name this moment mystery, as a number of more spiritually oriented ecofeminists have done (though Gaard does not). In many ecofeminist anthologies, there is a spirituality section; problematic though this inclusion may be on a number of counts (e.g., the rather individualistic suggestion that spirituality offers up a template for holistic human relations to nature), it suggests that ecofeminism places as central to its project the development of knowledges of nature that cannot be captured by the Symbolic. While it would be a mistake to place spiritual relations outside discourse, it would also be an error to dismiss the desire for such relations as simply discursive. Indeed, the notion of mystery bespeaks the need to develop and value a direct experience of wildness or strangeness that fosters human humility. It is through the cultivation of this kind of relationship that nature can appear in political discourse as a moment of the Real; from the experience of jouissance, trauma, limit, comes the retrospective resignification of nature as symptom.

In ecofeminism, the symptom appears as a respect for the unknowable Otherness of nature as an act of nature. To this point, let me quote from Catherine Keller:

> At any moment we meet an infinite plurality, most of which we do indeed screen out, bundle and reduce into manageable perceptual and cognitive categories. To attune ourselves to this plurality means to live with the untold, indeed unspeakable, complexity it poses for us. For as we take in the many, we ourselves are many.[49]

This passage suggests a recognition of a moment in nature that overflows our ability to describe it. It is wild. It is not simply the diversity of nature or our diversity as nature, but unspeakable complexity, a web of relations and experiences so complicated and diverse that it defies linguistic appropriation and can only be experienced as strange and wonderful. Like Gaard's wilderness, Keller's complexity requires that we sense differerently, out of a recognition of the limits of our habituation. The world overflows its signification; nature appears as unrepresentable and as reflecting and constituting the equally unrepresentable moments of specifically human existence. Nature here embodies both the Otherness "out there" and the Otherness in ourselves; even as we begin to sense differently, closure of human perception and identity becomes impossible, as there is always the stranger within us.

But to both Gaard and Keller, although nature might be specific in its suggestion of Otherness, it is always partly of humanity—artifactual, represented—and thus points to the recognition of limits within language, within humanity. We too are wild. To Keller, nature is a moment that prevents both individual and social closure; in its resistance to discursive construction, it is like a representational vortex around which language spins but that is actually inaccessible. We can never fully describe ourselves through a completed picture of the social, as that social is always already pierced by the impossibility of discourse to capture the truth of nature and ourselves. The rational (and other socially derived modes of knowing) is always already pierced by mystery, showing the necessity of wonder to our own movement.

Wonder, then, suggests an interpretation of the memory of the Real; as symptom, it is experienced as a remembrance of jouissance. Charlene Spretnak offers that she feels "that various intensities of mystery are revealed to us during the postorgasmic state and during certain kinds of meditation and . . . ritual, but the grandeur and majesty . . . I have found only in nature."[50] What is particularly interesting about Spretnak's words is that her mystery is remembered not as an embodiment of the majesty of nature, but as its trace; just as orgasm cannot be kept, held, or sustained in its full presence (and is thus remembered afterward as a sense of opening, as a shadow of past jouissance), so too is the full majesty of nature inaccessible through language and is thus remembered to consciousness as shadow, as fingerprint, as humbling awe. In her call for a spiritual remembrance of nature, Spretnak recognizes that her language fails to capture nature; her postorgasmic and meditative states are not the Real, but they gesture to its presence. As memories, as symptoms, these states signal the production of the space of the Real within human language, but never the Real itself.

The remembrance of trauma is also a basis for an ethical relation to the Real. Throughout her analysis of the increasingly invasive technologies and relations of late capitalism, ecofeminist Irene Diamond tells a number of stories that signal the importance of loss to the development of an ecological ethics. In particular, she describes her mother's technologically organized death and the ways in which Jewish burial rituals produce a swift and significant encounter with the facts of finitude that these technologies attempt to bypass. She writes:

> The ancient Jewish concepts of tumah, "the result of our confrontation with the fact of our own mortality," and taharah, "the result of our reaffirmation of our own immortality," were vivid reminders that "all things die and are reborn continually." I learned that one of the ways of making contact with tumah was through touching the inanimate shell of a human corpse. Tumah was not pollution; thus a corpse was not to be treated with dread and avoidance; indeed the care of the dead is a special mitzvah.[51]

For Diamond, the trauma of her mother's death signaled a recognition of the limits of control, the places where human language cannot capture the experience of bodily presence or finitude. Her response was to embrace tumah, the confrontation with mortality, to make a profoundly significant point about the ways in which death and birth technologies represent an attempt to avoid trauma, to avoid the experience of lack. While the burial rituals she described do not embody the experience of death, they encircle it in a way that promotes the recognition of human limit. (Taharah also speaks to human limit; immortality is not discursive.) That she has, from this experience, cultivated a sense of respect suggests the development of an ethical relation to the Real.

There are plenty of other examples. Ursula Le Guin writes of a wildness that cannot be expressed in the language of wilderness. Joanna Macy writes of the experience of being "spoken through." Dolores LaChappelle writes of ritualized sexual practices that foster an experience of nonlinguistic opening. Corinne Kumar D'Souza writes of ecofeminism as "bringing to human consciousness a thought that is unthinkable."[52] The point is not to enumerate the encounters but to show the variety of places where they are traced as significant relations to lack, as symptoms, and from which a sense of ethics emerges. Despite its occasionally ideological quest for fullness through identity with nature, ecofeminism is amply permeated by encounters with the Real. Insofar as these encounters are not covered over by statements about their truth or essential and graspable presence, and insofar as they are understood as tracings around an experience of lack, they signal a distinctly ethical relation.

In an even more sustained and self-critical way, Karen Warren's and Jim Cheney's writing on the parallels between ecofeminism and ecosystem ecology explicitly attach an agenda of democratizing and contextualizing knowledges of nature to a necessary recognition of the limits of that knowledge. Their "science" of nature is antihierarchical and inclusive, and it acknowledges the situatedness of all claims to know nature; "what counts as a tree, river, or animal, how natural 'objects' are conceived, described, and treated, must be understood in the context of broader social and institutional practices."[53] But perhaps more importantly, it juxtaposes an embodied objectivity with the idea (from Haraway) that "the 'object' of knowledge is an active agent in the construction of knowledge"[54] and the idea that the language the Other speaks may not be immediately understood by even the most sensitized and inclusive listener. Thus, their desire for an ethical system based on the understanding of beings in relationships includes spaces of both knowing and unknowing, both a democratized epistemology in which nonhuman natures are active participants and a sense of the inherent limits of language to describe the totality of any entity within ecosystemic relationships.

The very act of caring about or for nature suggests a desire to preserve something that is not entirely human. By locating the connections between humanity and nature partly in a realm of nature that lies perpetually beyond human construction, ecofeminism invokes the Real as central to the continuation of the planet. If this caring is not rendered symbolic through the assumption of natural identity (or scientific or any other human claim to its full and known positivity), then the preservation of nature suggests its place in democratic gaze to the Real as limiting all human discourse, including democracy. While I will not argue that ecology is thus absolutely central to the continuation of democracy, I will hold that part of ecofeminism's project—showing nature's moments of wildness and humanity's need for humility—suggests a politics oriented to the preservation of the possibility of relations to the Real against the trend toward ideological totality.

If we understand that part of ecofeminism's project is to show the connections between humanity and nonhuman nature outside of the realm of human discourse (i.e., to show that wildness is within us as much as without), it seems quite apparent that there is an incipient ethics of the Real going on, an undercurrent by which the possibility of fullness is undermined for both human and nonhuman nature. This is ecofeminism's tremendous moment of promise out of which a specifically democratic politics is emerging. The impossibility of capturing nature propels ecofeminists to "take the place where the symptom once was"; the question is then about creating a democratic discourse in which that place can be recognized. Put differently, an ecofeminist democratic politics must include at its center the limits of its own action if it is to remain democratic; a democratic politics, as a limited sphere, must reflect its own limits. An ethical relation to the Real is not *of* democracy, but it plays a part in constituting democracy as democratic from the places inside that signal the perpetual presence of the outside.

A Symptom and a Metaphor for Ecofeminists

It is possible to see in ecofeminism a variety of places where the limits of human discourse are viewed as central to the appearance of nature in that discourse; indeed, the appearance of nature can never be complete if it is to remain wild. It seems clear that the recognition of nature as symptom requires abandoning the idea of nature as female, or as feminine space comfortably inhabited; these ideas turn attention away from lack and point the way to the colonization of all nature by discourse. For nature to be experienced instead in all the wonder or trauma of its overflowing, there must be spaces opened up for the resignification of nature as symptom. The holes in human speech are significant presences in ecofeminist discourse, for they show not only the impossibility of reconciling our speech with the nonhuman but the impossibility of discourse to capture our own presence as parts of nature.

Thus in ecofeminism an ethics of the Real is central to the inclusion of nature in politics. Nature always already defies its construction; it is always Other, uncatchable. It can never perfectly appear through politics, because it embodies a moment that defies its constitution in discourse. This very Otherness is what keeps it going and what keeps democratic conversation from authoritarian closure. It is impossible to "get it right"; its constant Otherness prevents the full closure of human language upon itself. Nature shows the perpetual failure of culture to paint the whole picture; it is a constant that sticks in the gullet of phallogocentrism. Nature is gloriously strange; it is an unrepresentable kernel around which discourse circulates but which language can never fully apprehend, and which thus keeps the democratic conversation going. A space is left open for other experiences, for Otherness, for the recognition that discourse, no matter how democratic, cannot be complete.

I hold out great hope that this ongoing recognition of limit—nature as jouissance, nature as trauma, remembrance as openness, remembrance as loss—will continue to proliferate, will continue to call into question ecofeminism's look to nature for identity. Beyond the Symbolic is lack, not as guarantor of identity but as failure of its possibility; through identifying with the traces this lack leaves in discourse, it is possible to envision a politics in which the scar of the Real causes a more overt recognition of the empty place at the center of democracy, a center that includes nature's enigmatic presence.

Carol Bigwood offers a good example with which to conclude this analysis. The broadly phenomenological task of her *Earth Muse* is to create a text that moves toward an ecofeminist ethic of place that disrupts dominant (what she calls phallic) languages of women and nature. She writes that her book is an "attempt to think back to the beginnings of this uncanny erection [i.e., of phallocentric languages of nature and women], to disrupt and undermine relations of dominance, to find ways of opening up new spaces where differences can be."[55] Her philosophical text is periodically disrupted by scattered thoughts on the nonhuman nature in and on which she is writing, on art, and on her pregnancy. Thus the narrative of domination she wishes to expose is opened both by her careful deconstruction of its central tenets and by the anarchic appearance of parts of her life that she carefully inscribes as "somewhere else."

Bigwood writes of these experiences through a careful process of not explaining them away. It is not that they are random; they are a crucial part of the phenomenon. But they are not to be captured in a singular narrative; they overflow the story, they halt the reader's seamless perusal of its historical contours, they interrupt and remind us of a being (her usage) that is elsewhere. Bigwood writes to show the limits of language even as she uses language to create the spaces in which the recognition of this limit is possible.

Interestingly, she also chooses the term *home* to describe the place from which an ecological ethic can emerge. But her home is not familiar. "Home," as she understands it, "is a nomadic place, an unfinished place of variable historical and geographical boundaries, but a belonging-place nonetheless."[56] To Bigwood, challenging the familiarity of home requires challenging the notion of personal identification and Cartesian subjectivity that it carries in other home discourses. "Home is not," she writes, "the site of a privileged subject or a self-same identity that excludes Otherness but a complex, contextualized multiplicity traversed by differences of race, gender, and personal histories. . . . We must get beyond . . . self-certain identity . . . to be even conscious of home as a crossroads of difference."[57]

For Bigwood, an ecological ethics must begin with the *here*, but the here must be understood as traversed by our limits to explain it away. That she chooses to begin at home shows that even this most domestic of spaces is transgressed by unfamiliarity, by uncertainty, by the limits of subjectivity and representation. Thus, she points to home as containing the mark of the Real; her own careful construction of a narrative permeated by experiences of limit (some traumatic, others inexpressibly joyful) suggests a political project that places the symptom centrally in a democratic reconstruction of human relations to nature. If home is marked by limit, if it is a nomadic space in which the appearance of difference can be fostered, then this metaphor can signify a relation to the remembrance of lack that lies at the core of nonideological democratic representation.

The description of her response to the trauma of encountering a beloved forest, now clearcut, is exemplary. In this understanding of her trauma, she signals precisely the ethics of the Real that I believe underscores ecofeminist politics. Her encirclement of the Real stands as a resistance to the transparency of human discourse and shows that the elsewhere must be remembered in an ecological democracy.

> It seems to me . . . that in our human-dominated, world-dominated clearings, the playful flux of concealment, density, mystery, darkness, silence, and depth are taken for granted, as though this background were inexhaustible and will remain eternally waiting to be of service for our revealing. But maybe the earth's forests, for example, are no longer so dense that they can provide the background for human clearings. Perhaps the earth's density is losing its thickness; the deep of the sky, its depth; silence and concealment, its harbouring; and even withdrawal, its "with." It is ironic that we in the evening land, the land of the setting sun, should so culturally fear, hate, repress, and conquer black silence to which even the most articulate and privileged of us return.[58]

The question remains, though: How can this appreciation of the limits of discourse not lead to a renunciation of democracy? What tools do we have to guide us through the difficult negotiation of keeping both the political and the limit of politics at the center of our attention? I find part of my answer in the phrase *political animal*, an underutilized metaphor, I think. To me, the phrase signals the sociality of our animal-ness, the place where nature—ours and Others'—appears in political discourse. It also signals the animality of our politics, the place where political discourse finds its limits in nature's strangeness, the place where we are animals and not simply representations of animals to ourselves. Neither *political* nor *animal* contains the irreducible truth of the other; they only exist through their juxtaposition, and the relationship is one of varied movement. *Political* describes the moment where our animal desires are produced discursively, and *animal* describes the equally productive moment that politics cannot apprehend. This is no simple, essential statement from identity; it is not a claim to being a political speaker of a transparent nature, independent of the specifically constitutive qualities of political speech. Instead, it is a phrase that recognizes that we are constituted simultaneously as creatures of discourse, as creatures that discourse can never entirely describe, and as the paradox itself.

The double movement in *political animal* captures my attention, and its ambiguity leads me to ask questions. Perhaps that is the first step of any politics or philosophical inquiry. But I think it offers us more: it leads us to preserve and foster the specific possibility of each moment, both political and animal, knowing that each is crucial to the other. I think it also leads us to consider how the moment of wildness is a crucial part of a democratic project, even if it cannot appear in democratic politics except as a negativity.

To recognize that political speech can never approximate the truth of nature is to recognize the necessary humility of the democratic project. Certainly, such a humility is a guard against the possible claim that nature's interests are perfectly served in human democratic discussion; it leads us to an attitude of carefulness, of respect, of fallibility. To respect the limits of discourse is to avoid the authoritarian and totalizing claim that we "got it right"; it is to keep different forms of conversation going, to preserve the lack of closure that democracy requires. At the same time, such a recognition kindles in us the desire to experience the something else, the wild, the strangeness of nature beyond the political but recognizing the political's centrality in allowing wildness to continue.

Political animals are not confined to living through a static bifurcation of these moments; the two are contingent and mutually constitutive, not polarized and dualistic. Experiences of wildness might enrich our political discourses insofar as we become able to speak differently about nature, if not as nature; such is a vital part of democracy. In turn, democratic politics might create the possibility of the experience of wildness by preserving and enriching ecosystems, by recognizing the limits of the social and taking up a less arrogantly exploitative stance. Wildness and politics are not stagnant realms of life, demarcated by clear and impermeable boundaries; they are characters of diverse possibilities, each enhancing the other. That, I think, is the democratic promise of paradox: essence eludes us, and openness is preserved in the contingent specificity of two interdependent moments.

Conclusion

The Lack of Conclusiveness

Women's concern for the natural environment is rooted in our concern for the health and well being of our family and community. . . . Because we have traditionally been mother, nurse, and guardian for the home and community, women have been quick to perceive the threat to the health and lives of our families and neighbours that is posed by nuclear power proliferation, polluted waters, and toxic chemicals.

Ontario Advisory Council on Women's Issues, *Women and the Environment*

It doesn't sound quite so bad the second time around, does it? There is promise in this kind of statement; it is such a simple description of apparently everyday reality that it really could represent a founding awareness for an ecofeminist politics. The trouble comes when this kind of description, through the creation of some grand crosscultural narrative of women's identity with nature, begins to appear as a fact, not as a contingent element in a broader and far more complex discursive creation. As fact, it leads to reifying the identity "women" in relation to an equally static "nature" through a statement about essential difference. It leads to universalizing a white Western heterosexual middle-class notion of femininity as embodying the kind of environmental consciousness that all people should strive for. It leads to prioritizing the private sphere as the place where environmental consciousness is generated and environmental change practiced. It leads to bypassing the limits of our understanding of nature when it is their recognition that should inform an ecological-democratic politics.

But if you insert some questions, the statement offers something else. Read this instead: Why is women's concern for the natural environment (whatever that is) grounded or said to be grounded (by whomever) in our concern for the health and well-being of our family and community (whoever "we" are)? If the statement is read as a story, as a particular interpretation of a set of practices for a particular context, then what is revealed is not a truth out of which a politics emerges but a representation that is shown to be a crystallization of past and current interpretive moves. Asking questions about such stories is what I think ecofeminism is about, and this book has been about pushing ecofeminism to ask them.

The particular story I have told about ecofeminism concerns my sense that it needs to be involved in a more strongly radical democratic project. Identity and the belief in its truthfulness, solidity, presociality, and completion is a barrier to this involvement. What should replace identity is the democratic openness that comes with a recognition of the impossibility of identity. Such an openness is better for women, as gender can then be subjected to question as part of a political strategy; it is better for nature, as its enigmatic presence can then be shown to appear in politics without the essentializing and anthropocentric tendencies of identification; it is better for democracy, as it requires not only that we converse but invite new conversations.

If nothing else, I hope this book will invite new conversations. Of course, I am not alone in my desire for new voices; shortly after I finished writing this manuscript, two books appeared that engage with precisely my call for democratic questioning: Karen Warren's edited collection *Ecofeminism: Women, Culture, Nature* and Noël Sturgeon's *Ecofeminist Natures*.[1] Although I do neither text even remote justice in these brief words, allow me to end by welcoming them to the forum. The former text invites a variety of new philosophical and activist voices to cohabit the ecofeminist terrain and to interrogate from that ground issues ranging from environmental justice politics in India and Canada's Eastern Arctic to potential conversations between ecofeminism and Kant and Wittgenstein. Warren's determination to clear a space for theoretical speculation, empirical research, and activist self-reflection is commendable; the collection of these diverse pieces of the ecofeminist puzzle in one place shows a crucial willingness to engage ecofeminism in a wider conversation, which is, after all, its critical promise.

But it is the latter text that most captivates my imagination. Sturgeon—herself both a theorist and an activist—considers the meaning and import of ecofeminism as a social movement that challenges calcified practices of academic theorizing and grassroots activism. Fully aware of the political limits of essentialist critiques and of the risks involved in deploying essentialism strategically, she insists that the practice of ecofeminism in both realms must converse in specific opposition to the rigidity of the divide between ideal and strategy. As ontological and epistemological points in a radical democratic tension or conversation, the realms of theory and practice reveal their mutually constitutive qualities; in their combined orientation, they delineate a "fertile location for imagining the deployment of a new strategic and embodied politics."[2] Thus, for Sturgeon and for me, ecofeminism marks a political intervention that is simultaneously radically deconstructive and viscerally constructive, for all its contradictions and vicissitudes; the practice of ecofeminism should "fully engage in the interweaving of humor, irony, grace, resistance, struggle, and transformation that constitutes the best of political action."[3]

If democratic conversation is the horizon, then what better attitude can we take toward its envisioning?

Notes

INTRODUCTION

1 Jan R. McStay and Riley E. Dunlap, "Male-Female Differences in Concern for Environmental Quality," *International Journal of Women's Studies* 6, no. 4 (1983), 291. There are many more in this genre, but the classic piece is probably Dorothy Nelkin, "Nuclear Power as a Feminist Issue," *Environment* 23, no. 1 (1981).

2 See Catriona Sandilands, "On 'Green' Consumerism: Environmental Privatization and 'Family Values,'" *Canadian Woman Studies* 13, no. 3 (1993).

3 See Tim Luke, "Green Consumerism: Ecology and the Ruse of Recycling," in *In the Nature of Things: Language, Politics, and the Environment*, ed. Jane Bennett and William Chaloupka (Minneapolis: University of Minnesota Press, 1993). Except for the rather important fact that he ignores gender, Luke has some interesting ideas about green lifestyle manuals and the disappearance of corporate responsibility behind the screen of private action.

4 The Ontario Advisory Council's 1990 document *Women and the Environment* is quite fascinating, as it maintains no consistent view of feminism at all. After the opening valorization of women's knowledge of nature, it includes a range of biographies of famous women, all of whom are involved in some sphere of public life, to give authority to the connection between women and the environment. Then it proceeds to tell presumably ordinary women what they can do, generally valorizing private activities above public ones. At the very end there is a list of strategies for organizing, but it tells the budding activist that her first task should be to find an expert to act as spokesperson! Apparently, women's knowledge is enough to guide lifestyle changes, but we still need experts for public representation.

5 Think, for example, about the logic of selling so-called green cleaners. Aren't bacteria nature? Nobody is talking about rethinking how standards of cleanliness may be related to an antinature stance. The household is a site for a purified, "nice" nature only.

6 Helen MacDonald, "Heeding Rachel Carson's Call: Reflections of a Home-Making Eco-Crusader," *Alternatives* 20, no. 2 (spring 1994), 23.

7 Indeed, a maternal epic narrative informs the public appearances of women in forestry communities who want to defend their families against *environmentalists*.

8 The ritual citation of Rachel Carson as the foremother of motherhood environmentalism is an interesting exception. Carson was a scientist and author; ironically, she spent her life trying to overcome the assertions of feminine particularity that motherhood environmentalism heaped upon her. Carson may have cared deeply about human and nonhuman life, but it was not a care reducible to household activities.

9 For an elaboration of this question, see Robyn Eckersley, *Environmentalism and Political Theory: Toward an Ecocentric Approach* (Albany, N.Y.: State University of New York Press, 1992).

10 Barbara Epstein, "Ecofeminism and Grass-Roots Environmentalism in the United States," in *Toxic Struggles: The Theory and Practice of Environmental Justice*, ed. Richard Hofrichter (Philadelphia: New Society Publishers, 1993), 149–50.

11 Joni Seager, *Earth Follies: Coming to Feminist Terms with the Global Environmental Crisis* (New York: Routledge, 1993), 239.

12 Karen Warren, "Feminism and Ecology: Making Connections," *Environmental Ethics* 9, no. 1 (spring 1987), 6, emphasis added.

13 Donna Haraway, "Overhauling the Meaning of Machines," interview with Marcy Darnovsky, *Socialist Review* 21, no. 2 (April–June 1991), 67, 69.

14 Janet Biehl, *Finding Our Way: Rethinking Ecofeminist Politics* (Montreal: Black Rose Books, 1991), 1.

15 Tzeporah Berman, "Towards an Integrative Ecofeminist Praxis," *Canadian Woman Studies* 13, no. 3 (spring 1993), 17.

16 Susan Prentice, "Taking Sides: What's Wrong with Eco-Feminism?" *Women and Environments* 10, no. 3 (spring 1988), 9.

17 Lee Quinby, *Anti-Apocalypse: Exercises in Genealogical Criticism* (Minneapolis: University of Minnesota Press, 1994).

18 I use the term "U.S." intentionally. "America" refers to two continents' worth of cultures and politics (including Canada's); ecofeminism, as a body of political theory, has had a much firmer footing in the United States than it has anywhere else in America (including Canada), although a certain internationalization seems now to be taking place.

19 Carolyn Merchant, *Earthcare: Women and the Environment* (New York: Routledge, 1995), especially chapter 3; Karen Warren, *Ecological Feminist Philosophies* (Bloomington: Indiana University Press, 1996), especially the introduction.

20 See especially Ernesto Laclau and Chantal Mouffe, *Hegemony and Socialist Strategy: Towards a Radical Democratic Politics* (London: Verso, 1985); Ernesto Laclau, *New Reflections on the Revolution of Our Time* (London: Verso, 1990); Chantal Mouffe, *The Return of the Political* (London: Verso, 1993).

21 See Patrick Murphy, *Literature, Nature, and Other: Ecofeminist Critiques* (Albany: State Uni-

versity of New York Press, 1995); Val Plumwood, *Ecofeminism and the Mastery of Nature* (London: Routledge, 1993).

1. A GENEALOGY OF ECOFEMINISM

1 Elizabeth Dodson Gray, *Green Paradise Lost* (Wellesley, Mass.: Roundtable Press, 1979).

2 Merchant, *Earthcare*, 139.

3 Merchant's *Earthcare* provides a highly readable and informative historical examination of women's involvement in (and leadership of) U.S. environmental politics, in addition to some interesting comparisons to Sweden and Australia. Joni Seager's *Earth Follies* tells a somewhat different story and includes a necessary critique of the androcentrism of much mainstream environmentalism. For a fuller inclusion of class, race, and gender in the narrative of U.S. environmentalism, Robert Gottlieb's *Forcing the Spring: The Transformation of the American Environmental Movement* (Washington, D.C.: Island Press, 1993) is also very good.

4 Ynestra King disputes this "first," and was certainly active in the mid-1970s developing ecofeminism at the Institute for Social Ecology. For an English translation of excerpts from d'Eaubonne's text *Le Féminisme ou La Mort*, see "Feminism or Death," in *New French Feminisms: An Anthology*, ed. Elaine Marks and Isabelle de Courtivron (New York: Schocken Books, 1981), 64–67, 236.

5 Rosi Braidotti, Ewa Charkiewicz, Sabine Häusler, and Saskia Wieringa, *Women, the Environment and Sustainable Development: Toward a Theoretical Synthesis* (London: Zed Books, 1994), 62–63.

6 The origin stories told by Merchant, Seager, and Braidotti et al. all follow similar paths through the literature. Part of the reason I want to repeat this general—albeit highly selective—story is that it is so commonly accepted among writers on ecofeminism. As a history of who we are, what does it mean to trace our roots back along this particular path? What assumptions do we import without question? I will leave it to others—like Dorceta Taylor and Marcy Darnovsky—to provide some of the "stories less told."

7 Sherry B. Ortner, "Is Female to Male as Nature Is to Culture?" in *Woman, Culture and Society*, ed. Michelle Zimbalist Rosaldo and Louise Lamphere (Stanford, Calif.: Stanford University Press, 1974), 71–72.

8 Ibid., 87.

9 d'Eaubonne, *Le Féminisme ou La Mort*, 67. In her rejection of "power-to-the-women," d'Eaubonne was referring to what she considered "phallocratic" power and not an alternative notion of empowerment.

10 Alice Echols, *Daring to Be Bad: Radical Feminism in America, 1967–1975* (Minneapolis: University of Minnesota Press, 1989).

11 "Redstockings Manifesto," reprinted in Robin Morgan, *Sisterhood Is Powerful: An Anthology of Writings from the Women's Liberation Movement* (New York: Vintage, 1970), 533–34.

12 Shulamith Firestone, *The Dialectic of Sex: The Case for Feminist Revolution* (New York: Bantam, 1970), 9.

13 Ibid., 11, emphasis in original.

14 Ti-Grace Atkinson, *Amazon Odyssey* (New York: Links Books, 1974), 52.

15 Marge Piercy, *Woman on the Edge of Time* (New York: Fawcett Crest, 1976). Her utopia

may have been genderless but it was neither sexless nor raceless; only the essential connections between skin color and racial identity and between sex and gender identity were severed. Needless to say, there were no classes, only occupational diversity. The idea of gender, race, and sexuality as choices was fundamental to her utopia; differences existed, but not hierarchy. To her credit, even in the midst of all of this technologically engineered choice, Piercy's utopia did include the possibility that biotechnology was at least a source of debate.

16 Ibid., 105.

17 Mary Daly, *Gyn/Ecology: The Metaethics of Radical Feminism* (Boston: Beacon, 1978), 8.

18 Ibid., 9.

19 Ibid., 17–18.

20 Yolande Cohen, "Thoughts on Women and Power," in *Feminism: From Pressure to Politics*, ed. Angela Miles and Geraldine Finn (Montreal: Black Rose Books, 1989).

21 It is important to note that Daly understood that the process of Amazon dis-covery involved a lot of labor and that the patriarchal veneer was not thin. For Daly, "Gyn/Ecology requires a *constant effort* to see the interconnectedness of things" (20, emphasis added); identity may be natural, but its perception and realization are considerable achievements. Many critics miss this point.

22 Audre Lorde, "An Open Letter to Mary Daly" (1981), cited in Josephine Donovan, *Feminist Theory: The Intellectual Traditions of American Feminism* (New York: Frederick Ungar, 1985), 159.

23 Echols, *Daring to Be Bad*, 245.

24 Donovan, *Feminist Theory*, 163. Adrienne Rich divorced lesbian identification from sexual preference in her construction of a lesbian continuum.

25 As has been argued convincingly to me by Chaia Heller, the phrase *Judeo-Christian* is problematic on at least two counts. First, it conflates two significantly different religious traditions: although Christianity certainly emerged out of Judaism, the differences between them are sufficient to warrant considerable skepticism toward their unproblematic linkage. Second, it erases anti-Semitism (and its erasure can be seen as *part* of anti-Semitism). I use the phrase (hesitantly) in this work only because it is the way it is phrased in the texts whose arguments I recount.

26 Merlin Stone, *When God Was a Woman* (San Diego: Harcourt Brace Jovanovich, 1976). To her credit, Stone's agenda was not to recreate matriarchy but to uncover the historical roots of contemporary stereotypes of women and men.

27 Rosemary Radford Ruether, *New Woman/New Earth: Sexist Ideologies and Human Liberation* (New York: Seabury Press, 1975). Ruether is one of the few who does *not* conflate Judaism with Christianity.

28 Ibid., 186, 196.

29 Susan Griffin, *Woman and Nature: The Roaring Inside Her* (San Francisco: Harper and Row, 1978).

30 Susan Griffin, *Made from This Earth: Selections from Her Writing* (London: Women's Press, 1982), 82.

31 Ibid., 219. Partly because of its poetic form, it may be a mistake to interpret the text too literally. I recognize that there are many other interpretations of this text and that, like Daly's *Gyn/Ecology*, it speaks to the crucial feminist question of using language differently. In chapter 5, I make a case for a parodic form of repetition of the woman/nature connection, and it is quite possible that Griffin's and Daly's texts can

be situated in that type of approach. I am, however, not convinced that either text invokes the connection performatively, even if both do it beautifully.

32 Kathleen Barry, "West Coast Conference: Not Purely Academic," reprinted in Echols, *Daring to Be Bad*, 255.

33 Ynestra King, "The Eco-feminist Imperative (May 1981)," in *Reclaim the Earth: Women Speak Out for Life on Earth*, ed. Leonie Caldecott and Stephanie Leland (London: Women's Press, 1993).

34 Val Plumwood, "Ecofeminism: An Overview and Discussion of Positions and Arguments," *Australasian Journal of Philosophy* 64 (June 1986), 121.

35 Rosemary Radford Ruether, "Mother Earth and the Megamachine," in *Womanspirit Rising: A Feminist Reader in Religion*, ed. Carol Christ and Judith Plaskow (San Francisco: Harper and Row, 1979), 44.

36 These narratives also tend to assume a golden age, an era in which women—and, by extension, nature—were not oppressed. Often, this idea is centered on the notion that there was a point where humans did not understand the role of men in procreation and when the ability of women to give birth was considered a mystical process. With the comprehension of insemination came disenchantment and patriliny, and with patriliny came the domination of women. Fear of nature was also transformed into man's desire to dominate that which he now understood.

37 Joan Griscom, "On Healing the Nature/History Split," *Heresies* 4, no. 1 (1981), 4, emphasis in original. The other influential anthology on feminism and ecology appearing at about this time was Caldecott and Leland's *Reclaim the Earth*.

38 Ibid., 5.

39 For a good ecofeminist critique of liberal feminism, see Karen Warren, "Feminism and Ecology: Making Connections," *Environmental Ethics* 9, no. 1 (spring 1987).

40 Ynestra King, "Feminism and the Revolt of Nature," *Heresies* 4, no. 1, (1981), 12–16.

41 Ynestra King, "Healing the Wounds: Feminism, Ecology and the Nature/Culture Dualism," in Irene Diamond and Gloria Orenstein, *Reweaving the World: The Emergence of Ecofeminism* (San Francisco: Sierra Club Books, 1990), 110.

42 King, "Feminism and the Revolt of Nature," 13.

43 Ibid., 13.

44 Ibid., 15.

45 Carolyn Merchant, *The Death of Nature: Women, Ecology and the Scientific Revolution* (San Francisco: Harper and Row, 1980); Brian Easlea, *Science and Sexual Oppression: Patriarchy's Confrontation with Women and Nature* (London: Weidenfeld and Nicolson, 1981). Merchant's work is particularly significant and will be discussed in greater detail in chapter 3.

46 Plumwood considered Merchant's and Easlea's narratives to be sufficiently different from those primarily focused on hierarchical dualism to warrant a separate category (see her "Ecofeminism: An Overview"). While I agree that both accounts are considerably more materialist and historically nuanced than others, Merchant's story in particular accepts that hierarchical dualism was heavily influential in women/nature discourses both before and after the Scientific Revolution. Dualism provided, as it were, the conceptual framework into which developing mechanistic narratives were inserted.

47 Prudence Allen, *The Concept of Woman: The Aristotelian Revolution, 750 B.C.–A.D. 1250* (Montreal: Eden Press, 1985).

48 Take, for instance, St. Paul's "But I suffer not a woman to teach, nor to usurp authority over the man, but to be in silence. For Adam was first formed, then Eve. And
Adam was not deceived, but the woman being deceived was in transgression" (Tim-
othy 2:12–14) versus "There is neither Jew nor Greek, there is neither bond nor
free, there is neither male nor female: for ye are all one in Jesus Christ" (Galatians
3:28).

49 I am not averse to all grand narratives, as I think they are often useful as skeletal
structures for storytelling (one could argue that this book tells one). The reduction
of Western history to dualism, however, or even to the combination of dualistic
thought and technological change, no longer seems like a very incisive story.

50 It is my sense that origin stories fell out of feminist theoretical vogue sometime in
the middle of the decade, but this is a completely untested hypothesis.

51 Hazel Henderson, "The Warp and the Weft: The Coming Synthesis of Eco-
Philosophy and Eco-Feminism," in *Reclaim the Earth*, 207.

52 Warren, "Feminism and Ecology"; see also "Toward an Ecofeminist Ethics," *Studies in
the Humanities* 15, no. 2 (December 1988).

53 Apart from its historical significance, I include ecofeminist object relations here because I think psychoanalytic theory is an important tool with which to ask ecofeminist questions. The Lacanian account of language and subjectivity upon which my
questions rest, however, is dramatically different from the (American) object relations theory (or, as some have suggested, bastardizations of object relations theory)
that animated the ecofeminist analysis I recount here. While it is not the point of
this book to critique object relations in general (just its problematic extension to include nature), one primary difference concerns the focus on ego boundaries in object relations and on language and "lack" in Lacan. In my view, the Lacanian version
offers a far more promising, far more social view of subjectivity. For a fascinating
analysis of the difference between American and French appropriations of Freud,
see Sherry Turkle, *Psychoanalytic Politics: Jacques Lacan and Freud's French Revolution* (London: Guilford Press, 1992).

54 Nancy Chodorow, *The Reproduction of Mothering: Psychoanalysis and the Sociology of
Gender* (Berkeley and Los Angeles: University of California Press, 1978).

55 Ibid., 164–65.

56 Ibid., 166.

57 Ibid., 167.

58 Nancy Chodorow, "Gender, Relation, and Difference in Psychoanalytic Perspective," in *The Future of Difference*, ed. Hester Eisenstein and Alice Jardine (New Bruns-
wick, N.J.: Rutgers University Press, 1980), 16.

59 Ariel Salleh, "From Feminism to Ecology," *Social Alternatives* 4, no. 3 (1984), 8.

60 This argument bears similarity to Mary O'Brien's in *The Politics of Reproduction*
(Boston: Routledge, 1981).

61 Ariel Salleh, "The Liberation of Nature: A Circular Affair," *Environmental Ethics* 7
(summer 1985), 9.

62 Ariel Salleh, "Epistemology and the Metaphors of Production: An Eco-feminist
Reading of Critical Theory," *Studies in the Humanities* 15, no. 2 (December 1988), 134.

63 Carol Gilligan, *In a Different Voice: Psychological Theory and Women's Development* (Cambridge, Mass.: Harvard University Press, 1982).

64 Jim Cheney, "Eco-Feminism and Deep Ecology," *Environmental Ethics* 9, no. 2 (summer 1987), 143.
65 Isaac Balbus, "A Neo-Hegelian, Feminist, Psychoanalytic Perspective on Ecology," *Telos* 52 (summer, 1982).
66 Frank Adler, "A Reply to Balbus," *Telos* 52 (summer 1982), 157.
67 Patricia Jagentowicz Mills, "Feminism and Ecology: On the Domination of Nature," *Hypatia* 6, no. 1 (spring 1991), 167.
68 Warren, "Feminism and Ecology," 18.

2. IDENTITY

 1 Seager, *Earth Follies*, 247.
 2 Catriona Sandilands, "Ecofeminism and Its Discontents: Notes toward a Politics of Diversity," *The Trumpeter* 8, no. 2 (spring 1991). Although many of the criticisms raised in this article are no longer relevant, I am still wary of some New Age thinking.
 3 Karl Marx and Friedrich Engels, *The Communist Manifesto* (New York: Simon and Schuster, 1964), 73.
 4 Antonio Gramsci, *Selections from the Prison Notebooks* (New York: International Publishers, 1971).
 5 As Laclau and Mouffe note in *Hegemony and Socialist Strategy*, the disjuncture between an actual class and the realization by that class of its historical interests has also prompted a number of more authoritarian solutions, notably Lenin's and Stalin's.
 6 Alain Touraine, *The Workers' Movement* (Cambridge: Cambridge University Press, 1987), 21, emphasis in original.
 7 Ibid., 22.
 8 Ibid., 9.
 9 Laclau and Mouffe, *Hegemony and Socialist Strategy*, 12.
10 Karl Marx and Friedrich Engels, *The Communist Manifesto*, cited in *Karl Marx: Selected Writings*, ed. David McLellan (Oxford: Oxford University Press, 1977), 222.
11 Touraine, *The Workers' Movement*, 281.
12 Carl Boggs, *Social Movements and Political Power: Emerging Forms of Radicalism in the West* (Philadelphia: Temple University Press, 1986), 62.
13 Claus Offe, "New Social Movements: Challenging the Boundaries of Institutional Politics," *Social Research* 52, no. 4 (winter 1985).
14 Ibid., 824.
15 Ibid., 826.
16 Ibid.
17 Alberto Melucci, "Social Movements and the Democratization of Everyday Life," in *Civil Society and the State: New European Perspectives*, ed. John Keane (London: Verso, 1988), 246.
18 Ibid., 247
19 Ibid., 249.
20 Nancy Hartsock, "The Feminist Standpoint: Developing the Ground for a Specifically Feminist Historical Materialism," in *Discovering Reality: Feminist Perspectives on Metaphysics, Methodology, and Philosophy*, ed. Sandra Harding and Merrill B. Hintikka (London: D. Reidel, 1983), 285.
21 Ibid., 299.
22 Ibid.

23 Ibid., 305.

24 Melucci, "Social Movements," 248.

25 Warren Magnusson and Rob Walker, "Decentring the State: Political Theory and Canadian Political Economy," *Studies in Political Economy* 26 (summer 1988), 57.

26 Ibid., 60.

27 Ibid., 62.

28 Alain Touraine, *The Return of the Actor: Social Theory in Postindustrial Society* (Minneapolis: University of Minnesota Press, 1988), 75.

29 Ibid., 80.

30 Ibid., 81.

31 Ibid.

32 Micheline de Sève, "Women, Political Action and Identity," in *Culture and Social Change: Social Movements in Quebec and Ontario,* ed. Colin Leys and Marguerite Mendell (Montreal: Black Rose Books, 1992), 128.

33 Laclau and Mouffe, *Hegemony and Socialist Strategy,* 113.

34 Ibid., 125.

35 Ibid.

36 Iris Marion Young, "The Ideal of Community and the Politics of Difference," in *Feminism/Postmodernism,* ed. Linda Nicholson (New York: Routledge, 1990), 300.

3. FROM DIFFERENCE TO DIFFERENCES

1 Michael Zimmerman, *Contesting Earth's Future: Radical Ecology and Postmodernity* (Berkeley: University of California Press, 1994), 233.

2 Ibid., 239–40.

3 Merchant, *Earthcare,* 15.

4 Donna Haraway, *Simians, Cyborgs, and Women: The Reinvention of Nature* (New York: Routledge, 1991), 173.

5 Charlene Spretnak, cited in Zimmerman, 257.

6 Wilmette Brown, "Roots: Black Ghetto Ecology," in *Reclaim the Earth,* ed. Caldecott and Leland.

7 Vandana Shiva, *Staying Alive: Women, Ecology, and Survival* (London: Zed Books, 1988).

8 Vandana Shiva, "Development as a New Project of Western Patriarchy," in *Reweaving the World,* ed. Diamond and Orenstein, 193.

9 See, for instance, Rachel Bagby, "The Power of Numbers," in *Healing the Wounds: The Promise of Ecofeminism,* ed. Judith Plant (Toronto: Between the Lines Press, 1989).

10 Ynestra King, "Healing the Wounds," 126.

11 Karen Warren, "Toward an Ecofeminist Ethic," 149–50, emphasis in original.

12 Nearly ten years after Warren's article, the Chipko movement has become probably the most often cited example of ecofeminist action. In my view, it is problematic not only to call it ecofeminist (it is, as Warren notes, an extension of Gandhian *satyagrabas*) but to call it feminist.

13 Irene Dankelman and Joan Davidson, *Women and the Environment in the Third World: Alliance for the Future* (London: Earthscan Publications, 1988). It is important to note here that gender and development literature tends to contain rather different discourses about women's relations to nature than does self-defined ecofeminist literature. Dankelman and Davidson's book is interesting in that it is somewhat of a

crossover between the two literatures; it contains a rather restrained interview with Vandana Shiva, but its primary focus is on women's rights in the context of ecological degradation.

14 Huey-li Li, "A Cross–Cultural Critique of Ecofeminism," in *Ecofeminism: Women, Animals, Nature,* ed. Greta Gaard (Philadelphia: Temple University Press, 1993).

15 Merchant, *The Death of Nature,* especially chapter 8.

16 Ibid., 193.

17 Carolyn Merchant, *Radical Ecology: The Search for a Livable World* (New York: Routledge, 1992), 195–96.

18 Merchant, *Earthcare,* 16. Although this 1995 text is more recent than most I am considering in this chapter, the section from which I am drawing my examples is actually a revision and amplification of the argument she presented in *Radical Ecology* in 1992.

19 Ibid., 17.

20 Ibid., 24.

21 Bina Agarwal, "The Gender and Environment Debate: Lessons from India," *Feminist Studies* 18, no. 1 (spring 1992). It is worth noting that Agarwal rejected the label *ecofeminist* altogether, citing its lack of materialist analysis and its Western-centrism. She proposes *feminist environmentalism* in its place, which, in the final result, seems largely indistinguishable from Merchant's *socialist ecofeminism.*

22 Ibid., 150.

23 Ibid., 151.

24 Merchant has herself engaged in a very detailed and locally specific analysis of ecological relations. Her *Ecological Revolutions* (Chapel Hill: University of North Carolina Press, 1989) is a wonderfully detailed historical account of human/nonhuman interactions in New England. I continue to think that this is her best book.

25 Mary Mellor, *Breaking the Boundaries: Towards a Feminist Green Socialism* (London: Virago, 1992).

26 Ibid.

27 Janet Biehl, *Finding Our Way,* 100–101. Biehl is actually quite scathing in her critique of ecofeminism and (even more forcefully than Agarwal) rejects the label in describing her own work, preferring to retain the political logic and label of social ecology. Despite my hesitation about including it as an ecofeminist text, I think that some of its central tenets lie at the heart of social ecofeminism and belong properly to this section.

28 On this Libertarian Municipalism, and on social ecology more generally, see Murray Bookchin, *Remaking Society* (Montreal: Black Rose Books, 1989). For a discussion of social ecology's relations to deep ecology and ecofeminism, see Zimmerman, *Contesting Earth's Future.*

29 Janet Biehl, "Problems in Ecofeminism," *Society and Nature* 2, no. 2 (1993), 59. This article is a condensation of the central critique of ecofeminism she presented in *Finding Our Way.*

30 Val Plumwood, "Feminism and Ecofeminism: Beyond the Dualistic Assumptions of Women, Men, and Nature," *The Ecologist* 22, no. 1 (January/February 1992), 11.

31 Ibid., 12.

32 Warren, "Feminism and Ecology," 19.

33 Karen Warren, "The Power and the Promise of Ecological Feminism," *Environmental Ethics* 12, no. 2 (1990), 142–43.

34 Plumwood, "Feminism and Ecofeminism," 12, emphasis in original.

35 Mary Mellor, "Eco-Feminism and Eco-Socialism: Dilemmas of Essentialism and Materialism," *Society and Nature* 2, no. 1 (1993), 111.

36 Brian Swimme, "How to Heal a Lobotomy," in *Reweaving the World,* ed. Diamond and Orenstein, 17.

37 Joanna Macy, "Awakening to the Ecological Self," in *Healing the Wounds,* ed. Plant, 210. It is this apoliticizing and so-called irrational tendency in ecofeminism to which critics like Seager and Biehl especially object.

38 Two exceptions are Janet Biehl and Chaia Heller, who draw on Bookchin's notions of first and second nature to create accounts of women's potential for full inclusion in humanity's second nature (Biehl) and women's specific second nature (Heller). While I think that neither eventually gets rid of the problem of dualism (Heller suggests that women's second nature includes an awareness of intersubjectivity), their ideas of nature cannot be reduced to the position I have outlined here. See Biehl, *Finding Our Way,* and Chaia Heller, "Toward a Radical Feminism: From Dua-Logic to Eco-Logic," *Society and Nature* 2, no. 1 (1993).

39 See, for example, Janis Birkeland, "Ecofeminism: Linking Theory and Practice," in Gaard, *Ecofeminism,* 22.

40 In this regard, I think that Braidotti et al.'s treatment obscures more than it clarifies. See *Women, the Environment, and Sustainable Development,* 74. Essentialism refers to any categorization of social life in which actors are understood to have an essence, and that essence can be sociological.

41 Denise Riley, *"Am I That Name?" Feminism and the Category of "Women" in History* (Minneapolis: University of Minnesota Press, 1988), 2.

42 Donna Haraway, "A Manifesto for Cyborgs: Science, Technology, and Socialist Feminism in the 1980s," in *Feminism/Postmodernism,* ed. Linda Nicholson (New York: Routledge, 1991), 223.

43 Lee Quinby, *Anti-Apocalypse,* 45. A shorter version of her argument also appears in *Reweaving the World,* ed. Diamond and Orenstein.

4. FROM NATURAL IDENTITY TO RADICAL DEMOCRACY

1 Marti Kheel, "Ecofeminism and Deep Ecology: Reflections on Identity and Difference," in *Reweaving the World,* ed. Diamond and Orenstein, 137.

2 Victoria Davion, "Is Ecofeminism Feminist?" in *Ecological Feminism,* ed. Karen Warren (London and New York: Routledge, 1994), 25.

3 Margot La Rocque, "Speaking Animals: Notes on the Human Voiceover in Wildlife Documentaries," *Undercurrents: A Journal of Critical Environmental Studies* 2 (1990), 3.

4 Neil Evernden, *The Social Creation of Nature* (Baltimore: Johns Hopkins University Press, 1992), 15. The spruce budworm population periodically explodes, decimates the balsam fir that is the budworm's favorite food (not to mention the favorite resource of the Eastern softwood forest industry), and permits an increase in spruce and birch, thus restoring a more balanced spruce-birch-fir forest. Evernden entertains the entirely plausible idea that ecologists might paint human beings as global budworms, renewing balance through our devastation.

5 Ibid., 15

6 La Rocque, "Speaking Animals," 3, emphasis in original.

7 I do not mean to belittle those who argue for the right of disenfranchised speakers to voice their own experiences (even if these experiences should be understood as social interpretations rather than as truths). Rather, following numerous feminist and other authors, I question the notion of the speaking subject that underlies identity politics more generally.

8 Emily Ellison and Jane B. Hill, ed., *Our Mutual Room: Modern Literary Portraits of the Opposite Sex* (Atlanta: Peachtree Publishers, 1987), xxv, referring to cross-gender writing.

9 Alan Hutcheon, "Giving Smaller Voices a Chance to Be Heard," *Globe and Mail*, 14 April 1992, A18.

10 It also opens the way for gross anthropomorphism, as is the case with much contemporary sociobiology (at least in its popularized form), which selectively appropriates the behaviors of particular species (especially primates) to justify particular human social arrangements as natural.

11 Bookchin might argue that humans have the potential to be "nature rendered self-conscious" and that nature would be thus de facto represented in all of human democratic life. Although an interesting attempt to address the problem of speech for non-speaking nature, I think the assumption of an equivalence between human nature and the rest of nature (however future) for purposes of political speech is part of the problem, not part of the solution.

12 Theodore Roszak, "The Voice of the Earth: Discovering the Ecological Ego," *The Trumpeter* 9, no. 1 (winter 1992), 9. The title alone is telling: the planet speaks in us, and so long as we know how to listen to it, we are its speakers.

13 Quoted in Joanna Macy, "Awakening to the Ecological Self," in *Healing the Wounds*, ed. Plant, 202.

14 Ellie Ragland-Sullivan, *Jacques Lacan and the Philosophy of Psychoanalysis*, (Urbana: University of Illinois Press, 1986), 1–2.

15 Some psychoanalysts, it could be argued, continue to idealize a Cartesian subject even as they suggest its impossibility (e.g., ego psychology). Lacan, however, suggests that this subject is neither attainable nor especially desirable.

16 This brief description of Lacan's version of the subject is by no means complete. The purpose of this chapter, rather, is to point to the political implications of this construction. For a more detailed reading of Lacan, see Jane Gallop, *Reading Lacan* (Ithaca: Cornell University Press, 1985); Slavoj Žižek, *The Sublime Object of Ideology* (London: Verso, 1989) and *Looking Awry: An Introduction to Jacques Lacan through Popular Culture* (Cambridge, Mass.: Massachusetts Institute of Technology Press, 1991).

17 Elizabeth Grosz, *Jacques Lacan: A Feminist Introduction* (London: Routledge, 1990), 35.

18 Žižek, *The Sublime Object*, 175.

19 Ibid., 175, emphasis in original.

20 Jacques Lacan, *The Four Fundamental Concepts of Psychoanalysis*, ed. Jacques-Alain Miller and trans. Alan Sheridan (New York: W. W. Norton and Company, 1973), 199. For a fuller discussion of the subject that includes the important concepts of desire, *jouissance*, and the Other, see "The Subversion of the Subject and the Dialectic of Desire in the Freudian Unconscious," in *Écrits: A Selection* trans. Alan Sheridan (London: Norton, 1977).

21 Slavoj Žižek, "Beyond Discourse-Analysis," in Laclau, *New Reflections*, 250–51.

22 Catriona Sandilands, "Ecology as Politics: The Promise and Problems of the Ontario Greens," in *Organizing Dissent: Contemporary Social Movements in Theory and Practice*,
ed. W. K. Carroll (Toronto: Garamond Press, 1992).

23 Both the conceptual practices and the strategic tools of political mobilization are
borrowed from movement to movement; for example, 1970s feminist strategies bear
a striking resemblance to the politics of the civil rights movements of the 1960s.

24 Žižek, "Beyond Discourse-Analysis," 259.

25 I would like to thank Matthew Trachman for helping me to see the following distinction between the two conceptions of limits as they appear in environmental
politics.

26 Will Wright, *Wild Knowledge: Science, Language, and Social Life in a Fragile Environment*
(Minneapolis: University of Minnesota Press, 1992).

27 William Irwin Thompson, interview with David Cayley, "The Age of Ecology: Part
Two," *Ideas*, Canadian Broadcasting Corporation, 1990, 10.

28 Evernden, *The Social Creation of Nature*, 32.

29 Chantal Mouffe, "Radical Democracy: Modern or Postmodern?" in *Universal Abandon? The Politics of Postmodernism*, ed. Andrew Ross, (Minneapolis: University of Minnesota Press, 1988), 41.

30 Witness, for example, an increasingly vocal Libertarian Municipalist moment in
green politics, which stresses ideals of radical democracy as set out by Murray
Bookchin that are somewhat similar to those of Laclau and Mouffe. While there are
problems involved in the Municipalists' reification of democracy as tied solely to a
sense of place, not to mention in their rather static notion of the public sphere, they
do employ a central notion of democracy rather than identity as the constitutive
element in their political-ecological consciousness.

31 Lori Gruen, "Toward an Ecofeminist Moral Epistemology," in *Ecological Feminism*, ed.
Warren, 132.

32 Ibid., 133.

5. CYBORGS AND QUEERS

1 Carl Boggs, "The New World Order and Social Movements," *Society and Nature* 2, no.
2 (1994).

2 My thanks to Brian Singer for this wonderfully evocative phrase.

3 The story is, of course, far more complicated than this enumeration of subject positions suggests. Among other things, local tourist operators, members of First Nations, and provincial and federal governments are involved as key actors in the conflict; the politics of coalition-building and identity formation have been both
critical and fascinating throughout. For a good overview of the conflict, see Ron
Hatch, ed., *Clayoquot and Dissent* (Vancouver: Ronsdale Press, 1994).

4 On the many convergences between psychoanalytic and postmodernist feminist
positions in this area, see Patricia Elliot, "Politics, Identity, and Social Change: Contested Grounds in Psychoanalytic Feminism," *Hypatia* 10, no. 2 (spring 1995).

5 Haraway, *Simians, Cyborgs, and Women*, 149.

6 See Riley, *Am I That Name?* 13.

7 Haraway, *Simians, Cyborgs, and Women*, 157.

8 Judith Butler, *Bodies That Matter: On the Discursive Limits of "Sex"* (New York: Routledge,
1993), 188.

9 Drucilla Cornell, "What Is Ethical Feminism?" in *Feminist Contentions: A Philosophical Exchange*, Seyla Benhabib, Judith Butler, Drucilla Cornell, and Nancy Fraser (New York: Routledge, 1995), 86.

10 Ibid., 97, emphasis in original.

11 Haraway, *Simians, Cyborgs, and Women*, 189.

12 Ibid., 157.

13 Butler, *Bodies That Matter*, 231.

14 Ibid., 241.

15 I do not wish to erase the specificity of queer struggles against the constraints of heteronormativity in my appropriation of "queering" for a broader performative project. Queer politics have, however, been a singularly fruitful ground for examples of performative and ironic action, and although I think ecofeminism can and should include specific resistances to heteronormativity—on this see Greta Gaard, "Toward a Queer Ecofeminism," *Hypatia* 12: 1 (winter 1997)—the lessons that can be learned from these examples can and should also be expressed in other kinds of resistance.

16 I seem obliged to return to Clayoquot Sound. The subject position "environmentalist," as already noted, is marked with its own incompleteness by many commentators through the increasing recognition that "the environment" is a widely contested and empty social creation. As a variety of differently and partially situated knowledges of nature—including those of loggers—come to be resignified as "environmental," the possibility of each subject position's coming to be influenced by the others becomes apparent.

17 Greta Gaard, ed., *Ecofeminism: Women, Animals, Nature* (Philadelphia: Temple University Press, 1993).

18 Greta Gaard, "Living Interconnections with Animals and Nature," in *Ecofeminism: Women, Animals, Nature*, ed. Gaard, 5.

19 Diana Fuss, *Essentially Speaking: Feminism, Nature, and Difference* (New York: Routledge, 1989).

20 Elizabeth Carlassare, "Destabilizing the Criticism of Essentialism in Ecofeminist Discourse," *Capitalism, Nature, Socialism* 5: 3 (September 1994), 52.

21 Ibid., 53.

22 Ibid., 58.

23 Ibid., 59.

24 Ibid., 64.

25 Carlassare might argue that her reading of Griffin points precisely to a parodic stance, but she does not emphasize the need to subvert the solidity or authenticity of the representation at the moment of its invocation. For example, I find it difficult to read *Woman and Nature* as a parody even if I might be convinced that its essentialism is strategic.

26 Whether this position will be explored in more than a single article remains to be seen. I note with pleasure that a version of Carlassare's article appears in Carolyn Merchant's recent anthology, *Key Concepts in Critical Theory: Ecology* (Atlantic Highlands, N.J.: Humanities Press, 1994), which suggests that some see it as an important part of an emerging canon.

27 Carlassare may be seen as confusing essentialism with biological determinism (e.g., on page 52), yet she herself notes that not all claims to essential unity are based on

biology. (Indeed, Butler argues convincingly that core identity is an at least equally important representation of gendered essence in contemporary discourses.) The point is to destabilize coherence, not just the imputed source of the coherence.

28 See Murray Bookchin, *The Philosophy of Social Ecology: Essays on Dialectical Naturalism* (Montreal: Black Rose Books, 1990).

29 See, for example, essays in William Cronon, ed., *Uncommon Ground: Toward Reinventing Nature* (New York: Norton, 1995).

30 Stacy Alaimo, "Cyborg and Ecofeminist Interventions: Challenges for an Environmental Feminism," *Feminist Studies* 20, no. 1 (spring 1994).

31 Ibid., 135.

32 Ibid., 140.

33 In a related vein, Barbara Noske asks, "Must we bend over backwards in order to escape from human animal continuity? Why not point out that men too are continuous with animals, no less than women?" See her *Humans and Other Animals* (London: Pluto Press, 1989), 117.

34 Alaimo also mentions that this particular project constructs whales as underprivileged individuals, specifically as children. The campaign is almost identical to the Foster Parents Plan strategy, which has individual Third World children write letters of thanks to their kind First World benefactors. The whales cannot (or will not) write, of course, but the scientists who monitor them individually can and do. There are, in both campaigns, lots of photographs.

35 Alaimo, "Cyborg and Ecofeminist Interventions," 141.

36 Haraway, cited in ibid., 145

37 Alaimo, 146.

38 Ibid., 149.

39 Ibid.

40 Gaard, "Toward a Queer Ecofeminism," 119–20. See also Catriona Sandilands, "Lavender's Green? Some Thoughts on Queer(y)ing Environmental Politics," *Undercurrents* (May 1994). This chapter clearly fails to sufficiently problematize the heteronormativity that pervades ecological discourse, or to build much on Gaard's and my past writing. Queering ecofeminism is, however, an ongoing project of my work.

6. ECOFEMINISM, UNIVERSALITY, AND PARTICULARITY

1 See in particular Wolfgang Sachs, ed., *Global Ecology: A New Arena of Political Conflict* (Halifax: Fernwood Publications, 1993).

2 Frederick Buttel and Peter Taylor, "Environmental Sociology and Global Environmental Change," in *Social Theory and the Global Environment*, ed. Michael Redclift and Ted Benton (London: Routledge, 1994), 243.

3 Charlene Spretnak and Fritjof Capra, *Green Politics: The Global Promise* (Santa Fe: Bear and Company, 1986), 165, emphasis added.

4 Karen Litfin, "Ecoregimes: Playing Tug of War with the Nation-State," in *The State and Social Power in Global Environmental Politics*, ed. Ronnie D. Lipschutz and Ken Conca (New York: Columbia University Press, 1993), 95.

5 This generally derogatory label is used rhetorically to suggest that people struggling about their "back yards" are paying insufficient attention to the common good. As many proponents of environmental justice argue, however, NIMBY is

often a precursor to more critical analyses of environmental degradation, including, for example, recognition of the tendency of governments to place particularly nasty environmental problems in the back yards of poor communities of color (PIBBY, Put It in Blacks' Back Yards).

6 The second contradiction, to O'Connor, consists of the relations by which capital destroys the natural/material basis of its own productive relations in order to produce surplus value. As accumulation accelerates, natural resources become scarcer, raising production costs in the short term and undermining the possibility of human survival (including capitalism, of course) in the long term. See James O'Connor, "Conference Papers on Capitalist Nature," pamphlet 1, Santa Cruz, Center for Ecological Socialism (1991).

7 Michael Clow, "Ecological Exhaustion and the Global Crisis of Capital," *Our Generation* 23, no. 1 (winter 1992), 21, emphasis added.

8 The Brundtland Report (*Our Common Future*), while radical in its attention to the extent of environmental problems, was careful to argue that there was no contradiction between continued economic growth and environmental caretaking.

9 Clow, "Ecological Exhaustion," 21.

10 Ibid., 25.

11 Carl Boggs, "The New World Order and Social Movements," 99.

12 There is a rich and varied literature surrounding this concept, which most notably brings into state-centric discussions of international relations the strong presence of transnational NGO's and networks of grassroots movements. See, for example, Ronnie D. Lipschutz, "Reconstructing World Politics: The Emergence of Global Civil Society," *Millenium* 21, no. 3 (winter 1992).

13 Boggs, "The New World Order," 119.

14 Daniel Faber and James O'Connor, "Capitalism and the Crisis of Environmentalism," in *Toxic Struggles*, ed. Hofrichter, 20.

15 Richard Falk, "The Making of Global Citizenship," in *Global Visions: Beyond the New World Order*, ed. Jeremy Brecher, John Brown Childs, and Jill Cutler (Boston: South End Press, 1993), 50.

16 Vandana Shiva, "The Greening of Global Reach," in *Global Ecology*, ed. Sachs, 155, emphasis added.

17 Ibid., 155, emphasis in original.

18 See Laclau and Mouffe, *Hegemony and Socialist Strategy*, especially chapter 3.

19 This formulation of the authority of the universal comes from Ernesto Laclau, "Universalism, Particularism, and the Question of Identity," *October* 61 (summer 1992).

20 Laclau, "Universalism, Particularism," 89.

21 Ibid., 90.

22 The World Women's Congress Action Agenda is a compilation of (or, depending on your perspective, compromise position among) the work, ideas, and values of 1500 women from around the world. It was produced under the auspices of the World Women's Congress for a Healthy Planet, held in Miami, Florida, in November 1991.

23 While Angela Miles argues that the articulation of specificity is a prerequisite for the genuine achievement of equality, her argument overlooks a number of crucial points, as this chapter will address. See "Ideological Hegemony in Political Discourse: Women's Specificity and Equality" in *Feminism: From Pressure to Politics*, ed. Angela Miles and Geraldine Finn (Montreal: Black Rose Books, 1989).

24 Maria Mies and Vandana Shiva, *Ecofeminism* (Halifax: Fernwood Publications, 1993). Unlike other ecofeminist texts, this book has no particular subtitle, implying a claim to represent ecofeminism as a whole rather than any specific construction of it.

25 Ibid., 318, emphasis in original.

26 In response to the charge that my work claims to offer such an existent universal to ecofeminism, I would respond that I do not consider myself to embody anything like an emancipatory standpoint (i.e., there is a great deal of tension betwen my desire and my practice) and that my concern is to help to create the conditions in which a broader conversation is possible. To the extent that Mies and Shiva's work does precisely this, I applaud it, but I also see its standpoint as closing off the possibility of debate.

27 Val Plumwood, *Feminism and the Mastery of Nature*, 36.

28 Plumwood, "Feminism and Environmentalism," 12, emphasis added.

29 Plumwood, *Feminism and the Mastery of Nature*, 36

30 King, "Feminism and the Revolt of Nature," 15.

31 Plumwood's agenda is very explicitly oriented toward keeping alive the "good" parts of other feminisms.

32 Martha McMahon, "From the Ground Up: Ecofeminism and Ecological Economics," *Ecological Economics* 20 (1997), 166.

33 See, for example, Mary Mellor, "Women, Nature, and the Social Construction of 'Economic Man,'" *Ecological Economics* 20 (1997).

34 McMahon, "From the Ground Up," 164.

35 Ibid., 172.

36 As Stabile's opening quotation suggests, it is not always successful in achieving this goal; it is worth noting, however, the number of supposedly ecofeminist works that appear in anthologies from the environmental justice movement and the obvious influence of gendered analyses on anti-racist environmental activists.

37 Quinby, *Anti-Apocalypse*, 46.

38 Compare a "critical ecological feminism . . . would contain no assumptions which were not acceptable from a feminist standpoint, and would represent a fuller development of feminist thought in taking better account of the category of nature" (*Feminism and the Mastery of Nature*, 39) with "This is not to assume that everyone makes [connections between personal and general moral concerns], but rather to shift the moral focus from supposed oppositional relations . . . to the conditions of social and political life which produce . . . opposition and which . . . hinder empathic generalisation" (ibid., 187–88). The former is clearly oriented to the development of a "better feminist mousetrap"; the latter is about interrogating the failure of the standpoint to produce by itself a solid foundation for a feminist ethics.

39. Ibid., 196.

40. Ibid., 40.

41. Plumwood would probably not agree with my use of the term *deconstruct* to describe her project.

42 *Taskforce on the Churches and Corporate Responsibility Bulletin* (March/April 1992), 1. Although I am aware that the process of creating the WAA 21 statement was, for many, deeply problematic (one of my friends called it a "farce"), the document itself is an excellent representation, and the conference did *try*.

43 Braidotti et al., *Women, the Environment and Sustainable Development*, 101, 103.

44 Ibid., 103–4.

45 Ibid., 104.

46 And, as Braidotti et al. note, the moments where its authorship was less than democratic.

47 *Taskforce on Churches*, 1.

48 The status of corporations at Rio is interesting: they were granted NGO status, which completely masked their specific influence on the official discourse at the same time it disrupted the NGOs' ability to present a united front.

7. ECOFEMINISM, PUBLIC AND PRIVATE LIFE

1 See especially Chantal Mouffe, *The Return of the Political* (London: Verso, 1993).

2 James Rusk, "Environmentalists Not Seen as Force in Next Ontario Election," *Globe and Mail*, 5 April 1994, A3.

3 After their election, they wasted no time in scrapping the Interim Waste Authority. While I do not believe this was an inherently negative development (there will be no mega-dump in Caledon), this decision has reopened the door for private sector waste incineration. In general, as is probably not surprising under a profoundly neo-conservative regime, environmental issues have suffered considerably at the hands of the Harris Tories.

4 The protest (on June 26, 1995) was organized by a variety of different groups concerned about workers' rights, welfare reductions, discrimination against gay men and lesbians, employment equity, and all of the other NDP initiatives that the Conservatives had vowed to cancel. It was called Embarrass Harris and attracted about a thousand people.

5 As reported by Douglas Lintula in "Trends: Environmental Priorities Shift," *Earthkeeper* IV, Issue IV (April/May 1994), 7–8.

6 Cited in Rusk, "Environmentalists Not Seen as Force," A3.

7 Tim Luke, "Green Consumerism," 155.

8 Brian Tokar, *Earth for Sale: Reclaiming Ecology in the Age of Corporate Greenwash* (Boston: South End Press, 1997), xiii.

9 Laurie Adkin, "Counter-Hegemony and Environmental Politics in Canada," in *Organizing Dissent*, ed. Carroll, 150.

10 Hannah Arendt, *The Human Condition* (Chicago: University of Chicago Press, 1957), 7.

11 From an ecological standpoint, it is worth noting that she is critical of the instrumentalization and mastery of nature apparent in work and its increasing importance; to ecologists who would argue for reconnection to biological processes, however, she argues that action, not labor, should be the model for humanity.

12 Ibid., 7. I continue Arendt's use of the terms *men* and *man* to preserve the tension around whether they include *women* and *woman*.

13 Ibid., 8.

14 Arendt argues that the fact of natality, that each human is born new into the world, grounds the inherent human capacity to be "born again," to make new possibilities come into being.

15 Ibid., 50, 52.

16 Seyla Benhabib, *Situating the Self: Gender, Community, and Postmodernism in Contemporary Ethics* (New York: Routledge, 1992), 90.

17 Mary G. Dietz, "Hannah Arendt and Feminist Politics," in *Feminist Interpretations and Political Theory*, ed. Mary Lyndon Shandley and Carol Pateman (University Park: Pennsylvania State University Press, 1991), 243.

18 Arendt, *The Human Condition*, 52–53.

19 O'Brien, *The Politics of Reproduction*, 99–110. I imagine that most ecofeminists would agree with O'Brien on this point.

20 Drucilla Cornell, "Gender Hierarchy, Equality, and the Possibility of Democracy," *American Imago* 48, no. 2 (1991); Nancy Fraser, *Unruly Practices: Power, Discourse, and Gender in Contemporary Social Theory* (Minneapolis: University of Minnesota Press, 1989).

21 Cornell, "Gender Hierarchy," 253.

22 Ibid., 262.

23 Nancy Fraser, *Unruly Practices*, 160 n. 32.

24 Benhabib, *Situating the Self*, 195.

25 Fraser, *Unruly Practices*, 76.

26 Arendt, *The Human Condition*, 179.

27 Bonnie Honig, "Toward an Agonistic Feminism: Hannah Arendt and the Politics of Identity," in *Feminists Theorize the Political*, ed. Judith Butler and Joan W. Scott (New York: Routledge, 1992), 219.

28 For Arendt, there is a true self created in public appearance; this individuality is the human condition of plurality. For Lacan, there is no true self to be captured in appearance; subject positions mask the inevitable lack in the subject. The similarity is not in their notions of the self, but in their common challenge to the notion that politics is an expression of self, subject position, and social location.

29 Hannah Pitkin, "Justice: On Relating Private and Public," *Political Theory* 9, no. 3 (1981), 342, emphasis added.

30 Notably, Arendt would have us judge political actions without reference to moral standards. If the essence of politics lies in its uncertainty, then to predefine its ends by imposing upon it particular standards of morality derived from contemplation, not action, is to lose its openness.

31 Valerie Burks, "Women's Place: An Arendtian Critique of Feminism," *Women and Politics* 14, no. 3 (1994). Honig's implicit response to the charge of elitism is to suggest that performance is also a private act, a more everyday practice than Arendt's analysis allows. While this may be true, I think an orientation toward a common world beyond private interests remains a crucial part of Arendt's vision.

32 See especially her *On Revolution* (New York: Viking Press, 1963) and *Crises of the Republic* (New York: Harcourt Brace Jovanovich, 1969). Seyla Benhabib, "Hannah Arendt and the Redemptive Power of Narrative," *Social Research* 57, no. 1 (1990).

33 Arendt, *On Revolution*, 268.

34 Benhabib, "Hannah Arendt," 194.

35 Maurizio Passerin d'Entrèves, *The Political Philosophy of Hannah Arendt* (London: Routledge, 1994), 97–99.

36 Kerry Whiteside, "Hannah Arendt and Ecological Politics," *Environmental Ethics* 16 (winter 1994).

37 Arendt, *The Human Condition*, 3, emphasis added.

38 Women and Life on Earth was a gathering of six hundred women in Amherst, Massachussetts, in March of 1980. Out of this conference grew a large U.S.-wide

network of women's groups. In November of 1980 and 1981, "women surrounded the Pentagon for two days of nonviolent direct action against all military violence and against the sexual and economic violence in the everyday lives of all women" (Caldecott and Leland, *Reclaim the Earth*, 15). These all-women protests are often considered the activist beginnings of North American ecofeminism.

39 Unity Statement of the Women's Pentagon Action, USA, in *Reclaim the Earth*, ed. Caldecott and Leland, 15–16.

40 There is an allusion in one of the ending paragraphs to a maternal connection to the earth, but it is immediately made political through its construction as a right. The sense is not that a woman/nature bond is the basis for politics, but that the possibility of developing this bond privately is eroded by existing political and corporate structures. I have not seen this particular inflection anywhere else.

41 Ibid., 17.

42 Ibid., 8, emphasis added.

43 Ibid., 6.

44 Celeste Watson, "Action from Tragedy: Women at Love Canal and Three Mile Island," *Heresies* 4, no. 1 (1981), 40–43.

45 Stephanie Lahar, "Ecofeminist Theory and Grassroots Politics," *Hypatia* 6, no. 1 (spring 1991), 35.

46 Seager, *Earth Follies*, 247.

47 Janet Biehl, *Finding Our Way*. I do not characterize it as a tirade lightly; it is absolutely dismissive of anything that does not sound to the author like orthodox (!) social ecology. That the book as a result is almost unreadable is a shame, as it contains some excellent critiques and is one of the few recent ecofeminist works that deals with democracy at all.

48 Ibid., 137.

49 King, "Healing the Wounds," 116.

50 Ibid., 117.

51 Biehl, *Finding Our Way*, 153–54, emphasis in original.

52 Ibid., 151.

53 Libertarian Municipalism is a model of confederated local democratic political institutions based on the writings of social ecologist Murray Bookchin.

54 Josephine Donovan and Carol Adams, ed., *Beyond Animal Rights: A Feminist Caring Ethic for the Treatment of Animals* (New York: Continuum Publishing, 1996), 11.

55 Donovan, "Attention to Suffering: Sympathy as a Basis for Ethical Treatment of Animals," in *Beyond Animal Rights*, ed. Donovan and Adams, 147.

56 Peter Singer, *Animal Liberation* (New York: Avon Books, 1975).

57 Ibid., xi.

58 Marti Kheel, "The Liberation of Nature," 144.

59 Ibid., 147.

60 "An Ecofeminist Statement Delivered at the Summit for Animals, April 8–10, 1994, Boston, Massachussetts," reprinted in *Feminists for Animal Rights* VIII, no. 1–2 (spring–summer, 1994), 7.

61 I should be quite clear, here, that vegetarianism and anti-vivisectionism can be profoundly political discourses; the problem is not the articulation of personal ethics with political activity, but the pretense that the former necessarily contains—or morally overrides—the latter.

62 Josephine Donovan, "Animal Rights and Feminist Theory," in *Ecofeminism*, ed. Gaard, 185. While it is certainly true that animals do not want to be treated this way, the idea that we can hear their needs if we only listen carefully enough would seem to lead away from creating the political relations in which their enigmatic voices may have an influence. To give Donovan credit, her writings are, in other places, quite clear about the need to insert politics into caring.

63 Deane Curtin, "Toward an Ecological Ethic of Care," *Hypatia* 6, no. 1 (spring 1991), 71.

64 Carol Adams, "Caring about Suffering: A Feminist Exploration," in *Beyond Animal Rights*, ed. Donovan and Adams, especially 179 and 192.

65 Again, it is worth noting that Adams—and, to a lesser extent, Donovan—calls into question the possibility of empathy as a basis for caring. For Adams in particular, caring requires both a personal (gendered?) experience of suffering and a principled condemnation of the systemic relations that cause suffering. In insisting on both, Adams leaves open a space for politics.

66 Joni Seager has a lovely analysis of some of the profound misogyny of many animal rights campaigns, especially the antifur lobby. She holds gendered relations to fur up to public scrutiny, thus taking the campaign away from getting women to stop buying fur—a private act—and toward a broader questioning of the ways in which representations of women as animals are used to market fur.

67 The language of justice is critical; it suggests overt politicality at the same time that it displays a strong reference to the need to link environmental issues with social justice.

68 Celene Krauss, "Blue-Collar Women and Toxic Waste Protests: The Process of Politicization," in *Toxic Struggles*, ed. Hofrichter, 73.

69 Ibid., 109.

70 This sentiment is similar to the one embedded in the quotation that began this book. The difference between them is partly one of context: Krauss's article is included in an anthology that is all about politicizing the environment, where the opening quote was the beginning of a call to reduce, reuse, and recycle. That Krauss's piece begins with a critique of existing policy frameworks is also important; her call to look to the experiences of working-class women is born from a critique of politics as usual. But the contingency of "the personal is political" should be noted in the fact of the similarity; there is nothing inherently political in the personal.

71 Tokar, *Earth for Sale*, 209.

72 Ibid., 186.

73 One manufacturer of non-chlorine-bleached tampons and sanitary napkins markets its products under the name Eco-femmes. The performative drag politics of chapter 5 could lead to a great deal of fun with this marketing strategy.

8. THE RETURN OF THE REAL

1 Marian Engel, *Bear* (Toronto: McClelland and Stewart, 1976), 119.

2 Ibid., 133–34.

3 Ibid., 121.

4 Donna Haraway, "Otherworldly Conversations: Terran Topics; Local Terms," *Science as Culture*, 3, no. 14 (1992), 66–67.

5 Ibid., 67.

6 Ibid., 73.

7 My interspecies interaction suggests that cat/human relations do not easily fit under the heading of "training." The fact that *cat training* is generally regarded as an oxymoron suggests that cats are very active in constructing their interactions with humans and that their "moral personhood" appears quite differently than that of dogs in dog/human training relations. Indeed, cats are often considered the ultimate self-interested rational actors; see, for example, Harry Miller, *The Common Sense Book of Kitten and Cat Care* (New York: Bantam Books, 1966).

8 Haraway, "Otherworldly Conversations," 74.

9 Ibid., 75.

10 Ibid., 76.

11 Alan Wittbecker, "Nature as Self," *The Trumpeter* 6, no. 3 (1989), 80.

12 Gary Snyder, *The Practice of the Wild* (San Francisco: North Point Press, 1990), 10.

13 I do not mean to suggest that nature is thus not amenable to politicization; I do mean that it is possible to reconsider the value of privacy and ineffability as necessary counterparts to publicity. While there is a large difference between Arendt's understanding of privacy and the nonlinguistic one I provide here, I will borrow a passage from her that alludes to this value: "The sacredness of this privacy was like the sacredness of the hidden, namely, of birth and death, the beginning and end of the mortals who, like all living creatures, grow out of and return to the darkness of an underworld" (*The Human Condition*, 62).

14 Claude Lefort, *Democracy and Political Theory* (Minneapolis: University of Minnesota Press), 17.

15 Ibid.

16 Ibid.; emphasis in original.

17 Ibid.

18 Ibid., 19.

19 He also argues that it is precisely the process of democratic disincorporation that renders *possible* ideology, the attempt to reestablish a common purpose born from the democratic distance between power and its embodiment.

20 Ibid., 19.

21 For an elaboration of this argument, see Lefort, *The Political Forms of Modern Society: Bureaucracy, Democracy, Totalitarianism* (Cambridge, Mass.: Massachusetts Institute of Technology Press, 1986), 185–89.

22 Lefort, *Democracy and Political Theory*, 19–20.

23 One might also want to ask how this fantasy is particularly engendered by the death of the political as the political. Indeed, Arendt's thought is as much a response to totalitarianism as Lefort's, and her desire to preserve democratic space is clearly about the preservation of plurality. Lefort acknowledges this aspect of her thought, along with her failure to outline the significance of organic fantasy.

24 Yannis Stavrakakis, "Split Subject and Split Object: Towards a Generalization of the Lacanian Logic of Lack," *Essex Papers in Politics and Government: A Sub-Series in Ideology and Discourse Analysis*, no. 7 (n.d.), 17.

25 Ibid., 17. The quoted passage is from Slavoj Žižek, *For They Know Not What They Do* (London: Verso, 1991), 272.

26 Žižek, *The Sublime Object*, 56.

27 Ibid., 57.

28 Stavrakakis, "Split Subject and Split Object," 13.

29 Ibid., 18.

30 Ernesto Laclau, "Minding the Gap: The Subject of Politics," in *The Making of Political Identities* (London: Verso, 1994), 36.

31 Engel, *Bear*, 140.

32 "The paradox (and perhaps the very function of the prohibition as such) consists of course in the fact that, as soon as it is conceived as prohibited, the [R]eal impossible changes into something possible, i.e. into something that cannot be reached, not because of its inherent impossibility but simply because access to it is hindered by the external barrier of a prohibition," Slavoj Žižek, *Tarrying with the Negative* Durham, N.C.: Duke University Press, 1993), 116.

33 Haraway, "Otherworldly Conversations," 71.

34 Ibid., 71–72.

35 Of course, this stance "between" reality and representation also invokes the space of parodic repetition outlined in chapter 5.

36 This work does not deal with Lacan's notion of female lack that centers around the phallus. In essence, if man desires the phallus (not the penis), and woman, in her lack, *is* the phallus, then all language revolves around this relation, given that the phallus constitutes the Symbolic. For Irigaray, this is why language cannot represent women. I use a version of lack that originates in the mirror stage rather than this one that originates in the Oedipal relation, although my call for a politics of alterity shows a clear parallel to French feminism.

37 Patricia Elliot, *From Mastery to Analysis: Theories of Gender in Psychoanalytic Feminism* (Ithaca, N.Y.: Cornell University Press, 1991), 167. Elliot does not argue that this position grants women privileged access to a realm outside language, only that phallic language does not contain women.

38 Brian Swimme, "How to Heal a Lobotomy," in *Reweaving the World*, ed. Diamond and Orenstein, 15

39 Janet Biehl, cited in Merchant, *Radical Ecology*, 194.

40 Chaia Heller, "For the Love of Nature: Ecology and the Cult of the Romantic," in *Ecofeminism*, ed. Gaard, 240.

41 Karen Warren, "Introduction," *Ecological Feminism* (New York: Routledge, 1994), 2.

42 Luanne Armstrong, "The Great Cosmic Metaphor: Thinking about the 'Earth Our Mother,'" *Alternatives* 21, no. 2 (1995), 32.

43 Ibid., 34.

44 On the earth as sister, see Ursula Le Guin, "A Very Warm Mountain," in *Celebrating the Land: Women's Nature Writings 1850–1991*, ed. Karen Knowles (Flagstaff, Ariz.: Northland Publishing, 1992).

45 Summer Fike and Sarah Kerr, "Making the Links: Why Bioregionalism Needs Ecofeminism," *Alternatives* 21, no. 2 (1995), 26.

46 Greta Gaard, "Ecofeminism and Wilderness," *Environmental Ethics* 19 (spring 1997).

47 Ibid., 15.

48 Ibid.

49 Catherine Keller, "Women against Wasting the World: Notes on Eschatology and Ecology," in *Reweaving the World*, ed. Diamond and Orenstein, 258.

50 Charlene Spretnak, "Ecofeminism: Our Roots and Flowering," in *Reweaving the World*, ed. Diamond and Orenstein, 8.

51 Irene Diamond, *Fertile Ground: Women, Earth, and the Limits of Control* (Boston: Beacon Press, 1994), 156.
52 All in Plant, *Healing the Wounds*.
53 Karen Warren and Jim Cheney, "Ecological Feminism and Ecosystem Ecology," *Hypatia* 6, no. 1 (spring 1991), 186.
54 Ibid., 192.
55 Carol Bigwood, *Earth Muse: Feminism, Nature, and Art* (Philadelphia: Temple University Press, 1993), 2. I do no justice to her argument here and apologize to her for my Lacanian overdetermination of her decidedly un-Lacanian text.
56 Ibid., 292.
57 Ibid. Here Bigwood points to the possible reconceptualization of home as a specifically political site; if it is a site of strangeness and difference, then it can be considered a site for plurality and action in an Arendtian sense. I am not sure I am willing to make this move; politics isn't everywhere.
58 Ibid., 303.

CONCLUSION

1 Karen J. Warren, ed., *Ecofeminism: Women, Culture, Nature* (Bloomington: Indiana University Press, 1997); Noël Sturgeon, *Ecofeminist Natures: Race, Gender, Feminist Theory and Political Action* (New York: Routledge, 1997).
2 Sturgeon, *Ecofeminist Natures*, 196.
3 Ibid.

Index

action: Arendt on, 155, 159; as creation of individual through performance, 160; public realm required by, 155–57
Action Agenda 21, UN (1992), 128, 136, 146
Adams, Carol, 170, 173, 174
Adkin, Laurie, 154
Adler, Frank, 26
affinity: cyborg view of, 107–8; ironic repetition as form of, 109; performative, 111–24
Agarwal, Bina, 60–61, 62, 136
Alaimo, Stacy, 116–20, 121, 224n34
alienation: ecofeminist methods of resolving, 195–203; of subject, fundamental, 83–85; of workers, 30
Allen, Prudence, 19
alternative definitions of sense, 37, 38, 39
Amazon dis-covery, process of, 214n21
American Broadcasting Company's Earth Day Special (1990), 117
Angus Reid poll, environmental trends indicated in, 152–54
Animal Liberation (Singer), 171
animal rights discourse, ecofeminist engagements with, 170–74, 230nn62, 66
antagonism, 85; Canadian worker-

environmentalist conflict as, 101; defined, xx; equivalence and, tensions between, xx, 104–9, 120–24, 190; ever increasing field of, 45
antagonism within, 102–4
antiessentialism, 110, 114
antifur campaign, 230n66
apolitical ennui, 28, 166
Arendt, Hannah, 151–52, 155–62, 165, 168, 169, 231nn13, 23
Armstrong, Luanne, 197
articulation, 92; incompleteness of any position captured in or animated through, 107; practice of, 44; radical democratic, 86–87
assimilation, politics of, 9–10
Atkinson, Ti-Grace, 8
authenticity of voice, 78–82
authority, voices of, 76–78

Bagby, Rachel, 53
Balbus, Isaac, 25–26
barre through language, 185–86, 189
Barry, Kathleen, 14
Bear (Engel), 182–83, 191
Beauvoir, Simone de, 7, 16
Benhabib, Seyla, 156, 158, 162

≈ 235 ≈

feminist racism, 10
Fike, Summer, 197–98
Finding Our Way (Biehl), 62–64
Firestone, Shulamith, 8, 9, 11
First Nations women, 53–54, 56
Fraser, Nancy, 157, 158, 159
freedom and necessity, distinction
    between, 157
Freud, Sigmund, 22
Fuss, Diana, 112

Gaard, Greta, 110, 111, 112, 123, 198–99,
    200
"gay" identity, 40–41
gay men, practices of drag for, 108–9
gender, environmental justice movement
    and, 175–76
gender differences, development of, 21–24
genealogy of ecofeminism, 3–27; eco-
    feminist identity and, 26–27; goddess-
    centered cultures, development of,
    11–15; object relations and, 21–26,
    216n53; quest for roots, 15–21; radical
    and cultural feminisms and, 5, 6–11
Gibbs, Lois, xiii, xiv, 5, 165–66
Gilligan, Carol, 24, 171
global and local, tension between, 126
global citizenship, 131–32, 149
global consciousness, call for new, 130–31
global-ecological working class, 130
globalization: from above, 128; from
    below, 128, 132, 133–34, 138, 143–44,
    146, 149; environmental, 126, 127–39;
    particularity and, 132–35; reorganiza-
    tion of global socioeconomic system,
    129–30
goddess-centered cultures, development
    of, 11–15
golden age, 215n36
Gramsci, Antonio, 31
grassroots ecological activism, democratic
    promise in, 177–78
green consumerism, xii
Green Paradise Lost, 3
green politics: libertarian municipalist
    moment in, 222n30; status of eco-
    feminism as, 136

Griffin, Susan, 13, 15, 113, 117, 119
Griscom, Joan, 17
Grosz, Elizabeth, 83
grounds up approach to addressing
    environmental degradation, 143–44
Gruen, Lori, 93–94
Gyn/Ecology (Daly), 9, 15, 113, 214n21
"gynocracy," creation of, 10–11

Haraway, Donna, 49, 72–73, 103–4, 107,
    116, 117, 118, 119, 122, 179, 183–85,
    191–93
Hartsock, Nancy, 38–39, 43, 58
Häusler, Sabine, 6, 147
Hayles, N. Katherine, 116
Healing the Wounds (Plant), 54
Heller, Chaia, 195–96, 214n25, 220n38
Henderson, Hazel, 21
Heresies, 17, 165–66
heteroglossia, cultivation of, 104
hierarchical dualism, 15–17, 19–21, 24
Hofrichter, Richard, 175
holistic health movement, 51
home: Bigwood's use of, 204–5; nature as,
    197–98
homophobia, feminist, 10
homosexuality: identity politics and
    origins of, 40–41; lesbianism, 10, 11,
    108–9; practices of drag, 108–9,
    122–23
Honig, Bonnie, 159–60
Human Condition, The (Arendt), 163
humility, methodological, 94
humility of democratic project, 206

ideal class subject, rise and fall of, 30–34
Ideas program (CBC), 90
identity, 28–47; based on difference, so-
    cialist ecofeminism and, 61; defensive
    moment of, 47; demise of myth of solid,
    103–4; democracy and, 41–47; emer-
    gence from politics, 84; misrecognition
    of, 45–46, 84, 92; proliferation of eco-
    feminisms and problem of, 66, 67–71;
    proliferation of social movements and,
    28–29, 34–38; speaking, xx, 87; stand-
    point epistemologies and identity

politics, 38–41; workers' movement and, 30–34

identity politics, xviii–xx, 4; chain of equivalential, 102; environmental, in deep ecology, 81–82; feminist postmodernist critique of, 49; foundational fantasy of presociality of, 102; idea of speech in, 80; limits of, 88–89; logic of, 27, 39–40; notion of subject at base of, 81–82; as problems for democracy, 188; problems with, 5; standpoint epistemologies and, 38–41; version of community underscoring, 46–47

ideology: desire for certainty in, 188–89; quest to ideological fullness, 198; resistance of democracy to hardening of, 187

India: Chipko movement of Northern, 55–56, 218n12; conditions affecting women and nature in, 60–61

"informatics of domination," 72–73

international eco-managerialism, 128, 134

International Joint Commission on Great Lakes Water Quality, 178

International Monetary Fund, 130

interrogative form of resistance, 73–74

interrogative potential of ecofeminism, 144–45

Irigaray, Luce, 193, 232n36

irony, 53, 107, 108, 109

jouissance, 185, 189, 190, 191, 192, 200

Keller, Catherine, 199–200

Kerr, Sarah, 197–98

Kheel, Marti, 75, 171

King, Ynestra, 15, 17, 20, 21, 24, 54, 64, 72, 125, 142, 163, 168, 175–76

Krauss, Celene, 176

labor, Arendt on, 155

Lacan, Jacques, xviii, 83–85, 189, 193

LaChappelle, Dolores, 201

lack, 201, 204, 232n36; at center of subjectivity, 189–90; encirclement of, 190, 192–93; experiences of, 191–93

Laclau, Ernesto, xx, xxi, 32, 40, 44, 85, 89, 92, 98, 99, 100, 101, 117, 133, 134, 139, 151, 157, 189–90

Lahar, Stephanie, 166

language: barre through, 185–86, 189; *écriture féminine*, 193–94; *écriture naturelle*, 194; limits of, 88, 180–81, 183–86, 200–201, 204

La Rocque, Margot, 76, 78, 79

Lefort, Claude, 186–87, 231n23

Le Guin, Ursula, 201

Leland, Stephanie, 163–65

lesbians/lesbianism, 10, 11, 108–9

Li, Huey-li, 56–57, 111

liberal feminism, 64

liberal individualism, 171

Libertarian Municipalism, 222n30, 229n53

limits of language, 88, 180–81, 183–86, 200–201, 204

limits of subjectivity, 91

limits of the social, 89–94

local and global, tension between, 126

local resistance, empowerment of, 132–33

Lorde, Audre, 10

Luke, Tim, 154

MacDonald, Helen, xiv

McMahon, Martha, 143–44

MacMillan Bloedel, 101

Macy, Joanna, 69, 201

Magnusson, Warren, 41–42

marginal consciousness, ecofeminist, 19

marginalization of ecofeminism, 136

Margulis, Lynn, 90

Marx, Karl, 8, 31, 38, 39, 47, 89

Marxism, 33, 34–35

Matuschka, 123, 124

mediators, women as, 4, 6, 13

Mellor, Mary, 61–62, 67, 97, 176

Melucci, Alberto, 36, 37, 40, 42

Merchant, Carolyn, xix, 4–5, 11, 19, 49, 57–60, 63, 213n3

methodological humility, 94

Mies, Maria, 136, 137–39, 142, 145, 146

Miles, Angela, 225n23

Mills, Patricia Jagentowicz, 26

mimetic identification, feminist enactment of, 106–7

mirroring, antagonism exposed through, 106, 107

mirror stage of development, 83

misrecognition of identity, 45–46, 92; "real" logic of, 84

monarchy, power in democracy vs., 186–88

M/Other, male separation from, 24–25

motherhood environmentalism, xiii, xiv–xv, xvii, 4

Mouffe, Chantal, xx, xxi, 32, 40, 44, 85, 89, 92, 98, 99, 100, 101, 117, 133, 151, 157

multiplicity, solidification of identity and, 47

mystery, notion of, 199, 200

National Organization for Women, 7

natural self, 69–71

nature: as active and unpredictable character, 118–19; alternative modes of "speaking," 78; assumption of stability of, 71–72; "authentic" voice of, 79, 80; as co-construction among humans and non-humans, 118; constant Otherness of, 203–4; construction of, in cultural feminism, 14–15; ecofeminism and destabilization of, 115–20; ecofeminist natures from domestication to trauma, 194–203; in Haraway's nature stories, 183–85; as horizon produced through the social, 90; limits of the social and, 89–94; objective, idea of, 90; performative woman/nature affinity, 111–24; as primary category linking diversity of oppressed and resistant social positions, 67–68; problem of identity in proliferation of ecofeminisms and, 67–71; problem of representation of, 88, 180–81; questioning the positivity of, 91; social construction of, 68–69; as symptom, 193, 194, 203; as terrain of female consciousness, 13–14; voices of authority on, conflicting, 76–78

nature feminists, 17

"nature question": in cultural feminism, 10–11; feminist responses to, 17–18; in radical feminism, 6–10

naturism, 17

necessity and freedom, distinction between, 157

neoconservatism, xiii, 4

New Woman/New Earth (Ruether), 12, 15

NIABY (Not In Anybody's Back Yard), 131

NIMBY (Not In My Back Yard), 129, 131, 224n5

Noske, Barbara, 224n33

object relations, ecofeminism and, 21–26, 216n53

O'Brien, Mary, 157, 167

O'Connor, James, 129, 131, 133, 225n6

Oedipal period, development of gender differences in, 22–23, 24

Offe, Claus, 35–36

oikos (household), 167,169

Ontario Advisory Council on Women's Issues, xi, xiii, 208, 211n4

ontology as politics, 142

openness, democratic, xx–xxi, 209

oppression of women: ecofeminist transference to ideas on nature, 16–17; radical feminism on, 7–9; source of, 8–9

organic dualisms, 72–73

organochlorines, 177–78

Ortner, Sherry, 6–7, 8, 11, 13, 16, 63

"Otherworldly Conversations" (Haraway), 183–85

Our Common Future (WCED), 127, 129, 225n8

ozone depletion, recent discussions of, 76

paradox, democratic promise of, 207

parody of performative woman/nature affinity, 120, 122–23

partiality of subject position, recognition of, 107–8, 109

particularity, xx; ecofeminism and, 139–49; globalization and, 132–35; universality and, xx, 132–35, 139–49, 190

patriarchal dualism, 61–63

patriarchal religion, destructive significance of, 9, 12

strategic essentialism, ecofeminist, 112–15

Students for a Democratic Society, 7

Sturgeon, Noël, 209, 210

subjectivity: Cartesian, xx; ecology and political, 85–89; lack at center of, 189–90; limits of, 91

subject position (Symbolic): inevitable disjuncture between subject (Real) and, 105–6; recognition of partiality of, 107–8, 109; *See also* Symbolic order

subject (Real): fundamental alienation of, 83–85; inevitable disjuncture between subject position (Symbolic) and, 105–6; Lacan on, 83–85; problem of voice as problem of, 79–82; *See also* Real, return of the

subsistence (survival) perspective, 137–39

subversion, drag and possibility of, 109

Summit for Animals (1994), 172

sustainable development, 128, 129

Swallow, Ellen, 5

Swimme, Brian, 67, 195

Symbolic order, 83

symptom, 189, 191, 201; as marker of the Real, 189, 190; nature as, 193, 194, 203

Taskforce on the Churches and Corporate Responsibility, 146

Taylor, Peter, 128

Thompson, William Irwin, 90, 91

Tokar, Brian, 154, 177

totalitarianism, democracy vs., 187–88

Touraine, Alain, 31–32, 33, 42, 43

Toxic Struggles (Hofrichter), 175

trade unionism, 31, 33, 34

transformative feminism, 64–65

transformative social movements, 92

transgression: embracing, 102–4; recreation of nature away from reductionist and determinist understandings and, 118–19; tensions between coalition and, 98

trauma, ecofeminist natures from domestication to, 194–203

United Nations Commission on Environment and Development (UNCED),

132; preparatory process, tension in, 147

United Nations Earth Summit (1992), 127–28; Action Agenda 21, 128, 136, 146

United States environmental movement, 131

unity, ecofeminist myths of, 70

Unity Statement of the Women's Pentagon Action, 163–65

universal, patriarchal, 141

universality, xx; ecofeminism and, 135–39; as fictitious representation of impossible wholeness, 134; orientation toward future, 149; particularity and, xx, 132–35, 139–49, 190; resurrection of, 126, 127–32; tension between universal as challenge and universal as standpoint, 135

utopia, 213n15

vita activa, 155, 159

voice(s): authenticity of, 78–82; of authority, 76–78; problem of, as problem of subject, 79–82

Walker, Rob, 41–42

Warren, Karen, xv, xix, 21, 54–56, 64–65, 112, 196, 202, 209

Watson, Celeste, 165–66

Whale Adoption Project, 118, 224n34

When God Was a Woman (Stone), 11–12

Whiteside, Kerry, 162–63

Wieringa, Saskia, 6, 147

wildness, 184–86, 190, 194, 206–7; resolution of alienation and, 198–203

Wittbecker, Alan, 185

Woman and Nature: The Roaring Inside Her (Griffin), 13–14, 15, 113, 117

woman/nature connection, origins of. *See* genealogy of ecofeminism

Woman on the Edge of Time (Piercy), 8–9, 213n15

women: of color, attempt to incorporate perspectives of, 53–54; involvement in ecological politics, perception of, xii–xiii; as mediators, 4, 6, 13

Catriona Sandilands is assistant professor in the faculty of environmental studies at York University (Toronto), where she teaches and advises in the areas of environmental politics, environmental thought, cultural studies, and social and political thought. She has published a range of academic and popular works on the intersections among environmentalism, feminism, and political theory.